SHARON REECE, M.A., J.D., LL.M.

MAX D. SIEGEL, J.D.

Employee Benefits Law

THE ESSENTIAL CASES

AMERICAN BAR ASSOCIATION

Senior Lawyers Division

Cover design by Mary Anne Kulchawik/ABA Publishing.

Printed in the United States of America.

18 17 16 15 14 5 4 3 2 1

ISBN: 978-1-62722-852-7

e-ISBN: 978-1-62722-853-4

Library of Congress Cataloging-in-Publication Data

Reece, Sharon, author.
Employee benefits law : the essential cases / Sharon Reece and Max D. Siegel.
pages cm
Includes index.
ISBN 978-1-62722-852-7 (softcover : alk. paper) — ISBN 978-1-62722-853-4 (e-book) 1. Employee fringe benefits—Law and legislation—United States—Cases. 2. Pension trusts—Law and legislation—United States—Cases. 3. United States. Employee Retirement Income Security Act of 1974. I. Siegel, Max D., author. II. Title.
KF3509.R44 2014
344.7301'255—dc23 2014036713

To my family with love.
—Sharon Reece

To my loving partner.
—Max D. Siegel

Contents

Acknowledgments

The authors wish to acknowledge and thank the publisher, the editorial staff, and Richard Paszkiet in particular for their patience in working with us in the preparation of this book. We also want to thank administrative staff Carole Marshall and researchers Susan McCarty and Anna Johnston for their support.

About the Authors

Sharon Reece is currently Visiting Associate Professor of Law at The University of Maryland School of Law. For the past 20 years she has been a law professor teaching courses (undergraduate and graduate levels) and has published in the areas of Taxation and Employee Benefits Law. Prior to starting her teaching career, she worked as a tax attorney at the law firm of Berchem and Moses in Connecticut. She is a graduate of the University of the West Indies, Jamaica (BA), Long Island University (MA), Hofstra University (JD), and New York University (LLM, Taxation). She is admitted to multiple state bars, including New York and Connecticut, the United States District Court of Connecticut, and the United States District Court for the Southern District of New York. Professor Reece is a member of the American Bar Association, Tax Section. Professor Reece recently coauthored the book *ERISA: The Essentials* with David Pratt, who is currently a professor of law at the Albany Law School.

Max D. Siegel is an Employee Relations and Compliance Specialist serving Holy Cross Health, a not-for-profit health system based in Montgomery County, Maryland. His recent scholarship has been featured in *Maryland Law Review*, *Cardozo Journal of Law & Gender*, *George Mason University Civil Rights Law Journal*, *William & Mary Policy Review*, and additional publications. His work has examined health as a matter of social justice, including health equity following passage of the Patient Protection and Affordable Care Act and the relationship between HIV/AIDS and identity-based social movements in the United States. He is a graduate of the University of Maryland School of Law, where he earned a certificate in law and health care and received the Joseph Bernstein Prize for Most Significant Piece of Legal Writing, among other recognitions.

Preface

There are literally thousands of cases that relate to the Employee Retirement Income Security Act (ERISA). Courts' relentless attention to ERISA is no surprise in light of the transformative consequences of employee benefits throughout society. This can be overwhelming for anyone whose work implicates ERISA but especially for those who are uninitiated to employee benefit law. The primary objective of this book is to present in as concise a manner as possible what the authors have agreed are the most essential cases and most frequently litigated issues under ERISA. This book provides a window into the approach the courts have taken to the most fundamental aspects of ERISA litigation.

This book begins by defining what constitutes an ERISA plan and by classifying parties to such plans. This book then proceeds into the other most litigated areas of ERISA: preemption and other procedural matters, fiduciary liability, remedies, disability benefits, disclosure requirements, and spousal protections, including the shifting treatment of sexual minorities under ERISA. This book concludes with an examination of the antialienation and antiassignment rules, vesting, and other less litigated participant protections.

We hope you find this book helpful. We welcome your comments, which you may send to Sharon Reece at sreece@law.umaryland.edu or to Max D. Siegel at maxdrewsiegel@gmail.com.

Chapter 1

ERISA Plans

Federal law is the primary regulator of employee benefit plans. In particular, the Employee Retirement Income Security Act of 1974 (ERISA), as amended, governs "an employee welfare benefit plan or an employee pension benefit plan or a plan which is both an employee welfare benefit plan and an employee pension benefit plan."[1] ERISA plans must be established by an employee organization, usually a labor union, or an employer to provide certain benefits to participants or beneficiaries when the employee organization or employer are engaged in commerce or in an industry or activity affecting commerce.[2]

Every major section of ERISA contains the word "plan"; therefore, defining an ERISA plan is critical. The federal circuits have split on whether the determination of the existence of an ERISA plan is required for federal jurisdiction.[3] In terms of remedies and enforcement, participants may only proceed in suit to recover ERISA plan benefits under ERISA's enforcement provisions.[4] Another important consequence of ERISA's governance of a

---

1. 29 U.S.C. § 1002(3) (2013).
2. 29 U.S.C. § 1003(a) (2013); *see also* Ed Miniat, Inc. v. Globe Life Ins. Grp., Inc., 805 F.2d 732, 738 (7th Cir. 1986).
3. For an assessment of this split and a court's recalibration of its reasoning based on the Supreme Court's decision in Arbaugh v. Y & H Corp., 546 U.S. 500 (2006), see Daft v. Advest, Inc., 658 F.3d 583, 588–94 (6th Cir. 2011).
4. *See* Pilot Life Ins. Co. v. Dedeaux, 481 U.S. 41, 54 (1987) (explaining that "[t]he policy choices reflected in the inclusion of certain remedies and the exclusion of others under the federal scheme would be completely undermined if ERISA-plan participants and beneficiaries were free to obtain remedies under state law" and stating that "the conclusion [that ERISA's civil enforcement remedies were intended to be exclusive] is fully confirmed by the legislative history of the civil enforcement provision").

plan is ERISA's preemption doctrine. ERISA preempts "any and all State laws insofar as they now or hereafter relate to any employee benefit plan."[5] There is an exception for state laws that regulate insurance, banking, or securities.[6]

Courts typically characterize the question of whether an arrangement is an employee pension benefit plan or an employee welfare benefit plan as a question of fact, not law,[7] which, in such instances, precludes pretrial disposition of a case. The umbrella term "employee benefit plan" under ERISA includes both employee welfare benefit plans and employee pension benefit plans. ERISA defines "employee pension benefit plan" as a plan, fund, or program that, whether expressly or as a result of surrounding circumstances, provides retirement income to employees or results in a deferral of income by employees for periods extending to the end of employment or beyond.[8] An "employee welfare benefit plan" pertains to any plan, fund, or program that is established or maintained to provide participants or their beneficiaries with medical, surgical, or hospital care or benefits; benefits in the event of sickness, accident, disability, death, or unemployment; vacation benefits, apprenticeships, or other training programs; day care centers, scholarship funds, or prepaid legal services; or other benefits that employers, associations of employers, and labor relations experts, advisers, and consultants may provide under federal law.[9] ERISA covers both defined contribution[10] and defined benefit[11] plans.

The statutory definitions cannot encompass and in fact were not intended to address the myriad of arrangements in the marketplace that could be ERISA plans. Therefore, courts have had to interpret ERISA's statutory

5. 29 U.S.C. § 1144(a) (2013).
6. 29 U.S.C. § 1144(b)(2)(A) (2013).
7. *See* Meredith v. Time Ins. Co., 980 F.2d 353 (5th Cir. 1993); Harper v. Am. Chambers Life Ins. Co., 898 F.2d 1432 (9th Cir. 1990).
8. 29 U.S.C. § 1002(2) (2013).
9. 29 U.S.C. § 1002(1) (2013); *see also* 29 U.S.C. § 186 (2013).
10. The Internal Revenue Code considers a defined contribution plan to be any "plan which provides for an individual account for each participant and for benefits based solely on the amount contributed to the participant's account, and any income, expenses, gains and losses, and any forfeitures of accounts of other participants which may be allocated to such participant's account." 26 U.S.C. § 414(i) (2013).
11. The Internal Revenue Code considers a defined benefit plan to be "any plan which is not a defined contribution plan." 26 U.S.C. § 414(j) (2013).

language as it relates to plans in operational contexts. Courts have consistently reiterated that ERISA governs employee benefit plans and not employee benefits in general.[12] In addition, courts have expressed what the phrase "established or maintained" requires. While examining all surrounding facts and circumstances, courts have found that employers "established" an ERISA plan when the employers engaged in some degree of implementation beyond conferring a single benefit. There must be a discernible intention to provide benefits on a regular basis over a long term.[13] Even when an employer has not established a plan, an employer may have "maintained" a plan, meaning that an employer has continued a plan by involving itself in the payment of benefits, changing a policy's critical terms, or performing administrative functions associated with the plan.[14] Factors equally relevant to determining if an employer "established or maintained" a plan are the employer's oral and documented representations, the employer's creation of a reserve to pay benefits, whether benefit payments were made, any deliberate failures to avoid the perception that a plan exists, employees' reasonable understandings, and the employer's intent.[15]

The issue of whether an ERISA plan exists and which kind of plan exists are strategically important for litigation. An employee may prefer an arrangement to be considered an employee pension benefit plan, whether of the defined benefit plan type or the defined contribution plan type. ERISA established several substantive provisions to regulate private voluntary employee pension plans to protect employees' interests. Problems in the retirement and pension area—not problems with welfare benefit plans—motivated ERISA's enactment. State insurance laws containing more substantive regulations of welfare benefit plans than pension benefit plans were already in place.

Even though an employee may prefer a plan to be of the pension variety and thus operate under the watchful, substantive governance of ERISA, such an employee may prefer state law remedies when a dispute arises. Remedies

12. *See* Wurtz v. Rawlings Co., LLC, No. 12-CV-1182, 2013 WL 1248631, at *15 (E.D.N.Y. Mar. 28, 2013) (citing Howard v. Gleason Corp., 901 F.2d 1154, 1156 (2d Cir. 1990)).
13. *See* Anderson v. UNUM Provident Corp., 369 F.3d 1257, 1264–65 (11th Cir. 2004) (citing Butero v. Royal Maccabees Life Ins. Co., 174 F.3d 1207, 1214 (11th Cir. 1999)).
14. *Id.* at 1265 (citing Postma v. Paul Revere Life Ins. Co., 223 F.3d 533, 538 (7th Cir. 2000)).
15. *Id.* (citing *Butero*, 174 F.3d at 1215).

under ERISA are generally more limited than state law remedies because ERISA does not typically provide for compensatory and punitive damages.[16]

ERISA was designed to protect employees but was carefully calibrated in order not to discourage employers from establishing plans under this voluntary system of private retirement savings. The law's congressional findings maintain that "employees and their beneficiaries have been deprived of anticipated benefits . . . and that it is therefore desirable in the interests of employees and their benefits . . . that minimum standards be provided assuring the equitable character of [employee benefit] plans and their financial soundness."[17] Courts have recognized that Congress sought to balance the protection of employees and beneficiaries with the need to create incentives for employers to establish plans. Some identifiable concessions in the provisions of ERISA include limited remedies and the allowance for employers to utilize nonneutral fiduciaries.

Until the Affordable Care Act was passed, there was no comprehensive regulation of health-care plans. The federal government had addressed health-care issues incrementally, becoming more heavily involved after passing the Medicare and Medicaid Acts in the 1960s. As examples, Congress passed the Health Maintenance Organization (HMO) Act in 1973[18] to curb health-care spending, the Consolidated Omnibus Budget Reconciliation Act (COBRA) in 1986[19] to provide health insurance for a period of time after employment and other events in an employee's life that could lead to loss of health care coverage, and the Health Insurance Portability and Accountability Act (HIPAA) in 1996[20] initially to enhance employees' health insurance plan options and increase plans' portability.

The Affordable Care Act now governs an important form of employee welfare benefits plans: health-care plans. If a plan is a group health-care plan, it will have the limited protections of ERISA and the more comprehensive protections of the Affordable Care Act, which incorporates many of the state law protections that, under ERISA, would not necessarily apply

16. Mass. Mut. Life Ins. Co. v. Russell, 473 U.S. 134, 138 (1985).
17. 29 U.S.C. § 1001(a) (2013).
18. Pub. L. No. 93-222, 87 Stat. 914 (1973).
19. Pub. L. 99-272, 100 Stat. 82 (1986).
20. Pub. L. 104-191, 110 Stat. 1936 (1996).

to health-care plans due to ERISA's preemption provisions. Significant overlap exists between ERISA and the Affordable Care Act, which incorporates ERISA's definition of employee welfare benefit plan to define "group health plans."[21]

Exemptions from ERISA

Regardless of whether a plan otherwise constitutes a welfare benefit plan or an employee pension benefit plan, ERISA exempts governmental plans, any plan governed by the Railroad Retirement Act, and plans belonging to a tax-exempt international organization, such as the United Nations.[22] In addition, ERISA does not govern church plans, including certain church-affiliated organizations like hospitals, nor does it apply to "plans maintained solely to comply with applicable workmen's compensation, unemployment compensation, or disability insurance laws."[23] Department of Labor regulations exempt "group or group type insurance programs,"[24] and ERISA also exempts "top-hat plans" from certain provisions. A top-hat plan is a plan that is "unfunded and maintained for the primary purpose of providing deferred compensation for a select group of management or highly compensated employees."[25]

Another important exception is employer payroll practices. In *Massachusetts v. Morash*,[26] the Supreme Court held that the practice of paying employees for unused vacation time upon discharge did not constitute an employee welfare benefit plan under ERISA.[27] The Court gave deference

21. 29 U.S.C. § 300gg-91(a)(1) (2013).
22. 29 U.S.C. §§ 1002(32), 1003(b)(1) (2013).
23. 29 U.S.C. §§ 1002(33), 1003(b)(2)–(3) (2013).
24. 29 C.F.R. § 2510.3-1(j) (2013). Group or group-type insurance programs offered by an insurer to employees or members in an employee organization are exempted when there are no contributions by an employer or employee organization, program participation is completely voluntary, the functions of the employer or employee organization with respect to the program are to permit the insurer to publicize the program and to collect premiums or dues to remit to the insurer, and the employer or employee organization receives no consideration in connection with the program except reasonable compensation for administrative services. *Id.*
25. 29 U.S.C. § 1051(2) (2013).
26. 490 U.S. 107 (1989).
27. *Id.* at 120–21.

to the Department of Labor regulations, which stated that various payroll practices do not constitute welfare benefit plans, including vacation benefits paid out of general assets.[28]

The *Dillingham* Approach

In 1982, the United States Court of Appeals for the Eleventh Circuit articulated what would become a widely utilized framework for assessing ERISA applicability. In *Donovan v. Dillingham*, the court held that the trustees of Union Insurance Trust (UIT) and the businesses that the trustees owned and operated were subject to the fiduciary responsibilities established by ERISA.[29] UIT was a group insurance trust intended to allow employers of small businesses to procure lower-cost health insurance coverage for their employees.[30] To this end, UIT purchased a group health insurance policy, and employers and employee organizations subscribed to UIT to receive coverage under UIT's policy.[31] At issue before the Eleventh Circuit was whether this scheme constituted an employee welfare benefit plan.[32]

After reciting ERISA's statutory definition of an employee welfare benefit plan,[33] the Eleventh Circuit observed that two of the prerequisites to ERISA—"plan, fund, or program" and "established and maintained"—are less clearly defined than the others.[34] First, the court elaborated that, "[a]t a minimum, . . . a 'plan, fund, or program' under ERISA implies the existence of intended benefits, intended beneficiaries, a source of financing, and

28. *Id.* at 117–18.
29. Donovan v. Dillingham, 688 F.2d 1367, 1375 (11th Cir. 1982) (en banc).
30. *Id.* at 1370.
31. *Id.*
32. *Id.*
33. *Id.* at 1370–71 (citing 29 U.S.C. § 1002(1)) ("[A]ny plan, fund, or program which was heretofore or is hereafter established or maintained by an employer or by an employee organization, or by both, to the extent that such plan, fund, or program was established or is maintained for the purpose of providing for its participants or their beneficiaries, through the purchase of insurance or otherwise, (A) medical, surgical, or hospital care or benefits, or benefits in the event of sickness, accident, disability, death or unemployment, or vacation benefits, apprenticeship or other training programs, or day care centers, scholarship funds, or prepaid legal services, or (B) any benefit described in s 302(c) of the Labor Management Relations Act, 1947 (other than pensions on retirement or death, and insurance to provide such pensions).").
34. *Id.* at 1372.

a procedure to apply for and collect benefits."[35] Second, the court found that "established or maintained" requires that a plan actually be established or maintained by an employer or employee organization and that it be established or maintained for the specified purposes.[36] Although the memorialization of a plan in a formal, written document is mandated by ERISA, such is not necessary for the creation or existence of an ERISA plan.[37] The court noted that ERISA's fiduciary package, which includes the reporting and disclosure provisions, requires that a plan be established pursuant to a written document, but this requirement does not create a prerequisite for coverage under ERISA.[38]

The court articulated the standard: "In determining whether a plan, fund or program . . . is a reality a court must determine whether from the surrounding circumstances a reasonable person could ascertain the intended benefits, beneficiaries, source of financing, and procedures for receiving benefits."[39] An ERISA plan requires intended benefits, such as an insurance policy; beneficiaries, like employees or members receiving benefits; financing, including the employers' and employee membership organization's premium payments in *Dillingham*; and procedures to apply and receive benefits analogous to UIT's policy and the policy's claim procedures.

In applying this standard, the court looked to the Agreement and Trust document establishing UIT, which stated that the purpose of subscribing to UIT was to provide hospital and other benefits that are common to ERISA employee welfare plans.[40] Further, the insurance plan that UIT purchased provided health insurance, another benefit typical of ERISA.[41] The court also noted that UIT's participation agreements demonstrated that those benefiting from the subscription to UIT were employees or members of employee organizations.[42] Finally, the court reasoned that employers and unions subscribed to UIT to establish welfare benefit plans, that others

35. *Id.*
36. *Id.*
37. *Id.*
38. *Id.* (citing 29 U.S.C. §§ 1022, 1102).
39. *Id.* at 1373.
40. *Id.* at 1374.
41. *Id.*
42. *Id.*

subscribed to UIT without any agreement concerning health benefits but still purchased benefits for many employees or group members, and that both groups of subscribers adhered to the terms of UIT's policy.[43] The court thus concluded that the many subscribers to UIT established ERISA employee welfare benefit plans.[44]

Following the Eleventh Circuit's decision, other circuits quickly incorporated the *Dillingham* approach and began looking to surrounding circumstances when answering the threshold question of ERISA applicability. However, not all courts have adopted the *Dillingham* approach in determining whether an ERISA plan exists,[45] and some have narrowed it.[46] The Supreme Court of the United States has not yet explicitly approved or rejected the *Dillingham* approach.

Despite the fact that *Dillingham* set a low bar for a finding of an ERISA plan, arrangements have regularly failed to satisfy *Dillingham*. The United States Court of Appeals for the Sixth Circuit did not find a plan in *Hughes v. Zurz* because there were no reasonable, ascertainable benefits or procedures.[47] In *Hughes*, the court applied the *Dillingham* test to determine whether ERISA governed a deferred compensation plan.[48] Both parties agreed that the intended beneficiaries of the plan and the source of funding for the plan were clearly in line with ERISA under *Dillingham*, but the parties disputed whether the intended benefits and the procedures for attaining benefits were ascertainable.[49] The court found that even though evidence supported the existence of an intention to pay an individual a salary and to allow the individual to defer salary payment, a reasonable person could not determine the amount of deferred compensation upon a favorable reading

43. *Id.*
44. *Id.* at 1375.
45. *See*, e.g., Robertson v. Gem Ins. Co., 828 P.2d 496, 502–03 (Utah Ct. App. 1992) (refusing to follow Dillingham and explaining that the "[e]xistence of an employee benefit plan is a question of fact, to be determined by an objective standard, in light of all the pertinent circumstances and purposes sought to be served by ERISA").
46. For example, some courts have refused to accept that oral amendments to existing agreements fall within ERISA's scope. See Anderson v. Resolution Trust Corp., 66 F.3d 956 (11th Cir. 1995).
47. Hughes v. Zurz, 298 F.App'x 404, 412–16. (6th Cir. 2008).
48. *Id.* at 411–12.
49. *Id.*

of the facts.[50] Thus, the benefits were not ascertainable.[51] Regarding the procedures, the court observed that a specific claims procedure need not be set out in writing and that courts have recognized a reasonably ascertainable claims procedure where prior requests for benefits had been awarded as the result of presenting claims to a plan administrator.[52] However, no ascertainable procedure for attaining benefits existed in *Hughes* because there were no clear specifications of the amount of deferred compensation, no indication of when the deferment would end, and no cognizable sign of how the benefits should be received.[53]

Ongoing Administration

In addition to the *Dillingham* factors, there must be an ongoing administrative process. The Supreme Court in *Fort Halifax Packing Co., Inc. v. Coyne* explained the parameters of this scheme. *Fort Halifax* concerned a state statute in Maine potentially requiring an employer to give severance pay to employees after laying them off from a poultry plant.[54] Specifically, the statute stated that "any employer that terminates operations at a plant with 100 or more employees, or relocates those operations more than 100 miles away, must provide one week's pay for each year of employment to all employees who had worked in the plant at least three years" unless the employee accepted work at the new location.[55] The Court considered whether ERISA preempted this statute.[56]

The Court affirmed the lower court's finding that ERISA did not preempt the Maine law, reasoning that ERISA's plain language, the underlying purpose of ERISA preemption, and the overall objectives of ERISA foreclosed

50. *Id.* at 412–13.
51. *Id.* at 413.
52. *Id.* at 414–15 (citing Deibler v. UFCW, 973 F.2d 206, 210 (3d Cir. 1992); Whitfield v. Torch Oper. Co., 935 F. Supp. 822, 828 (E.D. La. 1996)).
53. *Id.*
54. Fort Halifax Packing Co., Inc. v. Coyne, 482 U.S. 1, 5 (1987).
55. *Id.*
56. *Id.* at 6. Importantly, the Court also addressed whether the National Labor Relations Act preempted the Maine statute, but this aspect of the Court's analysis is outside the scope of this chapter.

the argument that ERISA regulates any ERISA benefit and therefore preempted the statute at issue.[57] Vital to the Court's analysis was the use of the term "plan" in ERISA's preemption provision, which preempts state laws that "relate to any employee benefit plan."[58] The Court found that the Maine statute did not create an impediment to the uniformity of benefit administration, nor did it force employers to integrate "a state-mandated benefit plan" into its existing plan or to create a separate plan to process or pay benefits required by the State of Maine.[59] Finally, the Maine statute did not create a "plan" within the purview of the regulatory concerns leading to the passage of ERISA, including that a plan be operated in the interest of its beneficiaries, because the single payment of a severance amount did not involve an administrative activity that employers could abuse.[60]

With respect to the issue of "ongoing administration," a deferred compensation arrangement established by a credit union required ongoing administration where the administrator was required to periodically update the reserve fund that related to the compensation agreement.[61] On the other hand, an employment agreement with a deferred compensation arrangement was not considered an ERISA plan because of the limited ongoing administration.[62]

In determining whether there was ongoing administration, some courts emphasize the quality of the administration and examine the level of discretion utilized. Administrator discretion does not overcome the need for ongoing administration, but it does greatly inform courts' determinations about the existence of ongoing administration. In *Donovan v. Branch Banking & Trust Company*, the plan administrator's discretion to decide whether

57. *Id.* at 7.

58. *Id.* at 8 (citing 29 U.S.C. § 1144(a)).

59. *Id.* at 14. In reaching this point, the Court distinguished the Maine statute from a preempted Hawaii law that had required employers to provide a comprehensive health-care plan to employees that did not comply with an employer's existing ERISA plan and that would have left open the possibility that other states could impose additional requirements if left intact. *Id.* at 12 (citing Standard Oil Co. of Cal. v. Agsalud, 633 F.2d 760 (9th Cir. 1980), *aff'd*, 454 U.S. 801 (1981)).

60. *Id.* at 16.

61. Kirkindoll v. Nat'l Credit Union Administration Bd., No. 3:11-CV-1921-D, 2013 U.S. Dist. LEXIS 165197 (N.D. Tex. Nov. 20, 2013).

62. Cantrell v. Briggs & Veselka Co., 728 F.3d 444, 452 (5th Cir. 2013), *cert. denied*, No. 13-824, 2014 WL 126061 (U.S. Mar. 10, 2014).

employees were eligible for benefits did not constitute ongoing administration and did not support a finding that ERISA governed the plan.[63] *Donovan* concerned a severance agreement in anticipation of a corporate acquisition that required the plan's administrator to determine whether an employee had committed an act giving rise to termination for "good cause."[64] The United States District Court for the Southern District of West Virginia found that this requirement did not constitute the degree of administrative discretion to bring the plan under ERISA.[65] The *Donovan* court found that the ability to terminate employment "for cause" did not constitute the level of discretion required of an ongoing administrative scheme.[66] The plan administrator's sole discretion to decide whether an employee resigned for good reason also did not bring the severance agreement under ERISA, even in conjunction with the "for cause" requirement, because the agreement thoroughly defined what could constitute good reason.[67]

In *Lettes v. Kinam Gold, Inc.*, the Tenth Circuit considered the critical features of an ERISA plan to include "whether the plan pays benefits triggered by several events, as opposed to a one-time event, and whether it requires regular periodic payments."[68] The *Lettes* court found that it was not enough for the lower court to focus on the discretionary application of a plan's terms because doing so did not adequately consider whether the plan was sufficiently "ongoing" to implicate ERISA.[69] Thus, even though the golden parachute agreement at issue in *Lettes* gave the plan administrator discretion over various aspects of the plan, it was not governed by ERISA in light of its narrow time period and dependence on a single triggering event that might never happen.[70]

63. Donovan v. Branch Banking & Trust Co., 220 F. Supp. 2d 560, 562 (S.D. W. Va. 2002).
64. *Id.* at 566.
65. *Id.*
66. *Id.* at 566–67.
67. *Id.* at 567.
68. Lettes v. Kinam Gold, Inc., 3 F.App'x 783, 786 (10th Cir. 2001).
69. *Id.* at 788.
70. *Id.* The district court had found that the plan gave the administrator significant discretion in giving the administration complete discretionary authority to construe and interpret it, correct defects, supply omissions, reconcile inconsistencies and ambiguities, and decide whether a change of control had occurred, eligible employees were entitled to benefits, eligible employees had been offered comparable employment, and eligible employees had performed their jobs satisfactorily and otherwise abided by the terms of the agreement. *Id.* at 786–87.

In contrast, Third Circuit cases have often emphasized plan administrators' discretion when determining if an ERISA plan exists. In *Darlin v. Consolidated Rail Corporation*, the United States District Court for the Eastern District of Pennsylvania relied on other Third Circuit decisions focusing on discretion when determining if an ERISA plan existed.[71] *Darlin* involved an employer's promise of a pension benefit either in the form of a lump sum or an annuity to employees who were terminated without cause.[72] The court invoked *Pane v. RCA Corporation*, in which the United States Court of Appeals for the Third Circuit upheld a district court's finding that ERISA governed a plan requiring its administrator to determine if an employee was terminated other than for cause. As the district court in *Pane* noted, "each employee's termination must be analyzed in light of [particular] criteria."[73] In contrast, the *Darlin* court explained that, in *Middleton v. Philadelphia Electric Company*, the United States District Court for the Eastern District of Pennsylvania had found that a severance plan requiring an administrator to apply objective criteria and calculate benefits based on a simple formula was outside ERISA.[74] The court found the plan in *Darlin* to involve the use of an administrator's subjective discretion, and the court therefore held that ERISA applied.[75]

The Seventh Circuit has similarly emphasized discretion. In *Collins v. Ralston Purina Company*, the United States Court of Appeals for the Seventh Circuit found that ERISA governed employee retention contracts in which the employer agreed to pay six months of salary and a year of COBRA benefits when the employer terminated or substantially reduced the duties of the employee.[76] The Seventh Circuit distinguished the agreements from the statute obligating employers to make a single, lump-sum payment at issue in *Fort Halifax* on the basis that the employer faced obligations to numerous employees under individual agreements of varying amounts and

71. Darlin v. Consol. Rail Corp., 93 F. Supp. 2d 599, 600–02 (E.D. Pa. 2000).
72. *Id.* at 600.
73. *Id.* at 601 (quoting Pane v. RCA Corp., 667 F. Supp. 168, 171 (D. N.J. 1987), *aff'd*, 868 F.2d 631 (3d Cir. 1989)).
74. *Id.* (citing Middleton v. Philadelphia Elec. Co., 850 F. Supp. 348, 353 (3d Cir. 1994)).
75. *Id.* at 601.
76. Collins v. Ralston Purina Co., 147 F.3d 592, 594, 597 (7th Cir. 1998).

at different times.[77] The court also emphasized the long-term possibility of employer obligations under the agreements as an indication of an ongoing administrative scheme.[78] However, the court devoted most of its analysis to the discretionary aspects of the agreements. The court did not find "substantially reduced" responsibilities to be an "easily discernible" standard, remarking to the contrary, that it resulted in an administrative scheme that must compare current and prior responsibilities and decide if the difference was "substantial reduction."[79] Careful record keeping of who received benefits and why those benefits were received could lead to a working definition of "substantially reduced," but this sort of ongoing administrative scheme was precisely what the court found to saliently distinguish the agreements from the statute in *Fort Halifax*.[80]

In the absence of clear guidance from a higher court, district courts in the Fourth Circuit have adopted factors from other circuits to consider when determining whether an ERISA plan exists under the ongoing administration requirement. The United States District Court for the Middle District of North Carolina listed other circuits' and its own generally accepted factors as follows:

> (1) the amount of managerial discretion granted in paying the benefits and whether a case-by-case review of employees is needed; (2) whether payments are triggered by a single, unique event in the course of business or on a recurring basis; (3) whether the employer must make a one-time, lump-sum payment or continuous, periodic payments; and (4) whether the employer undertook any long-term obligations with respect to the payments.[81]

77. *Id.* at 595–96.
78. *Id.* at 597.
79. *Id.* at 596.
80. *Id.*
81. Mullaly v. Ins. Servs. Office, Inc., 396 F. Supp. 2d 290, 295 (M.D. N.C. 2005) (citing Emery v. Bay Capitol Corp., 354 F. Supp. 2d 589, 594 (D. Md. 2005); Blair v. Young Phillips Corp., 158 F. Supp. 2d 654, 659 n.3 (M.D. N.C. 2001); Donovan v. Branch Banking & Trust Co., 220 F. Supp. 2d 560, 564–65 (S.D. W. Va. 2002)).

The Court's decision in *Fort Halifax* clarified the reach of ERISA by requiring an ongoing administrative scheme, but, as the lower courts' decisions have made clear, the Court did so without providing a bright-line rule. After *Fort Halifax*, lower courts have focused on whether narrow benefit arrangements fall short of an ongoing administrative scheme.

Vouchers as ERISA Plans

In *Musmeci v. Schwegmann Giant Super Markets, Inc.*, the United States Court of Appeals for the Fifth Circuit held that an employer's grocery voucher plan for employees constituted a pension plan, entitling participants to monetary relief under ERISA.[82] Each month beginning in 1985, Schwegman Giant Super Markets, Inc. (SGSM) offered $216 in food vouchers to retired employees who had completed 20 years of service, attained the age of 60, and were employed as supervisors for at least one year at retirement.[83] SGSM did not have a written procedure for its voucher plan but nonetheless carried out a systematic administration of the plan involving documentation from SGSM's human resources department and top-level decisions about plan implementation and retiree qualification.[84] SGSM sold its business in 1997 and, a week before the sale, informed its qualified retirees that the distribution of vouchers would be discontinued.[85] Former employees who were adversely affected by the cessation of the voucher plan brought suit under ERISA and Louisiana law, although the trial court dismissed the state law claims upon finding that the voucher plan was a pension plan necessitating relief under ERISA.[86]

While the *Musmeci* decision has been both widely praised and criticized, at its core, it stands for the surviving principle that the precise nature of benefits is frequently not dispositive when ascertaining whether or not an ERISA plan exists.

---

82. Musmeci v. Schwegmann Giant Super Markets, Inc., 332 F.3d 339, 355–56 (5th Cir. 2003).
83. *Id.* at 342.
84. *Id.* at 343.
85. *Id.*
86. *Id.* at 343–44.

Stock Options

The United States Court of Appeals for the Third Circuit reached a different conclusion from the *Musmeci* case when it examined stock option plans in *Oatway v. American International Group, Inc.*[87] In *Oatway*, the court found that discretionary stock options given in recognition of special service and awarded in addition to ordinary service did not constitute a pension plan and were therefore not governed by ERISA.[88] Although the issue of the status of incentive stock options plan was novel for the Third Circuit, most courts had already held that an incentive stock option plan was not an ERISA plan.[89]

Single Employee Contracts

Single employee contracts are executed with a single employee concerning future payments.[90] The United States Court of Appeals for the Eleventh Circuit found an ongoing administrative scheme in *Williams v. Wright.*[91] At issue in *Wright* was whether an ERISA plan arose from a letter promising to provide an employee with a vehicle, pay the employee $500 each month, and cover the employee's gasoline expenses, country club membership, and his and his spouse's medical and life insurance premiums.[92] In distinguishing the case from *Fort Halifax*, the Eleventh Circuit held that the agreement to issue checks monthly as well as a note in the letter stating that revisions to the arrangement would be considered at a later date constituted an ongoing administrative scheme.[93] The court also found that the agreement satisfied the requirement of ascertainable procedures required under the *Dillingham* approach, and ERISA therefore governed the benefits contract.[94]

87. 325 F.3d 184 (3d Cir. 2003).
88. *Id.* at 189.
89. *Id.* at 187.
90. Nagy v. Riblet Products Corp., 79 F.3d 572 (7th Cir. 1996).
91. Williams v. Wright, 927 F.2d 1540, 1545 (11th Cir. 1991).
92. *Id.* at 1542 n.3.
93. *Id.* at 1545.
94. *Id.*

Severance Agreements

Determining whether an arrangement is an ERISA plan is most commonly disputed in relation to severance agreements,[95] to which courts have applied *Fort Halifax* in a variety of fashions. For example, a recent United States District Court case in Puerto Rico, *Gautier-Figueroa v. Bristol-Myers Squibb Puerto Rico, Inc.*, concerned a severance agreement promising benefits to be paid at regular payroll intervals until completion of benefit payments unless the former employee found new employment, at which point the remaining severance benefits would be paid in one lump sum.[96] *Gautier-Figueroa* relied on a trilogy of cases informing the First Circuit's approach to interpreting *Fort Halifax*, ultimately concluding that the severance agreement fell outside ERISA.[97]

The *Gautier-Figueroa* court first turned to *Fort Halifax* for guidance, emphasizing the one-off nature of that case's plan, and then to *Simas v. Quaker Fabric Corporation of Fall River*.[98] In *Simas*, the United States Court of Appeals for the First Circuit affirmed a lower court's finding that ERISA preempted a Massachusetts "tin parachute" statute requiring severance payments when employees lost their jobs within a period prior to or following a corporate takeover.[99] The court observed that the Massachusetts statute was similar to the Maine statute at issue in *Fort Halifax* to the extent that both called for payments to employees based on a specific event.[100] However, the court identified differences between the statutes that demonstrated the administrative burden imposed by the Massachusetts statute and that supported the finding that the Massachusetts statute's requirements created an ongoing administrative scheme.[101] The court explained that "[i]t is a matter of degrees but under *Fort Halifax* degrees are crucial."[102] The court noted that, unlike the plant closure resulting in a one-time payment in *Fort*

95. "Severance agreements" cover employer payments to involuntarily terminated employees. Gautier-Figueroa v. Bristol-Meyers Squibb P.R., Inc., 845 F. Supp. 2d 444, 452 (D. P.R. 2012).
96. *Id.* at 448.
97. *Id.* at 447, 453–55.
98. *Id.* at 453.
99. Simas v. Quaker Fabric Corp. of Fall River, 6 F.3d 849, 851 (1st Cir. 1993).
100. *Id.* at 853.
101. *Id.*
102. *Id.*

Halifax, the Massachusetts statute resulted in a payment scheme for each employee based on that individual's termination and within one of several time periods before or after the takeover.[103] The Massachusetts statute also raised new requirements for employees relating to whether the individual would qualify for unemployment compensation, including that they not have been discharged for cause.[104] The court explained that the reasoning in *Fort Halifax* did not create certainty as to where the Supreme Court would draw the line but that other circuits "read *Fort Halifax* as emphasizing the mechanical, one-time nature of the severance payments, . . . applied the decision to protect schemes akin to the Maine statute, and . . . ceased to apply the decision where the state statute or employer promise involved ongoing obligations materially beyond those present in *Fort Halifax*."[105]

As the *Gautier-Figueroa* court next discussed,[106] two years after deciding *Simas*, the United States Court of Appeals for the First Circuit took up *Belanger v. Wyman-Gordon Co.* and found, in applying *Fort Halifax* to *Belanger*, that four early retirement offers spanning a four-year period did not constitute an ERISA plan.[107] Former employees brought suit in *Belanger* after they had accepted a third offer for early retirement and the employer subsequently made a better fourth offer to the remaining employees.[108] In determining whether ERISA applied, the court explained: "*Fort Halifax* is the beacon by which we must steer"—the upshot of which being that "the existence of a plan turns on the nature and extent of an employer's benefit obligations."[109] Of the many factors at play in determining if a plan existed, one very important one the court identified was whether a reasonable employee would expect a continuing commitment by the employer to provide benefits where the employer expressed an intent to provide benefits on a regular or long-term basis.[110] The court found that the individual

103. *Id.*
104. *Id.*
105. *Id.* at 853–54.
106. Gautier-Figueroa v. Bristol-Myers Squibb P.R., Inc., 845 F. Supp. 2d 444, 453 (D. P.R. 2012).
107. Belanger v. Wyman-Gordon Co., 71 F.3d 451, 452 (1st Cir. 1995).
108. *Id.* at 453.
109. *Id.* at 454.
110. *Id.* at 454–55 (citing Henglein v. Informal Plan for Plant Shutdown Benefits for Salaried Employees, 974 F.2d 391, 400 (3d Cir. 1992); Donovan v. Dillingham, 688 F.2d 1367,

retirement offers standing alone constituted the sort of one-time, lump-sum payment that the Court excluded from ERISA in *Fort Halifax*.[111] The sequence of offers also did not create an ERISA plan, the employer never represented the offers as being linked, and the offers did not create continuing obligations.[112]

Finally, the *Gautier-Figueroa* court turned to *O'Connor v. Commonwealth Gas Company* for guidance.[113] In *O'Connor*, the United States Court of Appeals for the First Circuit found that an early retirement incentive plan was similar to a lump-sum severance package and therefore was not governed by ERISA.[114] Upon reviewing *Fort Halifax*, the court emphasized that the degree of employer discretion in administering a plan is most frequently the determinative factor in deciding what constitutes an ERISA plan.[115] The severance package at issue in *O'Connor* offered a severance bonus in the form of a one-time payment calculated based on tenure in addition to up to $5,000 in educational assistance, a pension credit allowing employees to collect their other pension benefits sooner, and one year of payments of employees' COBRA premiums.[116] The court characterized the latter three benefits as being afterthoughts to the severance bonus.[117] Because the severance provision constituted the sort of one-time lump sum outside the purview of ERISA, the court held that the early retirement incentive plan was not governed by ERISA even though the other provisions, such as the COBRA payments, might implicate ERISA.[118] Addressing a separate argument, the court found that inconsistent indicators of the employer's intention to establish an ERISA plan did not outweigh the non-ERISA aspects of the plan even though an employer's less ambiguous intention had previously

1373 (11th Cir. 1982)).
111. *Id.* at 455–56.
112. *Id.* The sequence of offers did not constitute an ERISA plan because the administration of the offers did not require a special mechanism or require nonmechanical decision making.
113. Gautier-Figueroa v. Bristol-Myers Squibb P.R., Inc., 845 F. Supp. 2d 444, 454 (D. P.R. 2012).
114. O'Connor v. Commonwealth Gas Co., 251 F.3d 262, 264 (1st Cir. 2011).
115. *Id.* at 267.
116. *Id.* at 267–70.
117. *Id.* at 269.
118. *Id.* at 267.

factored into the court's finding that ERISA governed a plan in a previous case.[119]

Having reviewed *Simas*, *Belanger*, and *O'Connor*, the *Gautier-Figueroa* court rejected a lower court's finding that the severance plan at issue required an ongoing administration scheme and fell under ERISA as part of a pre-existing severance plan.[120] Relying on *Belanger*, the higher court held that a series of incentives based on years of service did not constitute an ERISA plan because these particular incentives did not require a complicated administrative apparatus to either calculate or distribute them,[121] and a reasonable employee would perceive the promised severance as a singular agreement between the terminated employee and employer.[122] As in *O'Connor*, the severance agreement was offered on a "take-it-or-leave-it" basis without the need for an ongoing administrative scheme and without leaving the employer room for subjective judgment once the employee had signed it.[123] Unlike the "tin parachute" statute in *Simas*, the severance agreement did not require individualized determinations of employee obligations but rather "an initial clerical determination devoid of any discretion."[124]

---

119. *Id.* at 272 (citing Wickman v. Nw. Nat'l Ins. Co., 908 F.2d 1077, 1083 (1st Cir. 1990)).

120. Gautier-Figueroa v. Bristol-Myers Squibb P.R., Inc., 845 F. Supp. 2d 444, 455 (D. P.R. 2012) (citing Gautier-Figueroa v. Bristol-Myers Squibb P.R., Inc., 792 F. Supp. 2d 240, 244–45 (D. P.R. 2011)).

121. *Id.* at 457 (citing Belanger v. Wyman-Gordon Co., 71 F.3d 451, 455 (1st Cir. 1995)).

122. *Id.* at 461–62 (citing Belanger, 71 F.3d at 455). The circumstances that the court found determinative in its assessment of what a reasonable employee would perceive included the lack of a provision of anything summarizing benefits under ERISA or any retirement plan, the notice of termination made no reference to any administrative process of the existing severance plan, and a general release accompanying the termination notice provided that the laws of Puerto Rico would govern the agreement and not ERISA, which was the only time ERISA was mentioned in the agreement. *Id.* at 462.

123. *Id.* at 458–59 (citing O'Connor v. Commonwealth Gas Co., 251 F.3d 262, 266–67, 269 (1st Cir. 2011)). The court also found that, as in *O'Connor*, even though the severance plan offered other benefits such as a health-care plan, these benefits were peripheral and did not impose a burden on the employer's administrative integrity. *Id.* at 463–64 (citing *O'Connor*, 251 F.3d at 270). The court noted that other circuits had reached the same conclusion when confronted with plans that temporarily extended health-care benefits. *Id.* (citing Angst v. Mack Trucks, Inc., 969 F.2d 1530, 1539 (3d Cir. 1992); Stokes v. Local 116 of Intern. Union of Electronic, Elec., Salaried, Mach. and Furniture Workers, Civ. A. No 92-3131, 1993 WL 23895, at *8 (E.D. Pa. Feb. 2, 1993)).

124. *Id.* at 460 (citing Simas v. Quaker Fabric Corp. of Fall River, 6 F.3d 849, 853–54 (1st Cir. 1993)).

Multibenefit Plans

When one specific benefit out of many is at issue in a case, parties may argue that the benefit is separate from the other benefits comprising an ERISA plan. Though plans clearly possess some points of separation,[125] arguments that benefits belong to separate plans frequently fail. The Supreme Court weighed in on this issue in *Shaw v. Delta Air Lines, Inc. Shaw*. The Court decided that multibenefit plans conceivably containing both an ERISA plan and a non-ERISA plan could not be considered outside ERISA.[126] The Court reasoned that applying aspects of state regulations to one part of a plan and federal regulations to others would be inefficient and cause administrative impracticality.[127]

The federal circuits have held that certain aspects of an employee benefit plan cannot be "severed" and have generally considered benefit programs as a whole.[128] An example of a case involving a multibenefit package plan from the United States Court of Appeals for the First Circuit, *Gross v. Sun Life Assurance Company of Canada*, concerned long-term disability coverage.[129] The defendant unsuccessfully urged the court to divorce this part of the plan from the larger benefits plan for the purpose of determining ERISA applicability.[130] Important to the *Gross* court was that the different aspects of the plan had been consistently treated as a unit by plan administrators and in communications to employees despite these aspects' different contribution requirements.[131]

---

125. *See* Chiles v. Ceridian Corp., 95 F.3d 1505 (10th Cir. 1996) (finding separate plans when each had a different ERISA identification number and did not share the same trust or trust administrator and when the plans' language clearly represented the company's intent to form different plans).
126. Shaw v. Delta Air Lines, Inc., 463 U.S. 85, 107 (1983).
127. *Id.* at 107–08.
128. *See* Boos v. AT&T, Inc., 643 F.3d 127 (5th Cir. 2011); Loren v. Blue Cross & Blue Shield of Mich., 505 F.3d 598 (6th Cir. 2007); Postma v. Paul Revere Life Ins. Co., 223 F.3d 533 (7th Cir. 2000); Gaylor v. John Hancock Mut. Life Ins. Co., 112 F.3d 460 (10th Cir. 1997).
129. Gross v. Sun Life Assurance Co. of Can., No. 12-1175, 2013 WL 4305006, at *5 (1st Cir. Aug. 16, 2013).
130. *Id.*
131. *Id.*

Life Insurance Policies

The United States District Court of the Eastern District of California decided in *Cox v. Reliance Standard Life Insurance Company* that a life insurance policy was an ERISA plan because it met all of the *Dillingham* factors.[132] As with *Gross*, the *Cox* court refused to sever benefits.[133] ERISA generally applies to life insurance plans unless ERISA is supplanted by a safe harbor. The safe harbor applies if the employer, without consideration, makes no contribution to the plan beyond deducting premiums from payroll and serves only as a conduit for a life insurer to publicize its plan to employees, for whom participation is completely voluntary.[134]

132. Cox v. Reliance Standard Life Insurance Co., No. 1:13-CV-00104AWIJLT, 2013 WL 2156546, at *7 (E.D. Cal. May 17, 2013).
133. *Id.*
134. *See* Glass v. United of Omaha Life Ins. Co., 33 F.3d 1341 (11th Cir. 1994).

Chapter 2

Classifying Parties to an ERISA Plan

ERISA's definition of an employee benefit plan requires the presence of "employers and employees." Therefore, an additional step when determining whether ERISA governs a plan is classifying the parties. Similar to the larger issue of whether an ERISA plan exists, a party's classification is strategically important for litigation. A party to a transaction may resist classification as an employee or independent contractor depending on the circumstances. An employee enjoys the substantive protections of ERISA, which includes vesting of benefits. On the other hand, when state legal protections are favorable, claimants may seek classification as an independent contractor in order to place the action outside ERISA's preemption and make state-law remedies available.

The Supreme Court has considered with some frequency the meaning of an "employee" within different statutory schemes.[1] In *Nationwide Mutual Insurance Company v. Darden*, the Court was called on to do so in the context of ERISA. The controversy in *Darden* was whether the benefits that Nationwide Mutual Insurance Company and others promised to a contractor, Robert Darden, vested under the terms of ERISA.[2] Darden had brought an action concerning the benefits pursuant to ERISA's enforcement provision, but the provision only applies to a "participant" of an ERISA plan, which ERISA defines as "any employee or former employee of an employer . . . who is or may become eligible to receive a benefit of

1. *See, e.g.*, Cmty. for Creative Non-Violence v. Reid, 490 U.S. 730 (1989) (applying the common law to determine the meaning of "employee" within the Copyright Act of 1976).
2. Nationwide Mut. Ins. Co. v. Darden, 503 U.S. 318, 320 (1992).

any type from an employee benefit plan."[3] Thus, Darden could only bring an ERISA claim if he qualified as an employee under ERISA, which defines an employee as "any individual employed by an employer."[4] As the Court explained, this definition "is completely circular and explains nothing" and at no other point does ERISA give clear guidance on the term's meaning.[5]

The Court applied a common-law test to define "employee" within ERISA, construing "employee" to incorporate the general features of the law of agency.[6] This test considers with equal weight "the hiring party's right to control the manner and means by which the product is accomplished, the skills required, the source of instrumentalities, the location of the work, the duration of the relationship, whether the hiring party has the right to assign additional projects to the hired party, the extent of the hired party's discretion over when and how long to work, the payment method, the hired party's role in hiring and paying assistants, whether the work is part of the hiring party's regular business, whether the hiring party is in business, the provision of benefits, and the hired party's tax treatment."[7] That is, the test is not a shorthand formula but instead requires an inspection of all incidents of the relationship.[8] After setting forth the proper test to determine whether Darden qualified as an employee, the Court remanded the case to the United States Court of Appeals for the Fourth Circuit for further proceedings.[9] The Fourth Circuit again remanded the case to the district court for the purpose of determining if Darden was an employee under the Court's common-law test.[10]

The ambiguity in the Court's approach to defining employee has been widely criticized, often in light of the potential it creates for the misclassification of independent contractors.[11] Interestingly, the common-law rule

3. *Id.* at 320–21 (citing 29 U.S.C. § 1002(7)).
4. *Id.* at 321 (citing 29 U.S.C. § 1002(6)).
5. *Id.* at 323.
6. *Id.* at 323 n.3 (citing Cmty. for Creative Non-Violence v. Reid, 490 U.S. 730, 740 (1989)).
7. *Id.* at 323–24 (citing *Reid*, 490 U.S. at 751–52 (citations omitted)).
8. *Id.* at 324 (citing NLRB v. United Ins. Co. of Am., 390 U.S. 254, 258 (1968)).
9. *Id.* at 328.
10. Darden v. Nationwide Mut. Ins. Co., 969 F.2d 76 (4th Cir. 1992).
11. *See, e.g.*, Richard R. Carlson, *Why the Law Still Can't Tell an Employee When It Sees One and How It Ought to Stop Trying*, 22 BERKLEY J. EMP. & LAB. L. 295, 360 (2001) (citing Vizcaino v. Microsoft Corp., 120 F.3d 1006, 1011 (9th Cir. 1997)) (asserting that any attempt

invoked by the Court in *Darden* evolved from an older right-to-control test, which more simply evaluated the actual power of a principal to control the physical aspects of an employee's work.[12] In the 1989 case, *Community for Creative Non-Violence v. Reid*, the Supreme Court explained that to discern whether a hiree was an employee, it would look to the hiring party's right to control the method and means of accomplishing the task.[13] The factors it noted as relevant to this inquiry were, among others, the required skills, the source of the instrumentalities and tools, the location of the work, the duration of the parties' relationship, the extent of the hired party's discretion over when and how long to work, the payment method, the hired party's role in hiring and compensating assistants, whether the work was part of the hiring party's regular business, whether the hiring party was in business, employee benefits, and the hired party's tax treatment.[14]

In its most recent tentative draft, the *Restatement (Third) of Employment Law* recommends a greatly abridged approach: an employee is one who serves the interests of the employer after the employer agrees to accept the individual's services and the employer precludes the individual from rendering services as part of an independent business.[15] According to the *Restatement*, an individual renders services as an independent trade or business when such an individual exercises business judgment and control over the manner and mechanism of services and has control over important decisions like hiring, equipment inventory, and whether and when to service other customers.[16]

Courts have treated the *Darden* factors with flexibility. In *Ernster v. Luxco, Inc.*, the United Court of Appeals for the Eighth Circuit applied *Darden* to a claim brought under the Age Discrimination in Employment Act and the Iowa Civil Rights Act because both define "employee in the same circular fashion."[17] The *Ernster* court held that a jury instruction need not

---

by an employer to skirt ERISA by utilizing independent contractors may become increasingly problematic the longer the duration of the business relationship).

12. *See generally* Singer Mfg. Co. v. Rahn, 132 U.S. 518 (1889).
13. Cmty. for Creative Non-Violence v. Reid, 490 U.S. 730, 751 (1989).
14. *Id.* at 751–52.
15. RESTATEMENT (THIRD) OF EMPLOYMENT LAW § 1.01 TD No. 2 (2009).
16. *Id.*
17. Ernster v. Luxco, Inc., 596 F.3d 1000, 1004 (8th Cir. 2010) (citing 29 U.S.C. § 630(f); 29 U.S.C. § 1002(6); IOWA CODE ANN. § 216.2(6)).

quote all the *Darden* factors straight from the Supreme Court's decision and may also list other factors relevant to determinations of employee status.[18] Recently, the United States District Court for the Northern District of Ohio, *Jammal v. American Family Insurance*, mirrored the *Ernster* approach in finding that "[t]he *Darden* factors must be weighed . . . in combination with all of the other nuances of the relationship between the parties in order to determine whether an employee/employer relationship exists."[19]

Current and Former Employees as Participants

The Supreme Court stated in *Firestone Tire and Rubber Company v. Bruch* that an individual qualifies as a participant when he or she is an employee currently in or reasonably expected to be in covered employment, or if he or she is a former employee reasonably expecting to return to covered employment or who has a colorable claim to vested benefits.[20] A showing that an individual will become eligible for benefits rests on a claimant being able to make a colorable claim that he or she will prevail in a suit for benefits or that eligibility requirements will be fulfilled in the future.[21]

In the 2013 decision *Clayton v. ConocoPhillips Company*, the United States Court of Appeals for the Fifth Circuit dismissed a former employee's argument that the court should not distinctly define "participant" for the purpose of determining ERISA preemption and for the purpose of recovering attorney fees based on a plan's provision for such fees.[22] While attorney fees can be available whenever ERISA governs an action,[23] the plan in *Clayton* provided an additional avenue for such an award.[24] The plan provided

18. *Id.* at 1005.
19. Jammal v. Am. Family Ins., No. 1:13-CV-437, 2013 WL 4049673, at *5 (N.D. Ohio Aug. 9, 2013). The court further remarked that it is not enough to label a worker an "independent contractor." *Id.*
20. Firestone Tire and Rubber Co. v. Bruch, 489 U.S. 101, 117 (1989) (citing Kuntz v. Reese, 785 F.2d 1410, 1411 (9th Cir. 1986); Saladino v. I.L.G.W.U. Nat'l Retirement Fund, 754 F.2d 473, 476 (9th Cir. 1985)).
21. *Id.*
22. Clayton v. ConocoPhillips Co., 722 F.3d 279, 298 (5th Cir. 2013).
23. *See* 29 U.S.C. § 1132(g)(1) (2013).
24. *Clayton*, 722 F.3d at 288.

for the recovery of attorney fees "incurred by a Participant as they become due" or incurred "as a result of the Participant seeking to obtain or enforce any right or benefit provided by this Plan."[25] In denying Clayton's argument that he should qualify for attorney fees, the lower court had explained:

> The definition of Participant for purposes of ERISA jurisdiction, which includes any former employee with a colorable claim to ERISA benefits, is much broader than the definition of Participant under the Plan, which is restricted to current employees and those employees who terminate their employment under circumstances where they are actually entitled to benefits under the Plan.[26]

Clayton, who had not fit into either of the employee categories in the plan, argued on appeal that distinguishing between the meaning of a "participant" for the purpose of ERISA preemption and for the purpose of recovering attorney fees was nonsensical.[27] He asserted:

> The Plan does not create any benefits for nonparticipants and it does not create any category of persons who could become beneficiaries in the future. Since no benefits are available under the Plan except to those who are "participants" as the Plan defines them, it would be impossible to be a "participant" for ERISA jurisdictional purposes without being a "participant" of the Plan.[28]

The Fifth Circuit flatly rejected Clayton's argument. It reasoned that "if a plan document alone could define 'Participant,' then it would have been redundant for ERISA to have done so as well."[29] The court refused to read out one of ERISA's fundamental provisions.[30] It concluded:

25. *Id.*
26. Clayton v. ConocoPhillips Co., No. H-08-3447, 2012 WL 175419, at *8 (S.D. Tex. 2012).
27. *Clayton*, 722 F.3d at 298.
28. *Id.*
29. *Id.*
30. *Id.*

> In addition, and perhaps more fundamentally, the instant Plan provides a substantive contractual right to recover attorneys' fees, but only for claims brought within the contours of [the provisions for attorney fees]. It would be strange indeed to say that the Plan could create a right to fees but not define the contours of that right.
>
> ERISA, through its civil enforcement mechanism, simply provides a statutory process for vindicating whatever substantive rights a covered plan creates (as well as standards, to ensure that vested benefits are properly safeguarded until those rights are vindicated). Thus, there is nothing at all discordant about Clayton qualifying as a "Participant" for purposes of ERISA preemption but not qualifying as a "Participant" for purposes of recovering attorneys' fees under the Plan.[31]

Physicians as ERISA Employees

In *Alexander v. Avera St. Luke's Hospital*, the United States District Court for the District of South Dakota highlighted the special need for flexibility when applying the *Darden* factors in the physician context. *Alexander* concerned whether a physician, Dr. Alexander, qualified as an employee of Avera St. Luke's Hospital, which he contended had terminated his employment in violation of the Americans with Disabilities Act, the Age Discrimination in Employment Act, the South Dakota Human Relations Act, and the Family and Medical Leave Act.[32] Acknowledging the issue of the hiring party's control over performance as a primary consideration,[33] the court explained that this factor is less useful in determining whether a physician is an employee because, even when the physician is an independent contractor, a hospital must assert some degree of control to carry out its responsibilities to its patients.[34] The court further noted that it gave little weight to the amount of skill required in a medical setting because other hospital physicians were

---

31. *Id.*
32. Alexander v. Avera St. Luke's Hosp., No. 12-1012, 2013 WL 3341051, at *1 (D.S.D. July 2, 2013).
33. *Id.* at *3 (citing Kramer v. Cash Link Sys., 715 F.3d 1082, 1088 (8th Cir. 2013)).
34. *Id.* (citing Glascock v. Linn County Emergency Med., PC, 698 F.3d 695, 698 (8th Cir. 2012)).

also highly skilled, the source of instrumentalities was irrelevant because the hospital provided instruments and tools to all staff, and the location of the work was also irrelevant because all staff worked within the hospital.[35] The factors the court deemed relevant were the length of the relationship between the parties, the right to add projects to the hired party's work load, the hired party's discretion over work-related matters like the duration of work hours, the method of payment, the hired party's role in hiring and paying assistants, the provision of employee benefits, the tax treatment of the hiree by the hiring party, and the method of conflict resolution.[36] The court concluded:

> Applying the relevant *Darden* factors to the undisputed material facts, Dr. Alexander was an independent contractor for Avera. The relevant factors that influenced this finding created a distinction in treatment between employees and independent contractors within the hospital. The tax treatment, benefits, right to assign additional projects, role in hiring assistants, method of payment, and discretion over how long to work were given substantial weight in this conclusion. Both parties were given sufficient information and knowledge of the relationship, and each party was consistent in treating the relationship as an independent contractor relationship. I cannot imagine a clearer case of "course of dealing." To quote an old saying, actions speak louder than words. The undisputed material facts show that Dr. Alexander was an independent contractor and Avera is entitled to summary judgment as a matter of law. No reasonable jury could find that the relationship was that of employer-employee.[37]

Insurance Agents

Controversy over employee status under ERISA commonly arises when insurance agents are parties to a dispute. Taking the multifactorial approach

35. *Id.* at *3–4.
36. *Id.* at *4–8.
37. *Id.* at *8.

to determining employee status, courts have repeatedly found that insurance agents are independent contractors.[38] In *Arnold v. Mutual of Omaha Insurance Company*, the Court of Appeal for California recently upheld a lower court's classification of a nonexclusive insurance agent as an independent contractor because the agent used her own judgment in determining which individuals to solicit and the manner and duration of the solicitation, the agent did not work for the hiring party exclusively, the agent was not subject to evaluation or supervision, training offered by the hiring party was optional beyond what state law required, a fee for workspace and telephone service was assessed, and the minimal performance required to avoid termination was to submit one application for the hiring party's products within 180-day periods.[39] In short, the hiring party had no significant right to control the manner and means of accomplishing the service.[40] However, the United States District Court for the Northern District of Ohio observed in *Jammal v. American Family Insurance* that the defendants had not presented law suggesting that a commissioned insurance agent could never be an employee.[41] Thus, the *Darden* approach must be taken even when the hired party is an insurance agent, and perhaps a certain combination of factors will one day tip the scales toward employee status of such agents.[42]

Company Employers and Partners as Employees

There are clearer rules concerning whether employers and partners may qualify as employees within the scope of ERISA. The Department of Labor has issued regulations stating that an employer and his or her spouse are not employees with respect to a business he or she owns, and neither a partner nor a partner's spouse may be an employee with respect to his or

38. *See, e.g.*, Weary v. Cochran, 377 F.3d 522 (6th Cir. 2004); Oestman v. Nat'l Farmers Union Ins., 958 F.2d 303 (10th Cir. 1992); Lozon v. Comm'r, 73 T.C.M. (CCH) 2914 (1997); Butts v. Comm'r, 66 T.C.M. (CCH) 1041 (1993), *aff'd*, 49 F.3d 713 (11th Cir. 1995).
39. Arnold v. Mut. of Omaha Ins. Co., 135 Cal. Rptr. 3d 213, 220 (Cal. Ct. App. 2011).
40. *Id.*
41. Jammal v. Am. Family Ins., No. 1:13-CV-437, 2013 WL 4049673, at *5 (N.D. Ohio Aug. 9, 2013).
42. *Id.*

her partnership.[43] These regulations prevent partners, employers, and their spouses from being counted as employees but only in determinations of whether an ERISA plan exists.[44] In *Yates v. Hendon*, the Supreme Court held that the sole shareholder, working owner, and president of a corporation could qualify as an ERISA pension plan participant as long as the plan covered employees in addition to himself and his wife.[45]

ERISA Employers and Employee Organizations

ERISA provides strong guidance on the meanings of employer and employee organization. Employer refers to "any person acting directly as an employer, or indirectly in the interest of an employer, in relation to an employee benefit plan; and includes a group or association of employers acting for an employer in such a capacity."[46] Courts have found signatories to collective bargaining agreements, including general contractors, to be ERISA employers when those agreements created the obligation to contribute toward employee benefits and the signatories were not active representatives of other entities.[47]

This definition's inclusion of a group or an association of employers has earned special attention in the courts. As an example, the United States Court of Appeals for the Second Circuit held in *Marcella v. Capital District*

43. 29 C.F.R. § 2510.3-3(c) (2012).
44. Vega v. Nat'l Life Ins. Servs., 188 F.3d 287, 294 (5th Cir. 1999); Madonia v. Blue Cross & Blue Shield, 11 F.3d 444, 449 (4th Cir. 1993).
45. Yates v. Hendon, 541 U.S. 1, 6 (2004).
46. 29 U.S.C. § 1002(5) (2012).
47. *See* Cement & Concrete Workers Dist. Council Welfare Fund, Pension Fund, Legal Servs. Fund and Annuity Fund v. Lollo, 35 F.3d 29, 36–37 (2d Cir. 1994); Ironworkers Local Union, 45 F. Supp. 2d 1332, 1334 (M.D. Fla. 1999). These rulings followed an amendment to ERISA by the Multiemployer Pension Plan Amendments Act of 1980, Pub. L. No. 93-364, 94 Stat. 1208 (codified at 29 U.S.C. § 1145), adding: "Every employer who is obligated to make contributions to a multiemployer plan under the terms of the plan or under the terms of a collectively bargained agreement shall, to the extent not inconsistent with law, make such contributions in accordance with the terms and conditions of such plan or such agreement." The obligation of nonrepresentative signatories flowed from the finding of jurists such as then-Circuit Judge Stephen Breyer that ERISA only applies to employers who are already obligated in the absence of ERISA to make ERISA contributions, which therefore leaves nonrepresentative signatories responsible for their own promises. Mass. Laborers' Health & Welfare Fund v. Starrett Paving Corp., 845 F.2d 23, 25 (1st Cir. 1988).

Physicians' Health Plan, Inc., in an opinion written by then-Circuit Judge Sonia Sotomayor, that a group health policy offered by the Latham Area Chamber of Commerce was not an ERISA plan because it was established and maintained by the Chamber, which did not qualify as an employer.[48] The Second Circuit emphasized that the Chamber was open to membership by non-employers, bringing the Chamber outside ERISA's inclusion of a group or association of employers.[49] In *Moideen v. Gillespie*, the Ninth Circuit held that a multiple employer trust was not an employer under ERISA because its participants, including members of any business with 500 or fewer employees in any industry, lacked an organizational relationship as well as a commonality of interest to sponsor an employee welfare benefit plan.[50]

The United States District Court of the Southern District of Mississippi held in *Nowell v. Central Service Association* that an association of utility distributors within the same electric distribution industry established and operated to help members obtain better quality and lower cost employee benefit plans constituted an ERISA employer.[51] The court relied on the following factors, previously articulated by the Fifth Circuit, in determining whether an "association of employers" existed within the meaning of ERISA:

> 1) [T]he process by which the association was formed and the purposes for which it was formed; 2) the existence, if any, of pre-existing relationships among the employer/members; 3) whether employer/members were solicited; 4) who is entitled to participate and who actually participates in the association; 5) the powers, rights, and privileges of employer/members; and 6) whether employer/members actually control and direct the activities of the benefit plan.[52]

The existence of employee organizations, on the other hand, has caused less controversy. Employee organizations are defined within ERISA to include

48. Marcella v. Capital Dist. Physicians' Health Plan, Inc., 293 F.3d 42, 47 (2d Cir. 2002).
49. *Id.* at 48.
50. Moideen v. Gillespie, 55 F.3d 1478, 1481 (9th Cir. 1995).
51. Nowell v. Cent. Serv. Ass'n, 106 F. Supp. 2d 888, 892–93 (S.D. Miss. 2000).
52. *Id.* at 892 (citing MDPhysicians & Assocs., Inc. v. State Bd. of Ins., 957 F.2d 178, 180, 186 n.9 (5th Cir. 1992)).

labor unions, organizations, agencies, employee representation committees, associations, groups, or plans in which employees participate and that exist to deal with employers concerning an employee benefit plan or other matters arising from the employment relationship, as well as any employee's beneficiary association organized to establish such a plan.[53]

Physician Practice Associations

Physician practice associations organize to provide care in the HMO context. To determine whether a physician practice association—or any multiple employer welfare arrangement—falls within ERISA, courts typically address whether the program constitutes a benefit plan and whether the association's participants have established a welfare benefit plan. The Fifth Circuit held in *MDPhysicians & Associates, Inc. v. State Board of Insurance* that a physician practice association that created, administered, funded, and advertised an employee benefit plan was not an ERISA employer because the association acted on its own behalf in relation to the plan at issue, which it tendered for profit to various Texan employers, and the plan's establishment and maintenance did not involve the subscribing employers, which were the sole entities with whom the employees shared economic and representational ties.[54]

53. 29 U.S.C. § 1002(4) (2012).
54. *MDPhysicians*, 957 F.2d at 180, 186.

Chapter 3

ERISA Preemption

ERISA reaches beyond the typical Supremacy Clause preemption that accompanies all federal laws by preempting "any and all State laws insofar as they now or hereafter relate to any employee benefit plan."[1] This language of express preemption is tremendously broad, reflecting Congress's intent to federalize and thus make uniform the laws governing employee benefit plans. The Supreme Court noted in *Aetna Health Inc. v. Davila* that "[t]he purpose of ERISA is to provide a uniform regulatory regime over employee benefit plans."[2] As a result, "ERISA includes expansive pre-emption provisions . . . , which are intended to ensure that employee benefit plan regulation would be exclusively a federal concern."[3]

The debate leading up to passage of ERISA has prompted some observers to characterize ERISA preemption as a concession to employers desiring to avoid further regulation, specifically state regulation, in addition to the regulation extensively present under ERISA.[4] Soon after ERISA's passage, the Supreme Court ruled that even indirect state action impacting employee benefit regimes, such as laws focused on workers' compensation concerns, face preemption.[5] In *Pilot Life Insurance Company v. Dedeaux*, the Supreme Court stated that there was "no dispute that the common law causes of action asserted in [the plaintiff's] complaint 'relate[d] to' an employee benefit

1. 29 U.S.C. § 1144(a) (2013).
2. Aetna Health Inc. v. Davila, 542 U.S. 200, 208 (2004).
3. *Id.*
4. *See, e.g.*, Donald T. Rogan, *ERISA: The Savings Clause, § 502 Implied Preemption, Complete Preemption, and State Law Remedies*, 42 Santa Clara L. Rev. 105, 117–18 (2001).
5. *See* Alessi v. Raybestoas-Manhattan, Inc., 451 U.S. 504, 523–25 (1981).

plan," bringing the causes of action within ERISA preemption.[6] The plaintiff had sought redress for the administrator's improper processing of benefit claims, and preemption left the plaintiff without a remedy because ERISA did not provide for a cause of action for this particular claim.[7] Preemption applies to both statutory and common-law claims, but common-law claims relating to underlying events like separation from employment are still viable.[8]

Courts have struggled to apply the preemption clause. The United States Court of Appeals for the Ninth Circuit explained in *Dishman v. UNUM Life Insurance Company*: "It is with great trepidation that we tread into the field of ERISA preemption. As we noted in *Rutledge v. Seyfarth, Shaw, Fairweather & Geraldson*, '[d]eveloping a rule to identify whether ERISA preempts a given state law has bedeviled the Supreme Court.'"[9]

Vital to ERISA preemption is whether a law "relates to" an employee benefit plan. The Supreme Court first encountered ERISA preemption in the uncontroversial 1981 case *Alessi v. Raybestos-Manhattan, Inc.*, where it unanimously held that ERISA preempted a New Jersey law prohibiting the reduction of employees' retirement pension benefits or payments by the amount of workers' compensation awards.[10] On its next encounter with ERISA preemption in 1983, the Supreme Court found in *Shaw v. Delta Air Lines* that both a human rights law prohibiting employers from discriminating on the basis of pregnancy in their employee benefit plans as well as a disability benefits law requiring employers to pay employees specific benefits clearly related to ERISA plans.[11] The Court reasoned:

> We have no difficulty in concluding that the Human Rights Law and Disability Benefits Law "relate to" employee benefit plans. The breadth

---

6. Pilot Life Ins. Co. v. Dedeaux, 481 U.S. 41, 47 (1987).
7. *Id.* at 57.
8. *See* Dishman v. UNUM Life Ins. Co. of Am., 269 F.3d 974, 984 (9th Cir. 2001) ("[T]he objective of Congress in crafting [ERISA's preemption provision] was not to provide ERISA administrators with blanket immunity from garden variety torts which only peripherally impact daily plan administration.").
9. *Dishman*, 269 F.3d at 980 (citing Rutledge v. Seyfarth, Shaw, Fairweather, & Geraldson, 201 F.3d 1212, 1216 (9th Cir. 2000), *as amended by* 208 F.3d 1170 (9th Cir. 2000)).
10. *Alessi*, 451 U.S. at 509.
11. Shaw v. Delta Air Lines, Inc., 463 U.S. 85, 97 (1983).

> of [ERISA preemption section's] preemptive reach is apparent from that section's language. A law "relates to" an employee benefit plan, in the normal sense of the phrase, if it has a connection with or reference to such a plan. Employing this definition, the Human Rights Law, which prohibits employers from structuring their employee benefit plans in a manner that discriminates on the basis of pregnancy, and the Disability Benefits Law, which requires employers to pay employees specific benefits, clearly "relate to" benefit plans. We must give effect to this plain language unless there is good reason to believe Congress intended the language to have some more restrictive meaning.[12]

The Court explained that it would be wrong to restrict ERISA preemption to only those state laws dealing with subjects explicitly covered by ERISA, including reporting, disclosure, and fiduciary responsibilities, because the original bill leading up to ERISA passage featured that type of limited preemption clause, and Congress rejected the clause in favor of broad preemption.[13] Still, the Court noted, "[s]ome state actions may affect employee benefit plans in too tenuous, remote, or peripheral a manner to warrant a finding that the law 'relates to' the plan."[14] In *Ingersoll-Rand Co. v. McClendon*, although finding the particular law providing alternative enforcement mechanisms to be preempted, the Supreme Court expounded on the sort of laws outside ERISA preemption: "a generally applicable statute that makes no reference to, or indeed functions irrespective of, the existence of an ERISA plan."[15]

The Narrowing of Preemption

The earliest cases saw the Supreme Court embrace a broadly sweeping application of ERISA's preemption provision. The trend continued until

12. *Id.* at 96–97 (citations omitted).
13. *Id.* at 97.
14. *Id.* at 100 n.21 (citing Am. Telephone and Telegraph Co. v. Merry, 592 F.2d 118, 121 (2d Cir. 1979)).
15. Ingersoll-Rand Co. v. McClendon, 498 U.S. 133, 139 (1990).

1995 when, in *New York State Conference of Blue Cross & Blue Shield Plans v. Travelers Insurance Company*, the Court initiated the narrowing of ERISA's preemption's scope—starting with health-care issues. *Travelers* concerned a New York statute that required hospitals to impose surcharges on patients insured by a commercial carrier but not by Blue Cross & Blue Shield. The law subjected select HMOs to surcharges based on the number of each HMO's Medicaid-recipient enrollees.[16] After noting that "[t]he governing text of ERISA is clearly expansive" and reciting the law's preemption provision, the Court emphasized "relate to" as an important limiting factor not yet fully realized in prior cases.[17]

> Since pre-emption claims turn on Congress's intent, we begin as we do in any exercise of statutory construction with the text of the provision in question, and move on, as need be, to the structure and purpose of the Act in which it occurs. The governing text of ERISA is clearly expansive. Section 514(a) marks for pre-emption "all state laws insofar as they . . . relate to any employee benefit plan" covered by ERISA, and one might be excused for wondering, at first blush, whether the words of limitation ("insofar as they . . . relate") do much limiting. If "relate to" were taken to extend to the furthest stretch of its indeterminacy, then for all practical purposes preemption would never run its course, for "[r]eally, universally, relations stop nowhere," H. James, Roderick Hudson xli (New York ed., World's Classics 1980). But that, of course, would be to read Congress's words of limitation as mere sham, and to read the presumption against pre-emption out of the law whenever Congress speaks to the matter with generality. That said, we have to recognize that our prior attempt to construe the phrase "relate to" does not give us much help drawing the line here.[18]

In retreating from the broad reach of the "relate to" phrase recognized in *Shaw*, the Court in *Travelers* made it clear that when the phrase "connection

16. N.Y. State Conference of Blue Cross & Blue Shield Plans v. Travelers Ins. Co., 514 U.S. 645, 649 (1995).
17. *Id.* at 655.
18. *Id.* at 657 (citations omitted).

with" is relied on for ERISA preemption, the objectives of ERISA must be examined.[19]

> In *Shaw*, we explained that "[a] law 'relates to' an employee benefit plan, in the normal sense of the phrase, if it has a connection with or reference to such a plan." The latter alternative, at least, can be ruled out. The surcharges are imposed upon patients and HMO's, regardless of whether the commercial coverage or membership, respectively, is ultimately secured by an ERISA plan, private purchase, or otherwise, with the consequence that the surcharge statutes cannot be said to make "reference to" ERISA plans in any manner. But this still leaves us to question whether the surcharge laws have a "connection with" the ERISA plans, and here an uncritical literalism is no more help than in trying to construe "relate to." For the same reasons that infinite relations cannot be the measure of pre-emption, neither can infinite connections. We simply must go beyond the unhelpful text and the frustrating difficulty of defining its key term, and look instead to the objectives of the ERISA statute as a guide to the scope of the state law that Congress understood would survive.[20]

The Court distinguished the law in *Travelers* from those at issue in *Shaw*, *Alessi*, and *Ingersoll-Rand*, which the Court characterized as laws controlling employee benefit structures, administration, or enforcement mechanisms.[21] In contrast, the Court characterized the New York statute in *Travelers* as "[a]n indirect economic influence" that did not bind plan administrators to a particular choice and therefore did not function as a regulation of an ERISA plan.[22] The law might affect a plan's shopping decisions, but it did not change the fact that every plan would shop for the best deal it could get regardless of the attached surcharges.[23]

19. *Id.* at 657–58 (citations omitted).
20. *Id.*
21. *Id.*
22. *Id.* at 659.
23. *Id.* at 660.

Travelers introduced the "presumption against preemption," especially in areas within the sphere of traditional state regulation:

> [W]e have never assumed lightly that Congress has derogated state regulation, but instead have addressed claims of pre-emption with the starting presumption that Congress does not intend to supplant state law. Indeed, in cases like this one, where federal law is said to bar state action in fields of traditional state regulation, we have worked on the assumption that the historic police powers of the States were not to be superseded by the Federal Act unless that was the clear and manifest purpose of Congress.[24]

The Court clarified that it was not holding that ERISA only preempted the state law that directly regulated ERISA plans; it could not do so while giving credence to its prior opinions.[25] The Court left open the possibility that a state law could create acute enough economic impacts to force an ERISA plan to adopt a plan of substantive coverage or restrict a plan's choice of insurers, thereby resulting in a law that was preempted.[26] The Court concluded that the New York law only indirectly affected the relative price of insurance policies, and this impact was similar to numerous other state laws Congress could not have intended to eliminate with ERISA.[27]

The Court continued to view controversies as existing outside ERISA preemption after *Travelers*. In *De Buono v. NYSA-ILA Medical & Clinical Services Fund*, the Court upheld a tax on gross receipts for patient services despite the tax's application to a facility owned and operated by an ERISA plan on the grounds that the tax burdened ERISA plans without actually relating to them.[28] Informed by its decision in *Travelers*, the Court strove to give appropriate respect to a state taxation law, noting that the tax could burden ERISA plans without actually relating to them.[29] The Court

24. *Id.* (quotation marks omitted).
25. *Id.* at 668 (citing Ingersoll-Rand Co. v. McClendon, 498 U.S. 133, 139 (1990); Pilot Life Ins. Co. v. Dedeaux, 481 U.S. 41, 47–48 (1987); Shaw v. Delta Air Lines, Inc., 463 U.S. 85, 98 (1983)).
26. *Id.*
27. *Id.*
28. De Buono v. NYSLA-ILA Med. & Clinical Servs. Fund, 520 U.S. 806, 815 (1997).
29. *Id.*

explained that ERISA funds do not own most hospitals, and the ERISA fund the tax burdened in *De Buono* could have escaped the tax by purchasing health-care services from a hospital instead of running hospitals directly.[30]

The narrowing of ERISA preemption eventually reached beyond health-care issues to California's prevailing wage law. In *Mackey v. Lanier Collection Agency & Service, Inc.*, the Supreme Court acknowledged that "lawsuits against ERISA plans for run-of-the-mill state-law claims such as unpaid rent, failure to pay creditors, or even torts committed by an ERISA plan" were not preempted.[31] In the 1997 Supreme Court decision *California Division of Labor Standards Enforcement v. Dillingham Construction*, the Court relied on *Travelers* and found that ERISA's preemption did not apply to a state prevailing wage law.[32] The Supreme Court observed in the 2013 case *Dan's City Used Cars, Inc. v. Pelkey*:

> [T]he breadth of the words related to does not mean the sky is the limit. We have refused to read the preemption clause of the Employee Retirement Income Security Act of 1974, 29 U.S.C. § 1144(a), which supersedes state laws relate[d] to any employee benefit plan, with an uncritical literalism, else for all practical purposes pre-emption would never run its course. And we have cautioned that § 14501(c)(1) does not preempt state laws affecting carrier prices, routes, and services in only a tenuous, remote, or peripheral . . . manner.[33]

Despite the narrowing of ERISA preemption, courts still recognize state laws as preempted where they bear a significant enough connection to ERISA plans. A recent example arose in *Merit Construction Alliance v. City of Quincy* in which the United States Court of Appeals for the First Circuit considered an ordinance requiring bidders on municipal public works

30. *Id.* at 816.
31. Mackey v. Lanier Collection Agency & Serv., Inc., 489 U.S. 825, 833 (1988).
32. Cal. Div. of Labor Standards Enforcement v. Dillingham Construction, N.A., Inc., 519 U.S. 316, 334 (1997) (finding a statute requiring contractors to pay a prevailing wage but allowing lower wages for apprentices in an apprenticeship program was not preempted even though a separately funded apprenticeship plan constitutes an ERISA plan).
33. Dan's City Used Cars, Inc. v. Pelkey, 133 S. Ct. 1769, 1778 (2013) (citations and quotation marks omitted).

projects to engage in an apprentice training program.[34] The court found it clear that the ordinance "related to" an ERISA plan and that preemption was therefore warranted:

> The Supreme Court has distilled the statute's "relate to" language into two independently sufficient alternatives: "a connection with or reference to" an ERISA plan will result in preemption. Under this two-sided rubric, ERISA's preemptive reach "is clearly expansive." But the Court has nevertheless cautioned against "an uncritical literalism" in applying this test, warning that "infinite connections" cannot supply the measure of preemption. Thus, we must consider "the objectives of the ERISA statute as a guide to the scope of the state law that Congress understood would survive." In the process, we must remain mindful that ERISA was not intended to supersede the state's historic police powers unless such supersession "was the clear and manifest purpose of Congress."
>
> The battle here, as waged by the parties, focuses on the "connection with" component of the two-sided ERISA preemption calculus. The district court concluded that the Ordinance's requirement that "every bidder . . . have an apprenticeship program meeting Massachusetts standards" supplied the requisite connection. We share this view.
>
> To begin, it is important to note that programs "established or . . . maintained for the purpose of providing . . . apprenticeship or other training" qualify as ERISA employee welfare benefit plans. Thus, ERISA will preempt the Ordinance's operation if and to the extent that the Ordinance bears a sufficient connection to such programs.
>
> Of course, not every conceivable connection will support preemption. For example, state laws that merely exert an "indirect economic influence" on a plan do "not bind plan administrators to any particular choice" and, thus, do not come within ERISA's preemptive reach.
>
> The path from influence to coercion amounts to a continuum and it is not always a simple task to determine where along this

34. Merit Construction Alliance v. City of Quincy, No. 13-2189, 2014 WL 3457605, at *1 (1st Cir. July 26, 2014).

continuum a particular state law falls. This case, however, does not greatly tax our capacity for discernment: the Ordinance categorically requires all contractors on Quincy public works projects to operate a Massachusetts-approved apprentice training program. Incorporating the state's standards imposes a raft of stringent conditions on would-be bidders including, among others, documentation of the program's terms and conditions; the location of the program's apprentice activities; training and instruction; wage rates; recordkeeping; instructor qualifications; apprentice enrollment; reporting; and termination. For good measure (or bad measure depending on one's point of view), the Ordinance separately requires a defined graduation rate.

With such a compendium of stipulations in place, we have no difficulty concluding that the Ordinance goes far beyond simply influencing ERISA apprentice training programs. It mandates an employee benefit structure and specifies how that structure must be administered. This is simply too intrusive to withstand ERISA preemption.[35]

Conflict Preemption and Complete Preemption

ERISA preempts state-law claims that conflict with an ERISA cause of action.[36] A law will be preempted under the principles of conflict preemption, "to the extent that it actually conflicts with federal law," making it impossible to comply with both state and federal law,[37] or when the state law "stands as an obstacle to the accomplishment and execution of the full purposes and objectives of Congress."[38]

The civil enforcement provisions of ERISA § 502 have an independent preemptive force under this principle of complete preemption. In *Aetna Health Inc. v. Davila*, the Supreme Court reaffirmed that "any state-law cause of action that duplicates, supplements, or supplants ERISA's civil

35. *Id.* at *3–4 (citations and quotation marks omitted).
36. *Id.* (citing *Ingersoll-Rand*, 498 U.S. at 140; Powell v. Chesapeake & Potomac Tel. Co. of Va., 780 F.2d 419, 422 (4th Cir. 1985)).
37. English v. Gen. Elec. Co., 496 U.S. 72, 79 (1990).
38. Hines v. Davidowitz, 312 U.S. 52, 67 (1941).

enforcement remedy, conflicts with the clear congressional intent to make the ERISA remedy exclusive and is therefore pre-empted."[39] Congress intended § 502 to exclusively provide remedies for ERISA violations. The principles of complete preemption will allow a cause of action to be removed to federal court even if the complaint, on its face, only alleges state law causes of action and no federal cause of action implicating ERISA. If the remedial provisions of § 502 are implicated, the claims will be completely preempted and removable to federal court on that basis.

The Supreme Court examined complete preemption in *Metropolitan Life Insurance Company v. Taylor*. In *Taylor*, an employee covered under General Motors' disability policy became injured in a job-related automobile accident.[40] He was granted workers compensation benefits and subsequently returned to work, but he later took a leave of absence due to emotional problems.[41] After successive medical examinations, the employee was terminated when a physician certified his fitness to work, but he nevertheless did not return to work.[42] Taylor brought an action in state court against General Motors and Metropolitan Life Insurance Company, through which General Motors insured its employees, seeking "compensatory damages for money contractually owed Plaintiff, compensation for mental anguish caused by breach of this contract, as well as immediate reimplementation of all benefits and insurance coverages Plaintiff is entitled to."[43] Taylor sought redress for wrongful termination and for failure to promote him, asserting that these actions were designed to retaliate against him for his worker's compensation claim.[44] General Motors and Metropolitan sought removal of the case to federal court even though Taylor asserted only state-law claims, based on the fact that the substance of his grievances related to disability benefits and were governed by ERISA.[45]

The Supreme Court held that Taylor's common-law contract and tort claims were preempted by ERISA because the case "related to" an employee

39. Aetna Health Inc. v. Davila, 542 U.S. 200, 200–01 (2004).
40. Metro. Life Ins. Co. v. Taylor, 481 U.S. 58, 60 (1987).
41. *Id.* at 61.
42. *Id.*
43. *Id.*
44. *Id.*
45. *Id.* at 61–62.

benefit plan, and "as a suit by a beneficiary to recover benefits from a covered plan, it falls directly under § 502(a)(1)(B) of ERISA, which provides an exclusive federal cause of action for resolution of such disputes."[46] In reconciling the well-pleaded complaint rule with the law relating to removal to federal court, the Court explained the preemptive force of § 502:

> The well-pleaded complaint rule is the basic principle marking the boundaries of the federal question jurisdiction of the federal district courts.
>
> Federal pre-emption is ordinarily a federal defense to the plaintiff's suit. As a defense, it does not appear on the face of a well-pleaded complaint, and, therefore, does not authorize removal to federal court. One corollary of the well-pleaded complaint rule developed in the case law, however, is that Congress may so completely pre-empt a particular area that any civil complaint raising this select group of claims is necessarily federal in character.
>
> . . .
>
> Congress has clearly manifested an intent to make causes of action within the scope of the civil enforcement provisions of § 502(a) removable to federal court. Since we have found Taylor's cause of action to be within the scope of § 502(a), we must honor that intent whether pre-emption was obvious or not at the time this suit was filed.
>
> Accordingly, this suit, though it purports to raise only state law claims, is necessarily federal in character by virtue of the clearly manifested intent of Congress. It, therefore, arise[s] under the . . . laws . . . of the United States and is removable to federal court by the defendants.[47]

ERISA's civil enforcement provision states that a civil action may be brought by a participant or beneficiary "to recover benefits due to him under the terms of his plan, to enforce his rights under the terms of the plan, or to clarify his rights to future benefits under the terms of the plan."[48] Subsequently, the Supreme Court observed in *Aetna Health Inc. v. Davila*: "any

46. *Id.* at 62.
47. *Id.* at 63–67 (citations and quotation marks omitted).
48. 29 U.S.C. § 1132(a)(1)(B) (2013).

state-law cause of action that duplicates, supplements, or supplants the ERISA civil enforcement remedy conflicts with the clear congressional intent to make the ERISA remedy exclusive and is therefore pre-empted."[49] The Court further explained that if an individual could at some point bring a claim under ERISA's civil enforcement provision, and if the defendant has no other freestanding legal duty, then ERISA preempts that cause of action.[50] The Court then applied this rule to state statutory causes of action brought by two individuals against their HMOs:

> To determine whether respondents' causes of action fall "within the scope" of ERISA § 502(a)(1)(B), we must examine respondents' complaints, the statute on which their claims are based (the [Texas Health Care Liability Act]), and the various plan documents. Davila alleges that Aetna provides health coverage under his employer's health benefits plan. Davila also alleges that after his primary care physician prescribed Vioxx, Aetna refused to pay for it. The only action complained of was Aetna's refusal to approve payment for Davila's Vioxx prescription. Further, the only relationship Aetna had with Davila was its partial administration of Davila's employer's benefit plan.
>
> Similarly, Calad alleges that she receives, as her husband's beneficiary under an ERISA-regulated benefit plan, health coverage from CIGNA. She alleges that she was informed by CIGNA, upon admittance into a hospital for major surgery, that she would be authorized to stay for only one day. She also alleges that CIGNA, acting through a discharge nurse, refused to authorize more than a single day despite the advice and recommendation of her treating physician. Calad contests only CIGNA's decision to refuse coverage for her hospital stay. And, as in Davila's case, the only connection between Calad and CIGNA is CIGNA's administration of portions of Calad's ERISA-regulated benefit plan.
>
> It is clear, then, that respondents complain only about denials of coverage promised under the terms of ERISA-regulated employee

49. Aetna Health Inc. v. Davila, 542 U.S. 200, 209 (2004).
50. *Id.* at 10.

benefit plans. Upon the denial of benefits, respondents could have paid for the treatment themselves and then sought reimbursement through a § 502(a)(1)(B) action, or sought a preliminary injunction.

Respondents contend, however, that the complained-of actions violate legal duties that arise independently of ERISA or the terms of the employee benefit plans at issue in these cases. Both respondents brought suit specifically under the THCLA, alleging that petitioners "controlled, influenced, participated in and made decisions which affected the quality of the diagnosis, care, and treatment provided" in a manner that violated "the duty of ordinary care set forth in §§ 88.001 and 88.002." Respondents contend that this duty of ordinary care is an independent legal duty. They analogize to this Court's decisions interpreting LMRA § 301, 29 U.S.C. § 185, with particular focus on *Caterpillar Inc. v. Williams* (suit for breach of individual employment contract, even if defendant's action also constituted a breach of an entirely separate collective bargaining agreement, not preempted by LMRA § 301). Because this duty of ordinary care arises independently of any duty imposed by ERISA or the plan terms, the argument goes, any civil action to enforce this duty is not within the scope of the ERISA civil enforcement mechanism.

The duties imposed by the THCLA in the context of these cases, however, do not arise independently of ERISA or the plan terms. The THCLA does impose a duty on managed care entities to "exercise ordinary care when making health care treatment decisions," and makes them liable for damages proximately caused by failures to abide by that duty. However, if a managed care entity correctly concluded that, under the terms of the relevant plan, a particular treatment was not covered, the managed care entity's denial of coverage would not be a proximate cause of any injuries arising from the denial. Rather, the failure of the plan itself to cover the requested treatment would be the proximate cause. More significantly, the THCLA clearly states that "[t]he standards in Subsections (a) and (b) create no obligation on the part of the health insurance carrier, health maintenance organization, or other managed care entity to provide to an insured or enrollee treatment which is not covered by the health care plan of the entity."

Hence, a managed care entity could not be subject to liability under the THCLA if it denied coverage for any treatment not covered by the health care plan that it was administering.

Thus, interpretation of the terms of respondents' benefit plans forms an essential part of their THCLA claim, and THCLA liability would exist here only because of petitioners' administration of ERISA-regulated benefit plans. Petitioners' potential liability under the THCLA in these cases, then, derives entirely from the particular rights and obligations established by the benefit plans. So, unlike the state-law claims in *Caterpillar*, respondents' THCLA causes of action are not entirely independent of the federally regulated contract itself.

Hence, respondents bring suit only to rectify a wrongful denial of benefits promised under ERISA-regulated plans, and do not attempt to remedy any violation of a legal duty independent of ERISA. We hold that respondents' state causes of action fall "within the scope of" ERISA § 502(a)(1)(B) and are therefore completely preempted by ERISA.[51]

The Savings Clause

The plaintiffs in *Davila* leveraged what is popularly known as the savings clause to argue that the Texas law fell outside ERISA preemption.[52] Previous chapters have discussed factors limiting ERISA preemption insofar that a law concerning employee benefits is not preempted if it does not implicate a "plan" within the meaning of ERISA. Moreover, ERISA sets out a series of exemptions from ERISA preemption. One exemption, frequently termed the insurance exception or savings clause, applies to "any law of any State which regulates insurance, banking, or securities."[53] However, ERISA's "deemer clause" prohibits the avoidance of ERISA preemption through simply deeming any employee benefit plan, otherwise governed by ERISA, to be an insurance company, insurer, bank, trust company, or investment

51. *Id.* at 211–14 (citations omitted).
52. *Id.* at 216–17.
53. 29 U.S.C. § 1144(b)(2)(A) (2013).

company or to be engaged in insurance or banking and thus subject to state laws.[54] Thus, as the Supreme Court noted in *Pilot Life Insurance Company v. Dedeaux*, the savings clause applies to laws "specifically directed toward" the insurance industry and not to generally applicable laws with only some bearing on insurers.[55] The plaintiffs' argument in *Davila* that the law was subject to the savings clause and therefore saved from preemption failed because, as the Court made clear, "even a state law that can arguably be characterized as 'regulating insurance' will be preempted if it provides a separate vehicle to assert a claim for benefits outside of, or in addition to, ERISA's remedial scheme."[56]

In the 1985 case *Metropolitan Life Insurance Company v. Massachusetts*, the Supreme Court turned to previous cases analyzing laws regulating insurance pursuant to the McCarran-Ferguson Act of 1945 to discern whether a plan fell within the savings clause.[57] The Court listed three criteria to consider when determining if a practice constituted the business of insurance: "whether the practice has the effect of transferring or spreading a policyholder's risk; . . . whether the practice is an integral part of the policy relationship between the insurer and the insured; and . . . whether the practice is limited to entities within the insurance industry."[58]

In the 1999 *UNUM Life Insurance Company of America v. Ward*, the Supreme Court rejected the assertion that a state law had to satisfy all three McCarran-Ferguson factors to fall within the insurance exemption to preemption.[59] The Court explained that the McCarran-Ferguson factors deserved weight but were not determinative, and two out of three of the factors in *UNUM* served to clarify the commonsense view that the state regulation warranted the insurance exception.[60]

The Supreme Court continued to muddy the application of the McCarran-Ferguson factors to the ERISA insurance exemption with the 2002 case *Rush Prudential HMO, Inc. v. Moran*. At issue in *Moran* was whether ERISA

54. 29 U.S.C. § 1144(b)(2)(B) (2013).
55. Pilot Life Ins. Co. v. Dedeaux, 481 U.S. 41, 50 (1987).
56. *Davila*, 542 U.S. at 217–18.
57. Metro. Life Ins. Co. v. Massachusetts, 471 U.S. 724, 743 (1985).
58. *Id.*
59. UNUM Life Ins. Co. of Am. v. Ward, 526 U.S. 358, 364 (1999).
60. *Id.* at 373–74.

preempted a statute that provided participants in HMO health-care plans with a right to independent medical review if certain benefits were denied.[61] The Court expressed a reluctance to "plot the exact perimeter of the saving clause" but summarized the existing rule as follows: "when insurers are regulated with respect to their insurance practices, the state law survives ERISA."[62] The Court found the statute in *Moran* saved from ERISA preemption despite determining only two of the three McCarran-Ferguson factors were satisfied, leaving open the question "whether the review mandated here may be described as going to a practice that 'spread[s] a policyholder's risk.'"[63] The Court explained that "the factors are guideposts" and that "a state law is not required to satisfy all three McCarran-Ferguson criteria to survive preemption."[64]

Finally, in its unanimous 2003 decision *Kentucky Association of Health Plans v. Miller*, the Supreme Court rejected its prior use of the McCarran-Ferguson case law in the ERISA context.[65] The *Miller* Court held two Kentucky statutes known as "Any Willing Provider" (AWP) statutes saved from ERISA preemption.[66] These statutes prevented health insurers from discriminating against providers located within plans' geographic areas when those providers were willing to satisfy the terms and conditions of participation in the plans.[67] In addition, the statutes permitted any licensed chiropractor to serve as a primary care chiropractic provider within plans offering chiropractic benefits when the chiropractor was willing to meet the appropriate stipulations and conditions of participation.[68] In holding the AWP statutes exempt, the Court initiated a clean break from the McCarran-Ferguson factors and set forth two requirements for state laws within the insurance exception: "the law must be specifically directed toward entities engaged in insurance, and the law must substantially affect the risk-pooling

61. Rush Prudential HMO, Inc. v. Moran, 536 U.S. 355, 359 (2002).
62. *Id.* at 366 (citing Group Life & Health Ins. Co. v. Royal Drug Co., 440 U.S. 205, 211 (1979)).
63. *Id.* at 373.
64. *Id.* (citing UNUM Life Ins. Co. v. Ward, 526 U.S. 358, 373 (1999)).
65. Ky. Ass'n of Health Plans v. Miller, 538 U.S. 329, 339–40 (2003).
66. *Id.* at 332.
67. *Id.* at 331–32.
68. *Id.* at 332.

arrangement between the insurer and the insured."[69] Interestingly, the latter requirement was the McCarran-Ferguson factor the Court had previously left open in *Moran*.[70]

The *Miller* Court explained:

> We believe that our use of the McCarran-Ferguson case law in the ERISA context has misdirected attention, failed to provide clear guidance to lower federal courts, and, as this case demonstrates, added little to the relevant analysis. That is unsurprising, since the statutory language of § 1144(b)(2)(A) differs substantially from that of the McCarran-Ferguson Act. Rather than concerning itself with whether certain practices constitute "[t]he business of insurance," 15 U.S.C. § 1012(a), or whether a state law was "enacted . . . *for the purpose of* regulating the business of insurance," § 1012(b), 29 U.S.C. § 1144(b)(2)(A) asks merely whether a state law is a "law . . . which regulates insurance, banking, or securities." What is more, the McCarran-Ferguson factors were developed in cases that characterized conduct by private actors, not state laws.
>
> Our holdings in *UNUM* and *Rush Prudential*—that a state law may fail the first McCarran-Ferguson factor yet still be saved from pre-emption under § 1144(b)(2)(A)—raise more questions than they answer and provide wide opportunities for divergent outcomes. May a state law satisfy *any* two of the three McCarran-Ferguson factors and still fall under the saving clause? Just one? What happens if two of three factors are satisfied, but not "securely satisfied" or "clearly satisfied," as they were in *UNUM* and *Rush Prudential*? Further confusion arises from the question whether the *state law itself* or the *conduct regulated by that law* is the proper subject to which one applies the McCarran-Ferguson factors. In *Pilot Life*, we inquired whether Mississippi's *law of bad faith* has the effect of transferring or spreading risk, whether *that law* is integral to the insurer-insured relationship, and whether *that law* is limited to the insurance industry. *Rush Prudential*,

69. *Id.* at 341–42.
70. Rush Prudential HMO, Inc. v. Moran, 536 U.S. 355, 373 (2002).

by contrast, focused the McCarran-Ferguson inquiry on the *conduct regulated* by the state law, rather than the state law itself.

We have never held that the McCarran-Ferguson factors are an essential component of the § 1144(b)(2)(A) inquiry. *Metropolitan Life* initially used these factors only to buttress its previously reached conclusion that Massachusetts' mandated-benefit statute was a "law . . . which regulates insurance" under § 1144(b)(2)(A). *Pilot Life* referred to them as mere "considerations [to be] weighed" in determining whether a state law falls under the saving clause. *UNUM* emphasized that the McCarran-Ferguson factors were not "'require[d]'" in the saving clause analysis, and were only "checking points" to be used after determining whether the state law regulates insurance from a "common-sense" understanding. And *Rush Prudential* called the factors "guideposts," using them only to "confirm our conclusion" that Illinois' statute regulated insurance under § 1144(b)(2)(A).

Today we make a clean break from the McCarran-Ferguson factors and hold that for a state law to be deemed a "law . . . which regulates insurance" under § 1144(b)(2)(A), it must satisfy two requirements. First, the state law must be specifically directed toward entities engaged in insurance. Second, as explained above, the state law must substantially affect the risk pooling arrangement between the insurer and the insured. Kentucky's law satisfies each of these requirements.[71]

The Insurance Exemption and Discretionary Clauses

The role of discretionary clauses in insurance policies is currently attracting widespread attention. A recent decision in an Illinois federal court, *Novak v. Life Insurance Company of North America*, applied the *Miller* requirements to an Illinois Department of Insurance regulation prohibiting insurers from granting fiduciaries the discretion to interpret plan terms.[72] The defendants in *Novak* argued that the regulation was not exempt from ERISA preemp-

71. *Miller*, 538 U.S. at 339–342.
72. Novak v. Life Ins. Co. of N. Am., No. 12-C-9434, 2013 WL 3455844, at *4 (N.D. Ill. July 9, 2013).

tion because it was directed toward plan sponsors and trust instruments rather than entities specifically engaged in insurance.[73] The court found that the fact entities other than insurance companies may be affected by a state action did not take the action outside the savings clause.[74] Thus, the regulation was clearly directed toward entities engaged in insurance even though it placed limitations on fiduciaries.[75] The court found that the regulation also substantially impacted the risk-pooling arrangement between insurers and the insured by effectively transforming federal courts' standard of review of claim determinations from arbitrary and capricious—applied when fiduciaries had the discretion to interpret plans—to de novo.[76]

While the highest court of the Seventh Circuit has not yet settled this area of the law, the Sixth Circuit and Ninth Circuit Courts of Appeals each held state laws banning discretionary clauses nearly identical to the regulation in *Novak* to be exempt from preemption.[77]

In *Hancock v. Metropolitan Life Insurance Company*, the Tenth Circuit addressed a similar but not identical state rule banning reservation-of-discretion clauses in insurance-policy forms.[78] The Tenth Circuit observed that the rule at issue did not cause the option of insurer discretion to be removed from the range of permissible insurance bargains in ERISA plans.[79] It also did not affect who gets in the risk pool and did not prescribe the conditions under which insurers must assume risk.[80] Instead, the rule authorized discretion-granting clauses accompanied by certain disclosures and in conformance with the rule's font requirement.[81] The rule addressed the form and not the substance of ERISA plans, and the Tenth Circuit held that it failed to meet the *Miller* requirements because it had no impact on risk pooling.[82] Therefore, it was preempted by ERISA.

73. *Id.* (citing *Miller*, 538 U.S. at 342).
74. *Id.* at *5.
75. *Id.*
76. *Id.* at *6.
77. Am. Council of Life Insurers v. Ross, 558 F.3d 600 (6th Cir. 2009); Standard of Ins. Co. v. Morrison, 584 F.3d 837 (9th Cir. 2009).
78. Hancock v. Metro. Life Ins. Co., 590 F.3d 1141, 1146 (10th Cir. 2009).
79. *Id.* at 1149.
80. *Id.*
81. *Id.*
82. *Id.*

Other Exemptions

Various other exemptions from ERISA preemption exist. State criminal law and all other federal laws, including the Patient Protection and Affordable Care Act as well as bankruptcy laws, are exempted from ERISA preemption, as are qualified domestic relations orders. ERISA also exempts plans "maintained solely for the purpose of complying with applicable workmen's compensation laws or unemployment compensation or disability insurance laws."[83] Plans otherwise qualified for this last exemption still face preemption when they are one part in multibenefit plans that extend beyond complying with workmen's compensation, unemployment compensation, or disability insurance laws.[84]

Federal Common Law

The Supreme Court of the United States has noted Congress's intent for courts to develop and rely on federal common law in disputes involving ERISA plans.[85] Accordingly, at times, courts have supplemented ERISA's explicit remedies and gaps in the legislation with federal common law to decide the outcome of disputes that were not predetermined by ERISA's statutory language. In *Nachwalter v. Christie*, the United States Court of Appeals for the Eleventh Circuit examined the reasoning for and the limits of federal common law in ERISA proceedings:

> The claim that Congress intended for the federal courts to create a body of federal common law to govern ERISA cases does not, as appellant suggests, give a federal court *carte blanche* authority to apply any prevailing state common law doctrine it chooses to ERISA cases. A federal court may create federal common law based on a federal statute's preemption of an area only where the federal statute does not expressly address the issue before the court. Furthermore, even

83. 29 U.S.C. § 1003(b)(3) (2013).
84. Shaw v. Delta Air Lines, 463 U.S. 85, 106–08 (1983).
85. Pilot Life Ins. Co. v. Dedeaux, 481 U.S. 41, 56 (1987).

> when it is appropriate for a federal court to create federal common law, it may use state common law as the basis of the federal common law only if the state law is consistent with the policies underlying the federal statute in question; federal courts may not use state common law to re-write a federal statute.[86]

In its 2009 decision *Cross v. Bragg*, the United States Court of Appeals for the Fourth Circuit turned to the federal common law of contracts to address a "scrivener's error."[87] The Fourth Circuit explained:

> In assessing the defendants' scrivener's error contention, we are guided by the principle that ERISA plans are contractual documents which, while regulated, are governed by established principles of contract and trust law. In reviewing benefits claims under ERISA, we turn to the federal common law of contracts. We may, however, use principles of state common law to guide our analysis. Importantly, we have recognized that a scrivener's error, like a mutual mistake, occurs when the intention of the parties is identical at the time of the transaction but the written agreement does not express that intention because of that error; this permits a court acting in equity to reform an agreement. Further, the power to recognize and correct a scrivener's error in an ERISA plan rests exclusively with the courts, and an administrator cannot simply reform a plan to correct what it unilaterally perceives to be a mistake or error contained in the plan's written terms.
>
> A primary purpose of ERISA was to require that participants and beneficiaries be fully advised of their rights under employee benefit plans. Consistent with congressional intent, the Supreme Court has held that a written [benefit] plan is to be required in order that every employee may, on examining the plan documents, determine exactly what his rights and obligations are under the plan. Thus, when the terms of an ERISA plan are clear and unambiguous, a federal court is obliged to apply it as written. In limited circumstances, however, a

86. Nachwalter v. Christie, 805 F.2d 956, 959–60 (11th Cir. 1986) (citations omitted).
87. Cross v. Bragg, 329 F. App'x 443, 453–54 (4th Cir. 2009).

> court is entitled to reform an ERISA plan to correct a mutual mistake or to mitigate a fraud scheme. Such an action requires that the party seeking reformation present clear and convincing evidence showing that the mistake [was] mutual, or if unilateral, it [was] accompanied by fraud on the part of the other contracting party.[88]

Other examples of courts applying federal common law in ERISA proceedings include courts creating a federal common-law rule of unjust enrichment,[89] recognizing a federal common-law rule of equitable estoppel,[90] and relying on federal common law to apportion liability for benefit payments.[91]

Typical State-Law Claims

ERISA's civil enforcement provision states that a civil action may be brought by a participant or beneficiary "to recover benefits due to him under the terms of his plan, to enforce his rights under the terms of the plan, or to clarify his rights to future benefits under the terms of the plan."[92] As previously noted, the Supreme Court observed in *Aetna Health Inc. v. Davila*: "any state-law cause of action that duplicates, supplements, or supplants the ERISA civil enforcement remedy conflicts with the clear congressional intent to make the ERISA remedy exclusive and is therefore preempted."[93]

In *Woodworker's Supply, Inc. v. Principal Mutual Life Insurance Company*, the United States Court of Appeals for the Tenth Circuit explicitly identified four state laws and causes of action within ERISA's preemptive reach:

> (1) laws regulating the type of benefits or terms of ERISA plans; (2) laws creating reporting, disclosure, funding, or vesting requirements for [ERISA plans]; (3) laws providing rules for calculating

88. *Id.* at 453–55 (citations and quotation marks omitted).
89. Provident Life & Accident Ins. Co. v. Waller, 906 F.2d 985 (4th Cir. 1990).
90. Kane v. Aetna Life Ins., 893 F.2d 1283 (11th Cir. 1990).
91. Winstead v. Ind. Ins. Co., 855 F.2d 430 (7th Cir. 1988).
92. 29 U.S.C. § 1132(a) (2013).
93. Aetna Health Inc. v. Davila, 542 U.S. 200, 208 (2004).

benefits to be paid under [ERISA plans]; and (4) laws and common-law rules providing remedies for misconduct growing out of [ERISA plan administration].[94]

However, the Tenth Circuit observed that ERISA does not preempt state laws and claims that do not bear on the relations among principal ERISA entities, the plan, plan fiduciaries, or beneficiaries, nor does ERISA preempt actions affecting relations between these parties and outsiders.[95]

Breach of Contract

The United States Court of Appeals for the Sixth Circuit aligned with the Tenth Circuit's approach in *Penny/Ohlmann/Nieman, Inc. v. Miami Valley Pension Corporation* and found that ERISA preempted a breach-of-contract claim, which was brought against the trustee of a plan but did not preempt a breach-of-contract claim against a nonfiduciary service provider.[96] The Sixth Circuit observed: "ERISA preempts state laws that (1) mandate employee benefit structures or their administration; (2) provide alternative enforcement mechanisms; or (3) bind employers or plan administrators to particular choices or preclude uniform administrative practice, thereby functioning as a regulation of an ERISA plan itself."[97] The court also observed that, in the wake of *Travelers*, the Second Circuit, Fourth Circuit, Ninth Circuit, and Tenth Circuit had each held that ERISA state-law claims leveled against nonfiduciary service providers to ERISA plans were not preempted by ERISA.[98]

94. Woodworker's Supply, Inc. v. Principal Mut. Life Ins. Co., 170 F.3d 985, 990 (10th Cir. 1999) (citing Airparts Co., Inc. v. Custom Ben. Servs. of Austin, Inc., 28 F.3d 1062, 1064–65 (10th Cir. 1994)).
95. *Id.* (citing *Airparts*, 28 F.3d at 1065; Hospice of Metro Denver, Inc. v. Group Health Ins. of Okla. Inc., 944 F.2d 752, 756 (10th Cir. 1991)).
96. Penny/Ohlmann/Nieman, Inc. v. Miami Valley Pension Corp., 399 F.3d 692, 697 (6th Cir. 2005).
97. *Id.* at 698 (citations and quotation marks omitted).
98. *Id.* (citing Gerosa v. Savasta & Co., 329 F.3d 317, 330 (2d Cir. 2003); Ariz. State Carpenters Pension Trust Fund v. Citibank, 125 F.3d 715, 724 (9th Cir. 1997); Coyne & Delany Co. v. Selman, 98 F.3d 1457, 1466, 1472 (4th Cir. 1996); Airparts Co. v. Custom Benefit Servs., 28 F.3d 1062, 1066 (10th Cir. 1994)).

Not all breach-of-contract claims are preempted. Whenever courts have found that ERISA does not preempt breach-of-contract claims, it is a situation where an agreement or contract existed that was separate and distinct from the ERISA plan and this separate contract formed the basis for the claim.[99] The *Penny/Ohlmann/Nieman* court found that ERISA preempted the breach-of-contract claim against the trustee because all of the trustee's obligations arose from the plan and the breach-of-contract claim was based on the fact that a fiduciary breached the terms of the plan.[100] However, ERISA did not preempt the breach-of-contract claim against the nonfiduciary service provider because the provider did not serve as a fiduciary; the state-law cause of action did not fall within the three categories that ERISA generally preempts.[101] Furthermore, the provider's record-keeping services did not differ from the typical consulting, custodial, actuarial, or legal services provided to ERISA plans, and claims based on such services have been allowed to proceed in state courts.[102]

The court was not persuaded by the argument that the breach-of-contract claim against the service provider should have been preempted even though the service provider asserted that the claimant was attempting, through its state-law claims, to recover plan benefits.[103] Courts view a suit to recover plan benefits from a nonfiduciary as an attempt to create an alternative ERISA enforcement mechanism, and such a suit is preempted.[104] Whereas the claimant in *Penny/Ohlmann/Nieman* was seeking benefits that were triggered on behalf of the participants, the damages being sought were more in the nature of compensatory damages caused by a breach of contract.[105] Not every suit mentioning plan benefits requires preemption, and the court allowed the claimant to recover damages due to the breach of contract.[106]

99. *Id.* at 699 (citing Marks v. Newcourt Credit Group, Inc., 342 F.3d 444, 453 (6th Cir. 2003); Gerosa v. Savasta & Co., Inc., 329 F.3d 317, 319 (2d Cir. 2003); *Ariz. State Carpenters*, 125 F.3d at 718; *Coyne & Delany*, 98 F.3d at 1471; *Airparts Co.*, 28 F.3d at 1066).
100. *Id.*
101. *Id.*
102. *Id.* at 699–701.
103. *Id.* at 702.
104. *Id.*
105. *Id.* at 702–03.
106. *Id.*

Negligent Misrepresentation

In addition, the *Penny/Ohlmann/Nieman* court found that the negligent-misrepresentation claim against the trustee was preempted but that the negligent-misrepresentation claim against the nonfiduciary service provider was not.[107] The court explained that if the misrepresentation claim requires an evaluation of the plan and the parties' performance with respect to the plan, the claim will be preempted.[108] Thus, preemption turns on the nature of issues underlying the claim and not the timing of the alleged misrepresentation.[109]

The claimant alleged that the trustee had negligently misrepresented its knowledge of the applicable law and its ability to administer the plan in conformity with the law, the plan, and the prevailing industry standards.[110] Resolving the negligent-misrepresentation claim against the trustee would require a court to assess the trustee's obligations under the ERISA plan in order to compare it with the trustee's representations as well as to determine the legality of the trustee's performance.[111] ERISA preempted the negligent-misrepresentation claim because it went to the heart of ERISA's exclusive regulation, and allowing "the claim to proceed would result in the use of state tort-law as an end run around ERISA's exclusive enforcement mechanism."[112] In comparison, ERISA did not preempt the claim against the non-fiduciary because the claim arose solely out of an agreement to provide record-keeping services and did not call on a reviewing court to determine if an ERISA-qualified plan had been violated.[113] In a later Fourth Circuit case, *Griggs v. E.I. DuPont de Nemours & Company*, the court held that ERISA preempted a negligence claim. *Griggs* concerned a negligent-misrepresentation claim against a pension plan's ERISA fiduciary after the fiduciary failed to inform the claimant that he was not able to defer taxes

107. *Id.* at 703.
108. *Id.*
109. *Id.*
110. *Id.*
111. *Id.*
112. *Id.*
113. *Id.* at 703–04.

on his early retirement benefit.[114] At issue by the time *Griggs* reached the United States Court of Appeals for the Fourth Circuit was whether ERISA preempted the negligent misrepresentation claim if ERISA afforded the claimant no other remedy because, according to the claimant, preemption would be inappropriate whenever Congress fails to provide relief.[115] To the contrary, the court explained that a state-law cause of action is preempted when it is premised on the existence of an employee benefit plan and requires the claimant to plead and the court to find that an ERISA plan exists.[116] The court found that the negligent-misrepresentation claim was preempted because it was a claim concerning an important obligation of an ERISA fiduciary, which was to provide information concerning plan benefits empowering beneficiaries to make informed choices about plan participation.[117] In *Farr II*, the Ninth Circuit addressed a set of facts similar to those in *Griggs* and found that ERISA preempted various claims, including fraud and misrepresentation claims, when those claims were based on an employer's failure to explain the tax implications of plan payments.[118] The Ninth Circuit observed in *Farr II* that the plan's tax consequences "clearly 'relate to' plan administration because they are part of the overall mix of information relied upon by Plaintiffs in making their decisions to participate in the plan."[119]

Negligence and Malpractice Claims

In *Custer v. Sweeney*, the United States Court of Appeals for the Fourth Circuit considered whether a malpractice claim was preempted by ERISA.[120] The plaintiff argued that professional negligence and malpractice claims against third-party service providers to ERISA plans were outside pre-

114. Griggs v. E.I. DuPont de Nemours & Co., 237 F.3d 371, 376–77 (4th Cir. 2001).
115. *Id.* at 377.
116. *Id.* at 378 (citing Ingersoll-Rand Co. v. McClendon, 498 U.S. 133, 140 (1990)).
117. *Id.* at 379 (citing Varity Corp. v. Howe, 516 U.S. 489, 502 (1996)).
118. Farr v. U.S. West Comms., Inc., 151 F.3d 908, 911–13 (9th Cir. 1998), *amended by* Farr U.S. West Comms., 179 F.3d 1252 (9th Cir. 1999).
119. *Id.* at 913.
120. Custer v. Sweeney, 89 F.3d 1156, 1166 (4th Cir. 1996).

emption because those claims did not implicate the essential functions of employee benefit plans.[121] The court agreed with the plaintiff, thereby joining a unanimous body of federal law in concluding that Congress did not intend ERISA to preempt professional malpractice claims under state law based on services rendered to ERISA plans.[122] The court emphasized that malpractice claims represent a traditional exercise of state authority, which creates a presumption against ERISA preemption, and that permitting state-law malpractice claims against such service providers to ERISA plans would not compromise the policies underlying ERISA.[123]

Denial-of-benefit claims cast as malpractice claims face preemption. The Supreme Court stated in *Davila*:

> [I]f an individual brings suit complaining of a denial of coverage for medical care, where the individual is entitled to such coverage only because of the terms of an ERISA-regulated employee benefit plan, and where no legal duty (state or federal) independent of ERISA or the plan terms is violated, then the suit falls "within the scope of" ERISA § 502(a)(1)(B).[124]

The United States Court of Appeals for the Fourth Circuit explained in the unreported case *Kuthy v. Mansheim*:

> In *Davila*, the plaintiffs brought malpractice claims for injuries allegedly arising from [their insurance companies'] decisions not to provide coverage for certain treatment and services recommended by [plaintiffs'] treating physicians. Because the plaintiffs' claims stemmed from their insurance companies' interpretations of ERISA-regulated plans, the Court ruled that their malpractice claims implicated the same duties contained in ERISA and were therefore completely preempted. The same is true here. Kuthy alleges that Appellees committed malpractice by failing to authorize an experimental bone marrow transplant

121. *Id.*
122. *Id.* at 1167.
123. *Id.*
124. Aetna Health Inc. v. Davila, 542 U.S. 200, 210 (2004).

recommended by his wife's treating physician. Appellees' decision to deny coverage was based upon their interpretation of a provision in the insurance plan that excluded experimental treatments. Kuthy's claim therefore falls within the scope of ERISA.[125]

Unclaimed Property

The Uniform Unclaimed Property Act, a version of which is in effect in most states, defines property as including:

> [A]n amount due and payable under the terms of an annuity or insurance policy, including policies providing life insurance, property and casualty insurance, workers' compensation insurance, or health and disability insurance; and . . . an amount distributable from a trust or custodial fund established under a plan to provide health, welfare, pension, vacation, severance, retirement, death, stock purchase, profit sharing, employee savings, supplemental unemployment insurance, or similar benefits . . . .[126]

Accordingly, unclaimed employee benefits are typically subject to unclaimed property laws. Courts have found that these state laws are preempted by ERISA.[127] Moreover, the Department of Labor stated in 1995 that ERISA preempted the Uniform Unclaimed Property Act and even stated that ERISA preempted the model law under a theory of implied preemption,[128] which, according to the Supreme Court, arises "when compliance with both federal and state regulations is a physical impossibility" or state action "stands as

125. Kuthy v. Mansheim, 124 F. App'x 756, 758 (4th Cir. 2004) (citations and quotation marks omitted).
126. UNIFORM UNCLAIMED PROPERTY ACT OF 1981 § 1(10)(vi–vii).
127. *See* Commonwealth Edison Co. v. Vega, 174 F.3d 870 (7th Cir. 1999); Manufacturers Life Ins. Co. v. East Bay Restaurant and Tavern Retirement Plan, 57 F. Supp. 2d 921 (N.D. Cal. 1999).
128. Letter from Robert Doyle, Department of Labor Director of Regulations and Interpretations, to Willis Sullivan III, Chair, Drafting Committee to Revise Uniform Unclaimed Property Act, of the National Conference of Commissioners on Uniform State Laws (NCCUSL) (Mar. 3, 1995).

an obstacle to the accomplishments and execution of the full purposes and objectives of Congress."[129]

Commonwealth Edison Company v. Vega concerned an Illinois law, The Illinois Uniform Disposition of Unclaimed Property Act (Uniform Act), that sought to apply the Uniform Act to benefits payable under the Commonwealth Edison Company's pension plan that were not claimed by a beneficiary within five years.[130] Chief Judge Richard Posner of the United States Court of Appeals for the Seventh Circuit explained the rationale for ERISA preemption:

> ERISA preempts any state regulation that "relates to" an ERISA plan. The Uniform Act, although it does not refer explicitly to ERISA plans, relates to the Com Ed plan directly and substantially. Remember that until the check to the beneficiary is actually presented to the plan for payment through the banking system, and paid, the money due to the beneficiary is an asset of the plan. The state thus wants to take a chunk of an ERISA Plan's assets and put it in the state treasury. After that happens, any beneficiary of the plan who wants his benefits will have to apply to the state for them. The state becomes the plan administrator with respect to those assets. Not only does the state become the custodian of the assets, in violation of ERISA's provisions regarding plan administration, it depletes those assets, by taking the interest that accrues on them. If the ERISA plan entitled a beneficiary to interest for the period between when benefits were due him and when he actually collected them, the state would actually be reducing his ERISA benefits. Even if the plan does not provide for interest, as Com Ed's does not, the state would still be reducing the plan's assets. Suppose the benefits due the participant in year *t* are $10,000, and he doesn't claim them until year *t* + 6, by which time $10,000 in plan assets would have grown through the operation of compound interest to $14,000. Then, were it not for the Uniform Act, the assets of the plan would be greater by $4,000. The Act is the device by which the state appropriates those assets for itself.

129. Metro. Life Ins. Co. v. Massachusetts, 471 U.S. 724, 738 (1985).
130. *Commonwealth Edison Co.*, 174 F.3d at 872.

> It depletes those assets in another way, by subjecting the plan to the varying laws of the different states. Participants in the Com Ed plan are scattered over 44 states. Though there are only two basic state-law regimes governing unclaimed property (the two uniform laws), states have tended to custom-tailor whichever uniform law they have chosen to their particular needs. The consequence is numerous variations in the amount of time before the state takes over the money (recall that Illinois has shortened the period of the Uniform Disposition of Unclaimed Property Act) and in the formalities for claiming the money from the state. Several states have not even modeled their unclaimed-property laws on either of the uniform laws, but have gone their own way completely.[131]

In an earlier decision, *Aetna Life Insurance Company v. Borges*, the Second Circuit had found that Connecticut's escheat law's impact on a welfare plan was too tenuous to elicit ERISA preemption.[132] The plan at issue in *Aetna* differed from the one in *Commonwealth Edison Company*, however, in that it was a fully insured plan—meaning a plan contracting with an insurance company to provide all benefits—and the state sought to escheat benefits from the insurance company rather than from the plan itself.[133] Aetna would presumably make administrative and accounting adjustments to avoid losing money to the state, but the adjustments would only have minor effects on beneficiaries.[134] Thus, the state action in *Aetna* was "too tenuous, remote, and peripheral to require preemption."[135]

Community Property Systems

The majority of states take a common-law approach to marital property, denying spouses shares in each other's property during marriage and

131. *Id.* at 873 (citations omitted).
132. Aetna Life Ins. Co. v. Borges, 869 F.2d 142, 149 (2d Cir. 1989).
133. *Id.* at 147.
134. *Id.*
135. *Id.*

engaging in equitable distribution of property upon divorce. A minority of states takes a community property approach to property allocation at divorce and recognizes, with some deviation, a present half interest shared by each spouse in the other's earnings. A community property system's two essential characteristics are (1) the transmissibility of a spouse's interest to his or her heirs such that the heirs take that to which a deceased spouse would have been entitled and (2) the partnering of spouses in terms of gains and losses during the marital relationship.

ERISA features survivorship interests as well as interests arising upon divorce that are out of sync with the community property approach to marital property. In 1997, the Supreme Court transformed Louisiana's community property law, and indeed the law of community property, with the case *Boggs v. Boggs*. The Court held that ERISA preempted a state law that would have allowed Dorothy Boggs, a former spouse of the deceased Isaac Boggs, to transfer a portion of the survivor's annuity belonging to Sandra Boggs, who was Isaac's wife upon death.[136] The Court explained:

> ERISA's solicitude for the economic security of surviving spouses would be undermined by allowing a predeceasing spouse's heirs and legatees to have a community property interest in the survivor's annuity. Even a plan participant cannot defeat a nonparticipant surviving spouse's statutory entitlement to an annuity. It would be odd, to say the least, if Congress permitted a predeceasing nonparticipant spouse to do so. Nothing in the language of ERISA supports concluding that Congress made such an inexplicable decision. Testamentary transfers could reduce a surviving spouse's guaranteed annuity below the minimum set by ERISA (defined as 50% of the annuity payable during the joint lives of the participant and spouse). In this case, Sandra's annuity would be reduced by approximately 20%, according to the calculations contained in the sons' state-court filings. There is no reason why testamentary transfers could not reduce a survivor's annuity by an even greater amount. Perhaps even more troubling, the recipient of the testamentary transfer need not be a family member. For instance,

136. Boggs v. Boggs, 520 U.S. 833, 835–36 (1997).

> a surviving spouse's § 1055 annuity might be substantially reduced so that funds could be diverted to support an unrelated stranger.
>
> In the face of this direct clash between state law and the provisions and objectives of ERISA, the state law cannot stand.[137]

As a result, the Court stripped the deceased participant's former spouse in *Boggs* of testamentary power over half of the benefits from an employee stock ownership plan. Despite advocates' calls for Congress to amend ERISA out of respect for states' community property approaches to marital property, ERISA preemption of these laws when they conflict with its entitlements remains absolute.

State Divorce Revocation Laws

In a similar vein as *Boggs*, the Supreme Court held in its 2001 decision *Egelhoff v. Egelhoff* that ERISA preempted a Washington statute, which upon divorce, automatically revoked the beneficiary status of an ex- spouse who was designated the beneficiary of a nonprobate asset.[138] The decedent in *Egelhoff* passed away two months after divorce, leaving two sons from his prior marriage as his heirs at law at the time of death.[139] The decedent's former wife was the named beneficiary on his pension and life insurance policies at the time of his death. The decedent's sons argued in court that they were the rightful heirs.[140] The Supreme Court of Washington had agreed with the sons, explaining that ERISA "does not apply immediately and exclusively to an ERISA plan, nor is the existence of such a plan essential to operation of the statute."[141]

The Supreme Court of the United States disagreed with the Supreme Court of Washington:

137. *Id.* at 833–34.
138. Egelhoff v. Egelhoff, 532 U.S. 141, 143 (2001).
139. *Id.* at 144.
140. *Id.* at 144–45.
141. *In re Estate of Egelhoff*, 989 P.2d 80, 89 (Wash. 1999).

The statute binds ERISA plan administrators to a particular choice of rules for determining beneficiary status. The administrators must pay benefits to the beneficiaries chosen by state law, rather than to those identified in the plan documents. The statute thus implicates an area of core ERISA concern. In particular, it runs counter to ERISA's commands that a plan shall specify the basis on which payments are made to and from the plan, and that the fiduciary shall administer the plan in accordance with the documents and instruments governing the plan, making payments to a beneficiary who is designated by a participant, or by the terms of [the] plan. In other words, unlike generally applicable laws regulating areas where ERISA has nothing to say, which we have upheld notwithstanding their incidental effect on ERISA plans, this statute governs the payment of benefits, a central matter of plan administration.

The Washington statute also has a prohibited connection with ERISA plans because it interferes with nationally uniform plan administration. One of the principal goals of ERISA is to enable employers to establish a uniform administrative scheme, which provides a set of standard procedures to guide processing of claims and disbursement of benefits. Uniformity is impossible, however, if plans are subject to different legal obligations in different States.

The Washington statute at issue here poses precisely that threat. Plan administrators cannot make payments simply by identifying the beneficiary specified by the plan documents. Instead they must familiarize themselves with state statutes so that they can determine whether the named beneficiary's status has been revoked by operation of law. And in this context the burden is exacerbated by the choice-of-law problems that may confront an administrator when the employer is located in one State, the plan participant lives in another, and the participant's former spouse lives in a third. In such a situation, administrators might find that plan payments are subject to conflicting legal obligations.

To be sure, the Washington statute protects administrators from liability for making payments to the named beneficiary unless they have actual knowledge of the dissolution or other invalidation of marriage,

> and it permits administrators to refuse to make payments until any dispute among putative beneficiaries is resolved. But if administrators do pay benefits, they will face the risk that a court might later find that they had actual knowledge of a divorce. If they instead decide to await the results of litigation before paying benefits, they will simply transfer to the beneficiaries the costs of delay and uncertainty. Requiring ERISA administrators to master the relevant laws of 50 States and to contend with litigation would undermine the congressional goal of minimiz[ing] the administrative and financial burden[s] on plan administrators—burdens ultimately borne by the beneficiaries.
>
> We recognize that all state laws create some potential for a lack of uniformity. But differing state regulations affecting an ERISA plan's system for processing claims and paying benefits impose precisely the burden that ERISA pre-emption was intended to avoid. And as we have noted, the statute at issue here directly conflicts with ERISA's requirements that plans be administered, and benefits be paid, in accordance with plan documents. We conclude that the Washington statute has a connection with ERISA plans and is therefore pre-empted.[142]

State Slayer Statutes

State slayer statutes prevent murderers from benefiting from the death of a victim via inheriting from the decedent's estate. The Supreme Court of the United States addressed ERISA preemption of state slayer statutes in *Egelhoff*'s dicta.[143] Responding to the argument that the Court's holding predicated preemption of state slayer statutes, the Court explained:

> Those statutes are not before us, so we do not decide the issue. We note, however, that the principle underlying the statutes—which have been adopted by nearly every State—is well established in the law and has a long historical pedigree predating ERISA. And because the

142. *Id.* at 147–50 (citations and quotation marks omitted).
143. *Id.* at 152.

> statutes are more or less uniform nationwide, their interference with the aims of ERISA is at least debatable.[144]

Whether state slayer statutes are "more or less uniform" is in fact a matter of interpretation, as some statutes require conviction while others require only probable cause to deny benefits, but courts have typically treated the statutes as being free from ERISA preemption. An example is *Mack v. Estate of Mack*, where the Nevada Supreme Court found that a slayer statute survived preemption.[145] The court observed that several federal courts had reached a similar conclusion.[146] The court remarked: "We conclude that the Nevada slayer statute is not preempted by ERISA, as the application of this statute will not affect the determination of an employee's eligibility for benefits or the impact on the method of calculating benefits due."[147]

State Probate Action

Despite probate's historical place as a matter of state law, courts have extended ERISA preemption to probate actions. In 2011, the United States Court of Appeals for the Eastern District of North Carolina held that ERISA preempted a state statute requiring that a beneficiary of a life insurance policy survive the decedent-policyholder by 120 hours.[148] The court reasoned that the statute had "a connection with or reference to" an ERISA

144. *Id.* (citations omitted).
145. Mack v. Estate of Mack, 206 P.3d 98, 110 (Nev. 2009)
146. *Id.* (citing UNUM Ins. Co. of America v. Locke, No. 2:06 CV 0861, 2006 WL 2457106 (W.D. La. Aug. 22, 2006); Atwater v. Nortel Networks, Inc., 388 F. Supp. 2d 610, 614 (M.D. N.C. 2005); Conn. Gen. Life Ins. Co. v. Riner, 351 F. Supp. 2d 492, 497 (W.D. Va. 2005); Administrative Committee for the H.E.B. v. Harris, 217 F. Supp. 2d 759, 761 (E.D. Tex. 2002); New Orleans Elec. Pension Fund v. Newman, 784 F. Supp. 1233, 1236 (E.D. La. 1992); Mendez–Bellido v. Bd. of Tr. of Div. 1181, A.T.U., 709 F. Supp. 329, 331 (E.D. N.Y.1989)).
147. *Id.* (citations omitted). The Ohio Court of Appeals' decision in *Ahmed v. Ahmed* represents the minority view that ERISA preempts state slayer statutes. Ahmed v. Ahmed, 817 N.E.2d 424, 432 (Ohio Ct. App. 2004). The court stated: "For all intents and purposes, slayer statutes affect the administration of ERISA plans in the same manner as the statute discussed in *Egelhoff*." *Id.* at 430. The court's decision may have stemmed from an intention for the two sons involved in the action to benefit equally from their decedent-mother's estate. *See* Peter S. Lin, *Murdering the Slayer Statute Under the Pretense of ERISA Preemption*: Ahmed v. Ahmed, 58 TAX LAW. 767, 779–80 (2005).
148. Harleysville Life Ins. Co. v. Harrelson, No. 7:10-CV-00051-DAN, 2011 WL 4544047, at *4 (E.D. N.C. Sept. 29, 2011).

plan because the statute would change the plan's beneficiary.[149] Similarly, different states' death acts are not uniform, and failing to rule that ERISA preempted the statute would impede Congress's goal for ERISA to foster national uniformity among employee benefit plans.[150]

Similarly, the United States Court of Appeals for the Ninth Circuit held in *Board of Trustees of Western Conference of Teamsters Pension Trust Fund v. H.F. Johnson, Inc.* that ERISA preempted a Montana statute preventing creditors from presenting claims in probate.[151] The court observed that "Congress expressly provided a period of limitations governing actions to collect withdrawal liability," indicating "that Congress considered the period of limitations applicable to such actions essential to enforcement of employer obligations under [ERISA]."[152]

Pay-or-Play Schemes

In the 2008 case *Golden Gate Restaurant Association v. City & County of San Francisco*, the United States Court of Appeals for the Ninth Circuit ruled that ERISA did not preempt a San Francisco "pay-or-play" ordinance.[153] Specifically, the court rejected the notion that the ordinance, which required certain employers to make expenditures to covered employees' health-care costs or else make payments directly to the city, created an ERISA plan.[154] In addition, the court refused to find that the ordinance related to an ERISA plan.[155] The court reasoned:

> The Ordinance does not require any employer to adopt an ERISA plan or other health plan. Nor does it require any employer to provide specific benefits through an existing ERISA plan or other health

149. *Id.*
150. *Id.*
151. Bd. of Trs. of W. Conference of Teamsters Pension Trust Fund v. H.F. Johnson, Inc., 830 F.2d 1009, 1016 (9th Cir. 1987).
152. *Id.*
153. Golden Gate Rest. Ass'n v. City & County of S.F., 546 F.3d 639, 661 (9th Cir. 2008).
154. *Id.* at 648–49.
155. *Id.* at 659.

> plan. Any employer covered by the Ordinance may fully discharge its expenditure obligations by making the required level of employee health care expenditures, whether those expenditures are made in whole or in part to an ERISA plan, or in whole or in part to the City. The Ordinance thus preserves ERISA's uniform regulatory regime. The Ordinance also has no effect on the administrative practices of a benefit plan unless an employer voluntarily elects to change those practices.
>
> A covered employer may choose to adopt or to change an ERISA plan in lieu of making the required health care expenditures to the City. An employer may be influenced by the Ordinance to do so because, when faced with an unavoidable obligation to make a payment at a certain level, it may prefer to make that payment to an ERISA plan. However, as *Travelers* makes clear, such influence is entirely permissible.[156]

The Ninth Circuit distinguished the case from *Retail Industry Leaders Association v. Fielder* based on the eligibility of employees of employers who made payments under the San Francisco ordinance to enroll in a publicly operated welfare program known as the Health Access Plan (HAP).[157] In *Fielder*, the United States Court of Appeals for the Fourth Circuit found that ERISA preempted a state law requiring "employers with 10,000 or more Maryland employees to spend at least 8 percent of their total payrolls on employees' health insurance costs or pay the amount their spending falls short to the State of Maryland."[158] The Fourth Circuit found that the law prescribed a payment that was "actually a fee or a penalty that [gave] the employer an irresistible incentive to provide employees with a greater level of health benefits."[159] Thus, according to the Fourth Circuit, "the voices given in the [law] . . . [were] not meaningful alternatives by which an employer [could] increase its healthcare spending to comply . . . without affecting its ERISA plans."[160]

156. *Id.* at 655–56 (citations and quotation marks omitted).
157. *Id.* at 659–61.
158. Retail Indus. Leaders Ass'n v. Fielder, 475 F.3d 189, 183 (4th Cir. 2007).
159. *Id.* at 194.
160. *Id.* at 196.

Without accepting or rejecting the Fourth Circuit's reasoning in *Fielder*, the *Golden Gate* court found the Maryland law in *Fielder* distinguishable from the San Francisco ordinance:

> In stark contrast to the Maryland law in *Fielder*, the City-payment option under the San Francisco Ordinance offers employers a meaningful alternative that allows them to preserve the existing structure of their ERISA plans. If an employer elects to pay the City, that employer's employees are eligible for free or discounted enrollment in the HAP, or for medical reimbursement accounts. In contrast to the Maryland law, the San Francisco Ordinance provides tangible benefits to employees when their employers choose to pay the City rather than to establish or alter ERISA plans. In its motion for summary judgment, the Association provided no evidence to demonstrate that San Francisco employers are, in practical fact, compelled to alter or establish ERISA plans rather than to make payments to the City.
>
> Because the City-payment option offers San Francisco employers a realistic alternative to creating or altering ERISA plans, the Ordinance does not effectively mandate . . . that employers structure their employee healthcare plans to provide a certain level of benefits. In the view of the Fielder court, Maryland legislators intended to force Wal–Mart to increase its spending on healthcare benefits rather than to pay monies to the State. Unlike the Maryland law, the San Francisco Ordinance provides employers with a legitimate alternative to establishing or altering ERISA plans. We therefore conclude that the San Francisco Ordinance does not compel covered employers to establish or to alter ERISA plans.[161]

161. *Golden Gate*, 546 F.3d at 660–61 (citations and quotation marks omitted).

The Department of Treasury has delayed the federal pay-or-play requirement in the Affordable Care Act (ACA),[162] known as the "shared responsibility for employers regarding health coverage,"[163] until 2015.[164]

Preemption and the Patient Protection and Affordable Care Act

In addition to ERISA's preemption of state regulation of ERISA plans, ERISA features a civil enforcement remedy that the Supreme Court has interpreted to be the sole means for enforcing ERISA.[165] Therefore, as previously covered, state-law claims are generally preempted. ACA builds on the remedy available under ERISA through its appeals process with external review. Under ACA, group health plans and health insurers must implement an appeals process for coverage determinations and claim denials.[166] ACA requires, at a minimum, that the plan or issuer provide notice to enrollees of the appeals process and of the availability of any consumer assistance and that the plan or issuer allow enrollees to review their file, present evidence and testimony, and receive coverage pending the outcome of the appeal.[167] Appeals review must be external and in compliance with states' external review processes.[168] The Secretary will set forth guidance if the state has no applicable external review processes, the state's process does not meet the minimum consumer protections detailed in the National Association

162. Patient Protection and Affordable Care Act of 2010, Pub. L. No. 111-148, 124 Stat. 119 (codified at 42 U.S.C. §§18001–18121 (2012)), *amended by* Health Care and Education Reconciliation Act of 2010, Pub. L. No. 111-152, 124 Stat. 1029.
163. 26 U.S.C. § 4980H (2013).
164. *See* Mark J. Mazur, *Continuing to Implement the ACA in a Careful, Thoughtful Manner*, Treasury Notes, July 2, 2013, http://www.treasury.gov/connect/blog/Pages/Continuing-to-Implement-the-ACA-in-a-Careful-Thoughtful-Manner-.aspx.
165. 29 U.S.C. § 1132 (2012); Mary Ann Chirba-Martin, *ERISA Preemption of State "Play or Pay" Mandates: How PPACA Clouds an Already Confusing Picture*, 13 J. Health Care L. & Pol'y 393, 402–03 (2010).
166. 42 U.S.C. § 300gg-19 (2012).
167. *Id.*
168. *Id.*

of Commissioners Uniform Model Act,[169] or the plan is self-insured and therefore not subject to state insurance regulation.[170]

In addition, ERISA's enforcement preemption is further implicated through states' or the Secretary's enforcement authority. ACA empowers states to require health insurance issuers to meet ACA's requirements with respect to individual health insurance coverage and group health plans.[171] Accordingly, ACA does not supersede state laws establishing, implementing, or continuing standards or requirements relating to health insurance issuers to the extent that these state laws do not prevent ACA's application.[172] At the same time, ACA does directly address ERISA preemption of state regulation of ERISA plans.[173]

The Secretary may supersede a state's enforcement authority upon a finding that a state failed to substantially enforce ACA.[174] In general, noncompliant group health plans and health insurance issuers are subject to a civil money penalty in an amount up to $100 for each day and for each individual, for lack of compliance.[175] The Secretary will take into account the offender's record of compliance.[176] A health issuer is liable for its own failure, a group health plan is liable for its own failure when the plan is sponsored by two or more employers, and an employer is liable for the failure of a group health plan when the plan is not sponsored by two or more employers.[177] An entity is not liable if the Secretary finds that it did not know of the failure while exercising reasonable diligence or if the failure resulted from reasonable cause and not willful neglect and the entity corrected the failure either within 30 days of knowing of the failure or within 30 days from when the entity reasonably should have known of the failure.[178] The Secretary may waive all or part of the penalty for a failure due to reason-

169. *See generally* "Uniform Health Carrier External Review Model Act," NAT'L ASS'N OF INS. COMM'RS (last accessed Aug. 14, 2013), http://www.dol.gov/ebsa/pdf/externalreviewmodelact.pdf.
170. 42 U.S.C. § 300gg-19 (2012).
171. 42 U.S.C. § 300gg-22 (2012). This does not extend to federal plans. *Id.*
172. 42 U.S.C. § 300gg-23 (2013).
173. *Id.*
174. 42 U.S.C. § 300gg-22 (2012).
175. *Id.*
176. *Id.*
177. *Id.*
178. *Id.*

able cause and not willful neglect, and such a penalty's amount may not exceed the lesser of either 10 percent of the aggregate amount paid by the employer for group health plans the previous year or $500,000.[179]

A liable entity may request a hearing within 30 days after the Secretary's issuance of a notice of assessment.[180] Without a hearing request, the assessment constitutes a final and unappealable order.[181] Following a request, the administrative law judge presiding over the hearing will issue an order that is final but subject to district court review unless the Secretary modifies or vacates the decision within 30 days after the judge's decision.[182] An entity subject to a civil money penalty may obtain review by the appropriate United States district court within 30 days of the administrative law judge's order.[183] A reviewing judicial body may only set aside the findings of the Secretary if they are unsupported by substantial evidence.[184] If an entity fails to pay the penalty, the Secretary shall refer the matter to the United States Attorney General for recovery of the amount in district court.[185]

State's enforcement authority, however, turns on ERISA preemption of state regulation of ERISA plans. One consequence of ERISA preemption of state regulation of ERISA plans is that it situated 2010's sweeping health-care reform at the federal level by preempting potential state-led changes to health coverage.[186] ACA only relates to ERISA preemption to the extent that ACA regulates private employers.[187] In many ways, ACA skirted ERISA preemption.[188] It did so through federal changes that do not require state

179. *Id.*
180. *Id.*
181. *Id.*
182. *Id.*
183. *Id.*
184. *Id.*
185. *Id.*
186. Mallory Jensen, *Is ERISA Preemption Superfluous in the New Age of Health Care Reform?*, 2011 COLUM. BUS. L. REV. 464, 503 (2011).
187. *Id.* at 476 ("It is only in ERISA's coverage of the private employer sphere that ERISA preemption concerns will intersect with the ACA.").
188. Abbe R. Gluck, *Instrastatutory Federalism and Statutory Interpretation: State Implementation of Federal Law in Health Reform and Beyond*, 1221 YALE. L.J. 534, 590 (2011) ("[I]n the ACA, Congress left ERISA's preemption essentially in place and enacted the new statute on top of it; in so doing, Congress limited the kinds of state innovation it purports to encourage mostly to those state experiments explicitly contemplated by the Act's text (which amounts primarily to experiments centered around the new insurance-exchange concept).").

action or implementing laws, such as the individual mandate and the federal taxation of large employers who fail to provide health insurance; by altering the coverage landscape outside the purview of employer-provided benefits, including modifications to Medicare and Medicaid; and with amendments to ERISA that do not reach its preemption clause.[189]

Still, significant aspects of ACA continuously implicate ERISA preemption. For instance, whether new laws and regulations that states create pursuant to ACA-required exchanges will survive ERISA preemption remains a live question.[190] ACA called for each state, by January 1, 2014, to have an American Health Benefit Exchange to enable the purchase of qualified health plans and facilitate a Small Business Health Options Program (SHOP) to assist small employers in enrolling their employees.[191] The SHOP exchange could be its own freestanding entity or, if the state had the requisite resources, be absorbed into the state's health insurance exchange.[192] When the Secretary determined that a state would not have an operational exchange by January 1, 2014, the Secretary assumed responsibility for implementing the exchange.[193] Seventeen states have state-based exchanges, 27 states have defaulted to federally operated exchanges, and 7 states have declared a partnership with the federal government in operating exchanges.[194]

ACA expressly preserves "State regulatory authority," declaring that nothing in its title pertaining to state health exchanges and enforcement "shall be construed to preempt any State law that does not prevent the application of the provisions of this title."[195] State-operated exchanges have a variety of obligations, including overseeing health plans' benefit design, marketing, and quality.[196] In addition, states must modify small-group and individual insurance regulation by eliminating exclusions for preexisting conditions,

189. *Jensen, supra* note 186, at 501–02.
190. *Id.* at 503.
191. 42 U.S.C. § 18041 (2012).
192. *Id.*
193. 42 U.S.C. § 18041 (2012).
194. *State Decisions for Creating Health Insurance Marketplaces, 2014*, KAISER FAMILY FOUNDATION, http://kff.org/health-reform/state-indicator/health-insurance-exchanges/ (last visited Aug. 2, 2014).
195. 42 U.S.C. § 18041 (2012).
196. Alan Weil & Raymond Sheppach, *New Roles for States in Health Reform Implementation*, 29 HEALTH AFFAIRS 1178, 1179 (2010).

removing rate variation based on sex and other factors, and increasing oversight of health insurance rate increases.[197] ACA does not expressly indicate the lawmaking and regulatory mechanisms for implementing these exchanges, leaving open a possible ERISA preemption challenge.[198] Legal scholars have characterized ACA's reliance on state-operated exchanges in the absence of further guidance as being inexcusable, calling for legislation to explicitly address ERISA preemption in the current health-care landscape.[199]

Looking ahead to 2017, ACA will empower states to apply for "state innovation waivers."[200] These waivers will allow states to depart from the state exchange model and develop innovative methods for facilitating health insurance so long as the new methods meet criteria set forth by the United States Department of Health and Human Resources and do not increase the federal deficit.[201] The Secretary may grant these waivers but cannot waive any law outside the jurisdiction of the Department of Health and Human Resources, including ERISA.[202] As they have with state implementation of the exchanges, legal scholars have questioned whether ERISA preemption will limit these state programs and hamstring ACA's enablement of state-led innovation in health care.[203]

ERISA preemption certainly threatens ACA-induced, state-based health-care innovation, but it does not necessarily end it. One potential answer to a charge of ERISA preemption is that states are acting pursuant ACA when regulating ERISA plans and are therefore safe from ERISA preemption due to the regulatory relation of their activity to federal law. Another argument in favor of state participation in health reform vis-à-vis ACA implementation is that short of state passage of novel health-care laws, such as new pay-or-play laws, state implementation efforts do not have an impermissible "relation to" ERISA plans. Both of these points are harder to make

197. *Id.* at 1179.
198. *Jensen*, *supra* note 186, at 507. Scholars remain skeptical that a challenge would be brought. *See, e.g.*, *id.* ("[A]lthough states might challenge the ACA's requirement that they implement parts of the reform . . ., it seems unthinkable that they or any business or individual will seriously bring an ERISA preemption challenge to these aspects of the ACA.").
199. *See, e.g.*, *Chirba-Martin*, *supra* note 165, at 421.
200. 42 U.S.C. § 18052 (2012).
201. *Id.*
202. *Id.*
203. *Gluck*, *supra* note 188, at 590 n.153; *Jensen*, *supra* note 186, at 508–12.

in the context of state innovation waivers, which allow states to behave fairly autonomously from the federal government and might even let states directly regulate ERISA plans. The best means of survival for these waivers is likely to be legislative. Representative Dennis Kucinich proposed an amendment to ACA that would have given states an automatic waiver of ERISA preemption, such as the one granted to Hawaii, if the state received an innovation waiver. Even though this amendment died, future amendments may not—especially in light of the contemporaneously palatable federalist flavor of allowing states to adopt a stronger role in health-care solutions.

Chapter 4

Procedural Concerns

Procedural matters with vital consequences for actions brought under ERISA include the standard of review, attorney fees, standing, and statutes of limitations. We previously discussed preemption of state law, and we will now contemplate these other matters.

Standard of Review

Standard of review issues arise very often in cases involving denial of disability benefits. An administrator's decision to deny disability benefits is one of the most litigated issues under ERISA. Two standards of judicial review are applicable to a review of an administrator's denial of a claim for benefits: the more plenary de novo review and a more deferential standard of review, which courts refer to as either an abuse of discretion or an arbitrary and capricious standard. With a de novo review, an administrator's decision will be overturned if the court deems it was incorrect, regardless of whether the administrator acted reasonably in reaching its decision. In other words, under de novo, the court substitutes its own judgment for the plan administrator's judgment. Under an abuse of discretion standard of review, a court gives more deferential treatment to the administrator's decision and will usually uphold a reasonable decision. Courts often treat an abuse of discretion review as interchangeable with the arbitrary and capricious review. However, the Fourth Circuit has recognized that the arbitrary and capricious standard is more deferential and has identified a review for an abuse of discretion as the appropriate standard.[1] In contrast, the Eleventh Circuit has employed de novo, arbitrary and capricious, and enhanced arbitrary and capricious standards of review, adopting the heightened arbitrary and capricious approach where there was a conflict of interest.[2] When applying a deferential standard, some courts take a predetermined, multifactorial approach.[3]

The plan language determines the standard of review that will be applicable if denial of benefits were to be challenged under ERISA. In *Firestone Tire & Rubber Co. v. Bruch*, the Supreme Court set forth four principles to be considered when deciding on the appropriate standard of judicial review of benefit determinations: (1) the principles of trust law guide the determination of the appropriate standard of review;[4] (2) a denial of plan benefits normally should be determined under a de novo standard of review;[5] (3) where the plan expressly grants the administrator or fiduciary discretionary authority to determine eligibility for benefits or to construe the terms of the plan, trust principles make a deferential standard of review appropriate;[6] and (4) where the deferential standard of review applies, if the administrator or fiduciary has operated under a conflict of interest, that

1. Booth v. Wal-Mart Stores, Inc. Assocs. Health & Welfare Plan, 201 F.3d 335, 341–42 (4th Cir. 2000).
2. Marecek v. BellSouth Telecomm., Inc., 49 F.3d 702, 705 (11th Cir. 1995).
3. *See* Helton v. AT&T Inc., 709 F.3d 343, 353 (4th Cir. 2013) (citing *Booth*, 201 F.3d at 342–43) (considering the language of the plan, the purposes and goals of the plan, the adequacy of the materials considered in the decision-making process and the extent the materials support the final decision, whether the interpretation was consistent with plan provisions and with earlier interpretations, whether the decision making was reasonable and principled, whether the decision was consistent with the requirement of ERISA, the external standard relevant to the exercise of discretion, and the fiduciary's motives and any conflict of interest); Finley v. Special Agents Mut. Benefit Ass'n, Inc., 957 F.2d 617, 621 (8th Cir. 1992) (employing a deferential standard of review to plan administrators' decisions and examining "whether their interpretation is consistent with the goals of the Plan, whether their interpretation renders any language in the Plan meaningless or internally inconsistent, whether their interpretation conflicts with the substantive or procedural requirements of the ERISA statute, whether they have interpreted the words at issue consistently, and whether their interpretation is contrary to the clear language of the Plan").
4. Firestone Tire & Rubber Co. v. Bruch, 489 U.S. 101, 110–11 (1989) (citing Cent. States, Se. & Sw. Areas Pension Fund v. Cent. Transp., Inc., 472 U.S. 559, 570 (1985)).
5. *Id.* at 112.
6. *Id.* at 115.

conflict must be weighed as a factor in determining whether there was an abuse of discretion.[7]

The Court endorsed and elaborated on *Firestone* in *Conkright v. Frommert* by dismissing the suggestion that an exception to *Firestone* deference may be necessary in certain circumstances.[8] In *Conkright*, the Second Circuit had overturned an administrator's interpretation of a plan that had granted the administrator interpretive discretion solely because a court had previously overturned a different interpretation by the same administrator.[9] The Supreme Court characterized this action as an impermissible, "one-strike-and-you're-out" approach.[10]

The *Firestone* case did not state, and subsequent Supreme Court cases have not thoroughly defined, what particular plan language is adequate to confer discretion, nor did the Court in *Firestone* state precisely how a conflict of interest should be weighed under the deferential standard. The Court's failure to specifically define the extent of the deference to be given to benefit determinations as well as what is needed to overturn those determinations has led the circuits to develop their own rules pertaining to the standards of review. The Fourth Circuit in *Cosey v. Prudential Insurance Company of America* joined five other circuits in holding that plan language requiring participants to submit claims "satisfactory to us" does not confer the requisite discretion to trigger deferential judicial review.[11]

Courts have typically found that general, nonspecific clauses granting administrators or fiduciaries power do not impart the level of discretionary authority intended by the Court in *Firestone*.[12] Courts have more often

7. *Id.*
8. Conkright v. Frommert, 559 U.S. 506, 513 (2010).
9. *Id.*
10. *Id.*
11. Cosey v. Prudential Ins. Co. of Am., 735 F.3d 161 (4th Cir. 2013); *see also* Gross v. Sun Life Assurance Co. of Canada, 734 F.3d 1 (1st Cir. 2013).
12. *See, e.g.*, Masella v. Blue Cross & Blue Shield of Conn., Inc., 936 F.2d, 98, 103 (2d Cir. 1991) (observing that every plan contains a provision describing administrative discretion, rejecting "that the discretion to establish the terms of a plan is the same as the discretion to interpret the terms later," and applying the de novo standard); Michael Reese Hosp. v. Solo Cup Emp. Health Benefit Plan, 899 F.2d 639, 641 (7th Cir. 1990) (applying the de novo standard despite a provision stating that "[t]he Company shall be the Named Fiduciary and Plan Administrator pursuant to the provisions of ERISA, and as such, the Company shall have authority to control and manage the operation and administration of the plan"); Cathey v. Dow Chem. Co. Med. Care Program, 907 F.2d 554, 559 n.6 (5th Cir. 1990) (applying the

characterized clauses such as "power to construe" and "power to interpret" as imparting discretionary authority.[13] For example, the Seventh Circuit ruled in *Herzberger v. Standard Insurance Company* that, in order to warrant deferential review, the plan must explicitly confer discretion on the administrator, such as with the clause: "Benefits under this plan will be paid only if the plan administrator decides in his discretion that the applicant is entitled to them."[14] In its 2013 decision *Thurber v. Aetna Life Insurance Company*, the Second Circuit declined to extend the standard set forth by the Seventh Circuit in *Herzberger* to require that such a reservation of discretion be specifically conveyed to all members of the plan in order to warrant an arbitrary and capricious standard of review.[15] Accordingly, the Second Circuit performed a deferential review of the administrator's decisions even though the plaintiff claimed that she never received the summary plan description or a copy of the plan itself when both unambiguously granted the administrator discretion.[16]

Discretionary language in the summary plan description is not enough. In 2012, the Seventh Circuit echoed prior decisions and observed in *Schultz v. Aviall, Inc. Long Term Disability Plan* that the discretionary language

de novo standard despite the administrative discretion "to correct any defect, supply any omission or reconcile any inconsistency in, and to control and manage the operation and administration of the plan").

13. *See, e.g.*, Hutchins v. Champion Int'l Corp., 110 F.3d 1341, 1344 (8th Cir. 1997) (reviewing an administrator's interpretation of its plan under an abuse of discretion standard where the administrator had "sole, absolute and uncontrolled" discretion to administer the plan, including the power to interpret the plan's provisions); Moos v. Square D Co., 72 F.3d 39, 40–41 (6th Cir. 1995) (applying the arbitrary and capricious standard because the plan expressly granted the administrator full discretion in interpreting the plan and in determining eligibility for benefits when it provided that the administrator had "sole authority in the exercise of its discretion to interpret, apply and administer the terms of the [plan] and to determine eligibility for benefits"); DeNobel v. Vitro Corp., 885 F.2d 1180, 1186 (4th Cir. 1989) (finding that the plan's provision giving administers the ability "[t]o determine all benefits and resolve all questions pertaining to the administration, interpretation and application of Plan provisions" warranted the arbitrary and capricious standard).

14. Herzberger v. Stand. Ins. Co., 205 F.3d 327, 331 (7th Cir. 2000) (citing Cozzie v. Metro. Life Ins. Co., 140 F.3d 1104, 1007 (7th Cir. 1998); Hightshue v. AIG Life Ins. Co., 135 F.3d 1144, 1147 (7th Cir. 1998); Terry v. Bayer Corp., 145 F.3d 28, 37 (1st Cir. 1998); Anderson v. Operative Plasterers' & Cement Masons' Int'l Ass'n Local No. 12 Pension & Welfare Plans, 991 F.2d 356, 358 (7th Cir. 1993)).

15. Thurber v. Aetna Life Ins. Co., 712 F.3d 654, 659 (2d Cir. 2013).

16. *Id.* at 658–59.

must be in the plan itself and not just the summary plan description.[17] The Eleventh Circuit agreed and, in *Shaw v. Connecticut General Life Insurance Company*, the court declined to give effect to discretionary language found only in the summary plan description.[18] Both decisions align with the Supreme Court's holding in *CIGNA Corporation v. Amara* that the terms of the summary plan description cannot be enforced as plan terms.[19]

Benefit determinations turn on factual determinations, such as whether a triggering event was accidental or a claimant was disabled. The United States Court of Appeals for the Fifth Circuit explained in *Pierre v. Connecticut General Life Insurance Company* that *Firestone* only governs plan interpretations and does not pertain to factual determinations, which always warrant deference in the Fifth Circuit.[20] Other circuits have ruled that a de novo review of factual determinations is appropriate where the plan does not reserve discretionary authority.[21] Thus, it is advisable for plan administrators and fiduciaries to insist that the plan specifically grant them discretion to make determinations concerning the facts of the case.

Courts generally consider the unambiguous terms of a plan according to their ordinary meanings.[22] Per the doctrine of contra proferentem, courts frequently resolve ambiguities against the drafter of the document.[23] The reservation of discretion to interpret plan language may permit administrators to resolve ambiguous terms, subject to deferential review.[24]

A recent example of a deferential analysis was *Kutten v. Sun Life Assurance Company of Canada*, in which the United States Court of Appeals for

17. Schultz v. Aviall, Inc. Long Term Disability Plan, 670 F.3d 834, 837 (7th Cir. 2012) (citing Schwartz v. Prudential Ins. Co. of Am., 450 F.3d 697, 699–700 (7th Cir. 2006)).
18. Shaw v. Conn. Gen. Life Ins. Co., 353 F.3d 1276, 1284 (11th Cir. 2003).
19. CIGNA Corp. v. Amara, 131 S. Ct. 1866, 1877 (2011).
20. Pierre v. Conn. Gen. Life Ins. Co., 932 F.2d 1552, 1557–58 (5th Cir. 1991).
21. Torres v. Pittston Co., 346 F.3d 1324, 1329 (11th Cir. 2003); Riedl v. Gen. Am. Life Ins. Co., 248 F.3d 753, 756 (8th Cir. 2001); Walker v. Am. Home Shield Long Term Disability Plan, 180 F.3d 1065, 1068 (9th Cir. 1999); Luby v. Teamsters Health, Welfare, & Pension Trust Funds, 944 F.2d 1176, 1178 (3d Cir. 1991).
22. *See* Kunin v. Benefit Trust Life Ins. Co., 910 F.2d 534, 541 (9th Cir. 1990); Brewer v. Lincoln Nat. Life Ins. Co., 921 F.2d 150, 154 (8th Cir. 1990).
23. *See* Billings v. UNUM Life Ins. Co. of Am., 459 F.3d 1088, 1095 (11th Cir. 2006); Mongeluzo v. Baxter Travenol Long Term Disability Benefit Plan, 46 F.3d 938, 943 (9th Cir. 1995); Phillips v. Lincoln Nat. Life Ins. Co., 978 F.2d 302, 310–11, 314 (7th Cir. 1992).
24. *See* Weber v. GE Group Life Assurance Co., 541 F.3d 1002, 1010–11 (10th Cir. 2008); Fox v. Fox, 167 F.3d 880, 883 (4th Cir. 1999).

the Eighth Circuit upheld an administrator's finding that a claimant's vitamin regimen constituted medical treatment for the purposes of a disability plan's pre-existing condition clause.[25] The court explained:

> This case turns on a narrow question. Was it reasonable for Sun Life to conclude that Kutten's vitamin A supplements constituted a medical treatment?
>
> . . .
>
> Our search is not for the best or preferable interpretation of the Pre-Existing Condition clause's terms. An interpretation of a term is reasonable if the interpretation conforms with ordinary meaning, which can be derived from the dictionary definition of the word and the context in which it is used. Webster's Third New International Dictionary defines Medical as, of, relating to, or concerned . . . with the practice of medicine. Medicine, as used in the definition of medical, is defined as the science and art dealing with the maintenance of health and the prevention, alleviation, or cure of disease, and medicine, as a substance, is defined as a substance or preparation used in treating disease. Treatment is defined as the action or manner of treating a patient medically or surgically, and to treat is to care for (as a patient or part of the body) medically. These definitions support the conclusion that the ordinary meaning of the phrase medical treatment would encompass Kutten's vitamin A supplements. The supplements are medical in the sense that they prevented or alleviated the progression of Kutten's retinitis pigmentosa. Further, Kutten's daily supplement regimen constituted a treatment because it was the manner, in fact the only manner, by which Kutten could care for his condition. Thus, each day he continued his doctor-recommended regimen, he received medical treatment.[26]

25. Kutten v. Sun Life Assur. Co. of Can., No. 13-2559, 2014 WL 3562784, at *2 (8th Cir. July 21, 2014).
26. *Id.* at *3 (citations and quotation marks omitted).

The Standard of Review with a Conflict of Interest

In its 2008 decision *Metropolitan Life Insurance Company v. Glenn*, the Supreme Court greatly clarified the effect of an identifiable conflict of interest on courts' standards of review. In *Glenn*, a participant in a long-term disability insurance plan brought suit against MetLife, which served simultaneously as the plan's administrator and insurer.[27] The Court concluded that an employer who both funds a plan and decides on the claims operates under a conflict of interest within the meaning of *Firestone*.[28] The Court reasoned:

> Indeed, *Firestone* itself involved an employer who administered an ERISA benefit plan and who both evaluated claims and paid for benefits. And thus that circumstance quite possibly was what the Court had in mind when it mentioned conflicted administrators. The *Firestone* parties, while disagreeing about other matters, agreed that the dual role created a conflict of interest of some kind in the employer.
>
> MetLife points out that an employer who creates a plan that it will both fund and administer foresees, and implicitly approves, the resulting conflict. But that fact cannot change our conclusion. At trust law, the fact that a settlor (the person establishing the trust) approves a trustee's conflict does not change the legal need for a judge later to take account of that conflict in reviewing the trustee's discretionary decisionmaking.
>
> MetLife also points out that we need not follow trust law principles where trust law is "inconsistent with the language of the statute, its structure, or its purposes." MetLife adds that to find a conflict here is inconsistent (1) with ERISA's efforts to avoid complex review proceedings, (2) with Congress' efforts not to deter employers from setting up benefit plans, and (3) with an ERISA provision specifically allowing employers to administer their own plans.
>
> But we cannot find in these considerations any significant inconsistency. As to the first, we note that trust law functions well with a

27. Metro. Life Ins. Co. v. Glenn, 554 U.S. 105, 108–09 (2008).
28. *Id.* at 112.

similar standard. As to the second, we have no reason, empirical or otherwise, to believe that our decision will seriously discourage the creation of benefit plans. As to the third, we have just explained why approval of a conflicted trustee differs from review of that trustee's conflicted decisionmaking. As to all three taken together, we believe them outweighed by "Congress' desire to offer employees enhanced protection for their benefits."

The answer to the conflict question is less clear where (as here) the plan administrator is not the employer itself but rather a professional insurance company. Such a company, MetLife would argue, likely has a much greater incentive than a self-insuring employer to provide accurate claims processing. That is because the insurance company typically charges a fee that attempts to account for the cost of claims payouts, with the result that paying an individual claim does not come to the same extent from the company's own pocket. It is also because the marketplace (and regulators) may well punish an insurance company when its products, or ingredients of its products, fall below par. And claims processing, an ingredient of the insurance company's product, falls below par when it seeks a biased result, rather than an accurate one. Why, MetLife might ask, should one consider an insurance company inherently more conflicted than any other market participant, say, a manufacturer who might earn more money in the short run by producing a product with poor quality steel or a lawyer with an incentive to work more slowly than necessary, thereby accumulating more billable hours?

Conceding these differences, we nonetheless continue to believe that for ERISA purposes a conflict exists. For one thing, the employer's own conflict may extend to its selection of an insurance company to administer its plan. An employer choosing an administrator in effect buys insurance for others and consequently (when compared to the marketplace customer who buys for himself) may be more interested in an insurance company with low rates than in one with accurate claims processing.

For another, ERISA imposes higher-than-marketplace quality standards on insurers. It sets forth a special standard of care upon a plan

> administrator, namely, that the administrator "discharge [its] duties" in respect to discretionary claims processing "solely in the interests of the participants and beneficiaries" of the plan, it simultaneously underscores the particular importance of accurate claims processing by insisting that administrators "provide a 'full and fair review' of claim denials," and it supplements marketplace and regulatory controls with judicial review of individual claim denials.
>
> Finally, a legal rule that treats insurance company administrators and employers alike in respect to the existence of a conflict can nonetheless take account of the circumstances to which MetLife points so far as it treats those, or similar, circumstances as diminishing the significance or severity of the conflict in individual cases.[29]

The Court stated in *Firestone* that a conflict of interest is just one factor to consider in its review of an administrator's decision under a deferential standard.[30] Subsequently, many lower courts applied different degrees of scrutiny to evaluate a conflicted administrator's decision to deny benefits, including a sliding-scale standard that provided less deference based on higher degrees of conflict.[31] The Court clarified in *Glenn* that a conflict of interest does not supplant the deferential standard with a de novo review, reiterating that the conflict of interest is one of multiple factors to be considered using the deferential approach.[32] The Court explained:

> We do not believe that *Firestone*'s statement implies a change in the standard of review, say, from deferential to *de novo* review. Trust law continues to apply a deferential standard of review to the discretionary decisionmaking of a conflicted trustee, while at the same time requiring the reviewing judge to take account of the conflict when determining whether the trustee, substantively or procedurally, has

29. *Id.* at 112–15 (citations omitted).
30. Firestone Tire & Rubber Co. v. Bruch, 489 U.S. 101, 115 (1989).
31. *See, e.g.*, Estate of Schwing v. Lilly Health Plan, 562 F.3d 522, 525 (3d Cir. 2009) (citing Pinto v. Reliance Standard Life Ins. Co., 214 F.3d 377, 392 (3d Cir. 2000)); Crowell v. Shell Oil Co., 541 F.3d 295, 311 n.66 (5th Cir. 2008) (citing MacLachlan v. ExxonMobil Corp., 350 F.3d 472, 478–79 (5th Cir. 2003)).
32. *Glenn*, 554 U.S. at 115.

abused his discretion. We see no reason to forsake *Firestone*'s reliance upon trust law in this respect.

Nor would we overturn *Firestone* by adopting a rule that in practice could bring about near universal review by judges *de novo*—i.e., without deference—of the lion's share of ERISA plan claims denials. Had Congress intended such a system of review, we believe it would not have left to the courts the development of review standards but would have said more on the subject.

Neither do we believe it necessary or desirable for courts to create special burden-of-proof rules, or other special procedural or evidentiary rules, focused narrowly upon the evaluator/payor conflict. In principle, as we have said, conflicts are but one factor among many that a reviewing judge must take into account. Benefits decisions arise in too many contexts, concern too many circumstances, and can relate in too many different ways to conflicts—which themselves vary in kind and in degree of seriousness—for us to come up with a one-size-fits-all procedural system that is likely to promote fair and accurate review. Indeed, special procedural rules would create further complexity, adding time and expense to a process that may already be too costly for many of those who seek redress.

We believe that *Firestone* means what the word "factor" implies, namely, that when judges review the lawfulness of benefit denials, they will often take account of several different considerations of which a conflict of interest is one. This kind of review is no stranger to the judicial system. Not only trust law, but also administrative law, can ask judges to determine lawfulness by taking account of several different, often case-specific, factors, reaching a result by weighing all together.

In such instances, any one factor will act as a tiebreaker when the other factors are closely balanced, the degree of closeness necessary depending upon the tiebreaking factor's inherent or case-specific importance. The conflict of interest at issue here, for example, should prove more important (perhaps of great importance) where circumstances suggest a higher likelihood that it affected the benefits decision, including, but not limited to, cases where an insurance company administrator has a history of biased claims administration. It

> should prove less important (perhaps to the vanishing point) where the administrator has taken active steps to reduce potential bias and to promote accuracy, for example, by walling off claims administrators from those interested in firm finances, or by imposing management checks that penalize inaccurate decisionmaking irrespective of whom the inaccuracy benefits.[33]

The Fifth Circuit and Tenth Circuit continue to apply a sliding-scale approach in weighing the conflict of interest as a factor.[34]

Discovery

Prior to *Glenn*, courts often restricted their review of an administrator's decisions to the administrative record,[35] occasionally allowing limited discovery in special circumstances when a conflict of interest was present.[36] Following *Glenn*, courts have generally expanded discovery when there is a conflict of interest.

The First Circuit stated in *Liston v. UNUM Corporation Officer Severance Plan* that the normal rule in denial-of-benefits cases when the plan had reserved administrator discretion "is that review for arbitrariness is on the record made before the entity being reviewed" and that "at least some very good reason is needed to overcome the strong presumption that the record on review is limited to the record before the administrator."[37] Relying on precedent from the Fourth Circuit and Sixth Circuit, the court elaborated that "[e]ven where de novo review exists under ERISA, it is at least doubtful that courts should be in any hurry to consider evidence or

33. *Id.* at 115–18 (citations omitted).
34. *See Crowell*, 541 F.3d at 311 n.66; Weber v. GE Group Life Assurance Co., 541 F.3d 1002, 1010–11 (10th Cir. 2008).
35. *See* Sandoval v. Aetna Life & Cas. Ins. Co., 967 F.2d 377, 380 (10th Cir. 1992) (citing Perry v. Simplicity Eng'ring, 900 F.2d 963, 967 (6th Cir. 1990); Voliva v. Seafarers Pension Plan, 858 F.2d 195, 196 (4th Cir. 1988); Danti v. Lewis, 312 F.2d 345, 349–50 (D.C. Cir. 1962)).
36. *See* Semien v. Life Ins. Co. of N. Am., 436 F.3d 805, 814 (7th Cir. 2006) ("When 'impartiality can fairly be questioned,' district courts should allow limited discovery.").
37. Liston v. UNUM Corp. Officer Severance Plan, 330 F.3d 19, 23 (1st Cir. 2003) (citing Leahy v. Raytheon Co., 315 F.3d 11, 17 (1st Cir. 2002)).

claims not presented to the plan administrator."[38] After *Glenn*, the United States Court of Appeals for the First Circuit observed in *Denmark v. Liberty Life Assurance Company of Boston* that "*Glenn* fairly can be read as contemplating some discovery on the issue of whether a structural conflict has morphed into an actual conflict."[39] Still, "any such discovery must be allowed sparingly and, if allowed at all, must be narrowly tailored so as to leave the substantive record essentially undisturbed."[40] The court continued:

> Conflict-oriented discovery will be needed only to the extent that there are gaps in the administrative record. If, say, the plan administrator has failed to detail its procedures, discovery may be appropriate, in the district court's discretion. Otherwise, discovery normally will be limited to the clarification of ambiguities or to ensuring that the documented procedures have been followed in a particular instance.[41]

The United States District Court for the Southern District of New York has struggled to delineate the boundaries of discovery after *Glenn*. In 2008, the court announced that *Glenn* had "[a]brogated the limitations on discovery unique to ERISA cases" and opened the door to any discovery that "appears reasonably calculated to lead to the discovery of admissible evidence."[42] In 2011, the court disagreed with its prior decision, stating that *Glenn* "does not afford plaintiff free reign over discovery in this case" during a challenge to a denial of disability benefits.[43] The latter holding is more reflective of the approach of other courts, which frequently permit limited discovery where there is no evidence of a structural conflict in the administrative record.

38. *Id.* at 24 (citing Wilkins v. Baptist Healthcare Sys., Inc., 150 F.3d 609, 616 (6th Cir. 1998); Quiesinberry v. Life Ins. Co. of N. Am., 987 F.2d 1017, 1025 (4th Cir. 1993)).
39. Denmark v. Liberty Life Assurance Co. of Bos., 566 F.3d 1, 10 (1st Cir. 2009).
40. *Id.*
41. *Id.*
42. Hogan-Cross v. Met. Life Ins. Co., 568 F. Supp. 2d 410, 414–15 (S.D. N.Y. 2008).
43. Joyner v. Cont'l Cas. Co., 837 F. Supp. 2d 233, 242 (S.D. N.Y. 2011).

Attorney Fees

ERISA § 502(g)(1) provides that in an action for civil enforcement by a participant, beneficiary, or fiduciary, "the court in its discretion may allow a reasonable attorney's fee and costs of action to either party."[44] In exercising this discretion, courts have used a "five-factor test" to determine whether attorney fees should be awarded. The factors are (1) the offending parties' culpability or bad faith, (2) the ability of the offending parties to satisfy an award of attorney fees, (3) the deterrent effect of an award of attorney fees against the offending parties, (4) the benefit conferred on members of the plan as a whole, and (5) the relative merits of the parties' positions.[45] In its 2010 decision *Hardt v. Reliance Standard Life Insurance Company*, the Supreme Court explained that "[b]ecause these five factors bear no obvious relation to [ERISA's] text . . . they are not required for channeling a court's discretion when awarding fees under this section."[46] Subsequent to *Hardt*, the five-factor test remains discretionary,[47] but the Second Circuit has recognized its abrogation and required more detailed explanations of awards beyond the test's application.[48]

The Supreme Court held in *Hardt* that "a court 'in its discretion' may award fees and costs . . . as long as the fee claimant has achieved 'some degree of success on the merits.'"[49] Relying heavily on the 1983 Clean Air Act case *Ruckelshaus v. Sierra Club*, the Court found "that a fee claimant need not be a 'prevailing party' to be eligible for an attorney's fees award."[50] After stating that the five-factor test is not required under ERISA, the Court

44. 29 U.S.C. § 1132(g)(1) (2012).
45. *See* Eddy v. Colonial Life Ins. Co. of Am., 59 F.3d 201, 206 (D.C. Cir. 1995); McPherson v. Employees' Pension Plan of Am. Re-Ins. Co., 33 F.3d 253, 255 (3d Cir. 1994); Armistead v. Vernitron Corp., 944 F.2d 1287, 1301 (6th Cir. 1991); McElwaine v. US West, Inc., 176 F.3d 1167, 1172 (9th Cir. 1999); Gray v. New England Tel. & Tel. Co., 792 F.2d 251, 257–58 (1st Cir. 1986); Ursick v. Bethlehem Mines, 719 F.2d 670, 673 (3rd Cir. 1983); Iron Workers Local No. 272 v. Bowen, 624 F.2d 1255, 1266 (5th Cir. 1980); Hummell v. S.E. Rykoff & Co., 634 F.2d 446, 453 (9th Cir. 1980); Eaves v. Penn, 587 F.2d 453, 465 (10th Cir. 1978).
46. Hardt v. Reliance Standard Life Ins. Co., 560 U.S. 242, 254–55 (2010).
47. *See* LifeCare Mgmt. Servs. LLC v. Ins. Mgmt. Adm'rs Inc., 703 F.3d 835, 846 (5th Cir. 2013); Raybourne v. Cigna Life Ins. Co. of N.Y., 700 F.3d 1076, 1080 (7th Cir. 2012).
48. Levitian v. Sun Life & Health Ins. Co., 486 F. App'x 136, 141 (2d Cir. 2012).
49. *Hardt*, 560 U.S. at 245, 247 (2010) (citing Ruckelshaus v. Sierra Club, 463 U.S. 680, 694 (1983)).
50. *Id.* at 252.

expanded on the newly articulated standard and applied it to Hardt's challenge to the denial of her long-term disability benefits:

> Instead [of the five-factor test], *Ruckelshaus* lays down the proper markers to guide a court in exercising the discretion that § 1132(g)(1) grants. As in the statute at issue in *Ruckelshaus*, Congress failed to indicate clearly in § 1132(g)(1) that it "meant to abandon historic fee-shifting principles and intuitive notions of fairness." Accordingly, a fees claimant must show "some degree of success on the merits" before a court may award attorney's fees under § 1132(g)(1). A claimant does not satisfy that requirement by achieving "trivial success on the merits" or a "purely procedural victor[y]," but does satisfy it if the court can fairly call the outcome of the litigation some success on the merits without conducting a "lengthy inquir[y] into the question whether a particular party's success was 'substantial' or occurred on a 'central issue.'"
>
> Reliance essentially agrees that this standard should govern fee requests under § 1132(g)(1), but argues that Hardt has not satisfied it. Specifically, Reliance contends that a court order remanding an ERISA claim for further consideration can never constitute "some success on the merits," even if such a remand results in an award of benefits.
>
> Reliance's argument misses the point, given the facts of this case. Hardt persuaded the District Court to find that "the plan administrator has failed to comply with the ERISA guidelines" and "that Ms. Hardt did not get the kind of review to which she was entitled under applicable law." Although Hardt failed to win summary judgment on her benefits claim, the District Court nevertheless found "compelling evidence that Ms. Hardt is totally disabled due to her neuropathy," and stated that it was "inclined to rule in Ms. Hardt's favor" on her benefits claim, but declined to do so before "first giving Reliance the chance to address the deficiencies in its" statutorily mandated "full and fair review" of that claim. Hardt thus obtained a judicial order instructing Reliance "to act on Ms. Hardt's application by adequately considering all the evidence" within 30 days; "[o]therwise, judgment will be issued in favor of Ms. Hardt." After Reliance

> conducted that court-ordered review, and consistent with the District Court's appraisal, Reliance reversed its decision and awarded Hardt the benefits she sought.
>
> These facts establish that Hardt has achieved far more than "trivial success on the merits" or a "purely procedural victory." Accordingly, she has achieved "some success on the merits," and the District Court properly exercised its discretion to award Hardt attorney's fees in this case.[51]

District courts possess wide discretion when determining what attorney-fees award is reasonable.[52] Often, courts calculate an attorney-fees award under § 502(a)(1) by multiplying the number of hours reasonably expended on the litigation by a reasonable hourly rate based on the market.[53] While attorneys representing themselves pro se are not entitled to attorney fees, courts have awarded attorney fees to in-house counsel.[54] Awards of attorney fees are typically limited to the participants, beneficiaries, or fiduciaries listed in a suit brought under ERISA.[55]

The First, Third, Fourth, Fifth, Sixth, Eighth, Eleventh, and D.C. Circuits have not accepted the notion of a presumption in favor of awarding attorney fees to a prevailing plaintiff.[56] However, the Seventh Circuit and

51. *Id.* at 255–56 (citations omitted).
52. Hensley v. Eckerhart, 461 U.S. 424, 437 (1983).
53. McElwaine v. US West, Inc., 176 F.3d 1167, 1173 (9th Cir. 1999).
54. Treasurer, Trustees of Drury Indus., Inc. Health Care Plan and Trust v. Goding, 692 F.3d 888, 898 (8th Cir. 2012); Baker & Hostetler LLP v. U.S. Dept. of Commerce, 473 F.3d 312, 324 (D.C. Cir. 2006); Bond v. Blum, 317 F.3d 385, 400 (4th Cir. 2003).
55. *See* Downey Cmty. Hosp. v. Wilson, 977 F.2d 470, 474 (9th Cir. 1992) (remanding to the district court to reevaluate an award of attorney fees so that the award represents only the costs of litigating against parties in federal court pursuant to ERISA and not to the costs incurred in state courts); Saladino v. I.L.G.W.U. Nat. Retirement Fund, 754 F.2d 743, 744 (2d Cir. 1985) (denying an award of attorney fees after finding the party seeking the fees was not a participant under ERISA); M & R Inv. Co., Inc. v. Fitzsimmons, 685 F.2d 283, 288 (9th Cir. 1982) (denying attorney fees to trustees because they did not qualify as participants, beneficiaries, or fiduciaries).
56. *See* Martin v. Ark. Blue Cross & Blue Shield; 299 F.3d 966, 971 (8th Cir. 2002); Cottrill v. Sparrow, Johnson & Ursillo, Inc., 100 F.3d 220, 226 (1st Cir. 1996); Eddy v. Colonial Life Ins. Co. of Am., 59 F.3d 201, 205–06 (D.C. Cir. 1995); Quesinberry v. Life Ins. Co. of N. Am., 987 F.2d 1017, 1030 (4th Cir. 1993); Ellison v. Shenango Inc. Pension Bd., 956 F.2d 1268, 1274 (3d Cir. 1992); Armistead v. Vernitron Corp., 944 F.2d 1287, 1302 (6th Cir. 1991); Iron Workers Local No. 272 v. Bowen, 624 F.2d 1255, 1266 (5th Cir. 1980).

the Ninth Circuit have in the past simultaneously applied the presumption and the five-factor test when assigning attorney fees.[57]

The Eighth Circuit and Ninth Circuit prefer not to award attorney fees against plaintiffs. In *Corder v. Howard Johnson & Company*, the Ninth Circuit reiterated its ongoing "disfavor of attorney's fees against individual ERISA plaintiffs who seek pension benefits to which they believe they are entitled," continuing its tendency against awarding attorney fees and thereby penalizing plaintiffs where beneficiaries sought recovery for errors that severely threatened the plan's ability to pay their benefits.[58] In *Maune v. International Brotherhood of Electrical Workers*, the Eighth Circuit explained that "an award of attorney's fees to the Fund may discourage others who are similarly situated from bringing claims for wrongful denial of benefits," which would conflict with ERISA's remedial purpose.[59]

Standing

The Supreme Court explained in *Firestone Tire & Rubber Company v. Bruch*:

> In our view, the term participant is naturally read to mean either employees in, or reasonably expected to be in, currently covered employment, or former employees who have . . . a reasonable expectation of returning to covered employment or who have a colorable claim to vested benefits. In order to establish that he or she may become eligible for benefits, a claimant must have a colorable claim that (1) he or she will prevail in a suit for benefits, or that (2) eligibility requirements will be fulfilled in the future. This view attributes

57. McElwaine v. US West, Inc., 176 F.3d 1167, 11172 (9th Cir. 1999); Little v. Cox's Supermarkets, 71 F.3d 637, 644 (7th Cir. 1995).
58. Corder v. Howard Johnson & Co., 53 F.3d 225, 231 (9th Cir. 1994) (citing Credit Managers Ass'n of S. Cal. v. Kennesaw Life & Acc. Ins. Co., 25 F.3d 743, 748 (9th Cir. 1994); Flanagan v. Inland Empire Elec. Workers Pension Plan, 3 F.3d 1246, 1253 (9th Cir. 1993); Tingey v. Pixley-Richards W., Inc., 958 F.2d 908, 909 (9th Cir. 1992)).
59. Maune v. Int'l Broth. of Elec. Workers, Local No. 1, Health & Welfare Fund, 83 F.3d 959, 964 (8th Cir. 1996).

> conventional meanings to the statutory language since all employees in covered employment and former employees with a colorable claim to vested benefits may become eligible. A former employee who has neither a reasonable expectation of returning to covered employment nor a colorable claim to vested benefits, however, simply does not fit within the [phrase] may become eligible.[60]

Even if the participant has received benefits by the distribution of an annuity contract, the participant maintains standing under ERISA § 502(a)(9) if the insurer later fails to meet its contractual obligations.[61] ERISA empowers the Secretary of Labor, a participant or beneficiary at the time of the alleged violation, or a fiduciary, to obtain appropriate equitable relief.[62] This relief includes "the posting of security if necessary, to assure receipt by the participant or beneficiary of the amounts provided or to be provided by such insurance contract or annuity, plus reasonable prejudgment interest."[63] The purchase of the annuity can be in connection with the termination of the plan or the termination of the individual's status as a participant. Punitive damages are not authorized by the legislation.

The circuits are split as to whether former participants may bring suit if, "but for" a defendant's actions, they would be entitled to additional benefits. The First, Second, Fifth, Sixth, and Eighth Circuits support "but for" standing.[64] The Fourth, Tenth, and Eleventh Circuits have rejected this approach, requiring that parties demonstrate that they reasonably expect to return to covered employment or can demonstrate a colorable claim for vested benefits.[65]

60. Firestone Tire & Rubber Co. v. Bruch, 489 U.S. 101, 117–18 (1989) (citations and quotation marks omitted).
61. 29 U.S.C. § 1132(a)(9) (2013).
62. *Id.*
63. *Id.*
64. *See* Swinney v. Gen. Motors Corp., 46 F.3d 512, 518–19 (6th Cir. 1995); Vartanian v. Monsanto Co., 14 F.3d 697, 702 (1st Cir. 1994); Mullins v. Pfizer, Inc., 23 F.3d 663, 666–68 (2d Cir. 1994); Howe v. Varity Corp., 36 F.3d 746 (8th Cir. 1994); Christopher v. Mobil Oil Corp., 950 F.2d 1209, 1221 (5th Cir. 1992).
65. *See* Felix v. Lucent Techs., Inc., 387 F.3d 1146, 1160-62 (10th Cir. 2004) (citing *Firestone*, 489 U.S. at 117–18; Sanson Gen. Motors Corp., 966 F.2d 618, 619, 621–22 (11th Cir. 1992); Stanton v. Gulf Oil Corp., 792 F.2d 432, 433–35 (4th Cir. 1986)).

The United States Court of Appeals for the Ninth Circuit held in *McBride v. PLM International, Inc.*, that a claimant may bring an ERISA § 510 claim after benefits have distributed.[66] Section 510 prohibits interference with protected rights, and it protects whistleblowers.[67] Section 510 is enforced through ERISA's remedial provisions.[68] The *McBride* court observed that "measuring ERISA standing at the time an action is filed is a judicially created requirement which is appropriate for most circumstances," but not in the case of a whistleblower.[69] The court continued:

> Depriving a plaintiff of standing to sue under ERISA for his employer's clear violation of section 1140 would, in effect, make standing contingent upon the occurrence of subsequent events entirely within the control of the employer. . . . Requiring that claimants like McBride be plan participants at the time of suit would create a race to the courthouse. Standing would depend upon which event occurred first: the plan's termination, or the claimant's filing of a lawsuit. In this case, McBride alleged that his discharge was caused by his criticism of PLM's proposed ESOP termination. Ironic it would be indeed to hold that the plan's termination itself then deprived McBride of standing to sue.
>
> When an individual alleges, as here, that he was discharged in violation of ERISA's whistleblower provisions, his employer cannot be allowed to evade section 1140 accountability simply by terminating the plan and distributing the benefits. Nothing in *Firestone* commands such a result. If an employee is a participant at the time of the alleged ERISA violation and alleges that he was discharged or discriminated against because of protected whistleblowing activities, we hold that such an employee has standing to sue under ERISA. To require that the claimant be a participant at the time of filing suit would undermine the very purpose of ERISA's whistleblower provision: to provide

66. McBride v. PLM Int'l, Inc., 179 F.3d 737, 743 (9th Cir. 1999).
67. 29 U.S.C. § 1140 (2012).
68. *Id.*
69. *McBride*, 179 F.3d at 743.

a federal remedy for discrimination against plan participants for exercising their protected rights under ERISA.[70]

The First, Third, Fourth, Sixth, Seventh, Ninth, and Eleventh Circuits have held that former employees who had received their individual pension account balances in full had standing under ERISA.[71] The United States Court of Appeals for the Fourth Circuit concluded in *In re Mutual Funds Investment Litigation* that cashed out former participants in a defined contribution plan who were cashed out remained "participants" for purposes of ERISA § 502(a)(2) when they sought to recover amounts that they alleged would have been in their accounts had it not been for fiduciary misconduct.[72] The Fourth Circuit relied on the Supreme Court's holding in *Larue v. DeWolff, Boberg & Associates, Inc.*, that a former employee who had cashed out a defined-contribution plan could still bring suit for a fiduciary breach that had generated a loss in his individual plan account.[73]

A designated beneficiary of a participant who is deceased, or an alternate payee under a qualified domestic relations order has standing to sue under ERISA, either for a § 502(a)(1)(B) claim for benefits or to redress other violations under § 502(a)(3). Courts have found that children of the deceased who are not named as beneficiaries do not qualify as beneficiaries by operation of law.[74] Similarly, in *Cobb v. Central States*, the United States Court of Appeals for the Fifth Circuit did not recognize an unnamed wife's standing to recover benefits from her estranged, deceased husband's pension plan.[75] The court underscored that the definition of a beneficiary for the purposes of standing under ERISA "requires something that the definition of participant does not: that the 'beneficiary' be 'designated' as

70. *Id.* (citations omitted).
71. *See* Evans v. Akers, 534 F.3d 65 (1st Cir. 2008); *In re* Mut. Funds Inv. Litig., 529 F.3d 207 (4th Cir. 2008); Vaughn v. Bay Envtl. Mgmt., Inc., 567 F.3d 1021 (9th Cir. 2008); Lanfear v. Home Depot, Inc., 536 F.3d 1217 (11th Cir. 2008); Bridges v. Am. Elec. Power Co., 498 F.3d 442 (6th Cir. 2007); Graden v. Conexant Sys. Inc., 496 F.3d 291 (3d Cir. 2007); Harzewski v. Guidant Corp., 489 F.3d 799 (7th Cir. 2007).
72. *In re Mut. Funds Inv. Litig.*, 529 F.3d at 210.
73. *Id.* at 214 (citing LaRue v. DeWolff, Boberg & Assocs., 552 U.S. 248 (2008)).
74. Crawford v. Roane, 53 F.3d 750, 755 (6th Cir. 1995); Coleman v. Champion Int'l/Champion Forest Prod., 992 F.2d 530, 533–34 (5th Cir. 1993).
75. Cobb v. Cent. States, Se. & Sw. Areas Pension Fund, 461 F.3d 632, 636 (5th Cir. 2006).

such by the participant or by the terms of the plan."[76] In *Sladek v. Bell System Management Pension Plan*, the Seventh Circuit allowed a surviving spouse to proceed when she was not named by a spouse with Alzheimer's disease based on the argument that her spouse's election was voidable due to incompetency.[77]

A plan may sue or be sued in its own capacity.[78] ERISA provides that a monetary award against a plan is "enforceable only against the plan as an entity and shall not be enforceable against any other person unless liability against such person is established in his individual capacity."[79] Thus, if a fiduciary breach led to the judgment against the plan, a separate enforcement action would have to be brought against the fiduciary to recover the loss incurred by the plan as a result of the judgment against it. The ERISA enforcement action against the fiduciary would have to be brought by a proper plaintiff, including a beneficiary, participant, fiduciary, or the Secretary of Labor, and the action could not be brought by the plan itself because a plan has no standing to bring an action under the enforcement provisions of ERISA. However, a plan may conduct business and acquire the same rights to causes of action under state law as any other entity. Courts have recognized that a plan can pursue a federal common-law action for restitution when plan funds are transferred from one plan to another because of an error in administration.[80]

In *Wilmington v. Shipping Company v. New England Life Insurance Company*, the United States Court of Appeals for the Fourth Circuit found that a participant bringing suit on the behalf of a plan still had Article III standing despite the fact that the plan was trusteed by the Pension Benefit Guaranty Corporation (PBGC), a U.S. agency created by ERISA.[81] The court recognized the dual role of the PBGC as both guarantor of unpaid, guaranteed benefits and statutory trustee, but the court rejected the argument that

76. *Id.* at 635.
77. Sladek v. Bell Sys. Mgmt. Pension Plan, 880 F.2d 972, 976 (7th Cir. 1989).
78. 29 U.S.C. § 1132(d)(1) (2012).
79. 29 U.S.C. § 1132(d)(2) (2012).
80. *See* State St. Bank & Trust Co. v. Denman Tire Corp., 240 F.3d 83, 89 (1st Cir. 2001); Luby v. Teamsters Health, Welfare, & Pension Trust Funds, 944 F.2d 1176, 1186 (3d Cir. 1991); Provident Life & Acc. Ins. Co. v. Waller, 906 F.3d 985, 989–90 (4th Cir. 1990).
81. Wilmington Shipping Co. v. New England Life Ins. Co., 496 F.3d 326, 335–36 (4th Cir. 2007).

"the overarching governmental interest in the solvency of ERISA's insurance program exempts the PBGC from the otherwise absolute duty that ERISA imposes on fiduciaries, including statutory trustees, to hold plan assets in trust for the benefit of plan participants."[82] The court explained:

> PBGC, acting as trustee, must hold plan assets in trust for the benefit of plan participants and pay all plan benefits, if possible, in accordance with the statutory order of priorities. Only after the PBGC as trustee has allocated plan assets and determined that the plan has insufficient funds to meet its obligations does the PBGC as guarantor "chip in" from ERISA funds to cover the unpaid guaranteed benefits. To be sure, ERISA provides that its insurance funds may be credited with the value of a terminated plan's assets administered under § 1342, but only to the extent that plan assets exceed plan liabilities (not to the extent they exceed guaranteed benefits), and only after the statutory trustee has satisfied all plan liabilities.[83]

The United States Court of Appeals for the Ninth Circuit rejected the *Wilmington* rationale in *Paulsen v. CNF Inc.*, finding that the PBGC's role as an independent actor negated redressability and therefore Article III standing.[84]

Statutes of Limitations

The only statute of limitations that ERISA provides is for breach of fiduciary duties. In such a case, a claimant must take action within six years of the last action that constituted a part of the breach or, in the case of an omission, since the latest date on which the fiduciary could have cured the breach.[85] In the case of fraud or concealment, the claimant must take action no later than six years after the date of discovery of the breach.[86] If

82. *Id.* at 331–33, 336.
83. *Id.* at 336.
84. Paulsen v. CNF Inc., 559 F.3d 1061, 1075 (9th Cir. 2009).
85. 29 U.S.C. § 1113(1) (2012).
86. 29 U.S.C. § 1113(2) (2012).

the claimant had actual knowledge of the breach of violation, the claimant must take action within three years after the earliest date he or she had actual knowledge of the breach or violation.[87]

Whether a plaintiff has "actual knowledge" of a breach, thereby triggering the three-year limitation when there is no fraud or concealment, is a question of fact with various standards across the circuits. The Third Circuit has required a plaintiff to "have actual knowledge of all material facts necessary to understand that some claim exists, which facts could include necessary opinions of experts, knowledge of a transaction's harmful consequences, or even actual harm."[88] Despite this standard being more stringent than others, in *Kurz v. Philadelphia Electric Company*, the United States Court of Appeals for the Third Circuit found the claimant had actual knowledge when the defendant had openly announced the contested changes providing certain employees with better benefits than others.[89] The court explained:

> For those who did not qualify, the "harmful consequences" of the change were obvious. No "opinions of experts" were needed. Legal consultation was not required. The plaintiffs had "knowledge of all relevant facts at least sufficient to give [them] knowledge that a fiduciary duty ha[d] been breached or ERISA provision violated." The plaintiff class therefore had actual knowledge . . . .[90]

The United States Court of Appeals for the Ninth Circuit applied a less stringent standard in *Blanton v. Anzalone* and considered the time limitation triggered by "knowledge of the transaction that constituted the alleged violation, not by . . . knowledge of the law."[91] The United States Court of Appeals for the Sixth Circuit aligned behind this approach in *Wright v. Heyne* and held that the trigger of a time limitation "is only the plaintiff's actual knowledge of the underlying conduct giving rise to the alleged vio-

87. *Id.*
88. Gluck v. Unisys Corp., 960 F.2d 1168, 1177 (3d Cir. 1992) (citations omitted).
89. Kurz v. Phila. Elec. Co., 96 F.3d 1544, 1551 (3d Cir. 1996) (citations omitted).
90. *Id.*
91. Blanton v. Anzalone, 760 F.2d 989, 992 (9th Cir. 1985) (citing United States v. Kubrick, 444 U.S. 111, 118–25 (1979); NLRB v. Don Burgess Construction Corp., 596 F.2d 378, 382 (9th Cir. 1979)).

lation . . . rather than the knowledge that the underlying conduct violates ERISA."[92] In *Wright*, trustees of the Wright, Goff, Krantx, Harmon, and Jones Profit Sharing Plan, which was a retirement plan, claimed that Vestax, a securities corporation, and Michael Heyne, Vestax's owner as well as the plan adviser, had violated ERISA through investment decisions and its handling of commissions.[93] The Sixth Circuit found *Wright* easily resolved under the less stringent standard:

> Wright, Goff and Krantz obtained actual knowledge that Vestax and Heyne allegedly "invested the assets" of the Plan "in high-risk investments" such as "junk bonds"; that Vestax and Heyne allegedly made "investment decisions that were imprudent" including "annuitizing an annuity, investing in certain limited partnerships, and purchasing both "A" and "B" shares of the same investment fund"; that Vestax and Heyne allegedly "caused" the Plan "to invest in and through companies in which the Defendants had a direct financial interest [AFA Financial]"; that Vestax and Heyne allegedly "caused" the "Plan to purchase or sell assets principally for the purpose of earning transaction commissions" for themselves; and that Vestax and Heyne allegedly "paid themselves commissions on certain securities transactions in which they engaged on behalf of the [Plan]." Further, Plaintiffs were, in several instances, specifically told that Heyne had invested their funds in a manner they had specifically instructed against.
>
> Plaintiffs obtained actual knowledge of all of those alleged facts from their own dealings with Vestax and Heyne during the period from 1992 through 1995 and from their consultations in 1993, 1994 and 1995 with four investment professionals—Phillip Shaffer, Denny Dicky, William Cseplo and Tom Wright—well outside the three-year limitations period established by § 1113(2). Further each of these consultants specifically and unequivocally informed Plaintiffs of the "harmful consequences" of Vestax's and Heyne's allegedly improper acts and at least one of them (Cseplo) advised that they should "seek

92. Wright v. Heyne, 349 F.3d 321, 331 (6th Cir. 2003).
93. *Id.* at 322.

> legal action" in early 1995. Indeed, it was based upon their actual knowledge of the foregoing material facts that all of the Plaintiffs fully terminated all of their relationships with Defendants by September 11, 1995. Notwithstanding this, Plaintiffs did not file their Complaint in this case until October 30, 1998. Because they did not file their action within three years after obtaining actual knowledge of the alleged facts upon which their claims for breach of ERISA fiduciary duties are based, their claims are time-barred by 29 U.S.C. § 1113(2).[94]

The standard used in *Martin v. Consultants & Administrators* by the United States Court of Appeals for the Seventh Circuit fell in between the most and least stringent standards. The court required that "a plaintiff must know of the essential facts of the transaction or conduct constituting the violation."[95] Recognizing the ambiguity of this standard, the *Martin* court expounded:

> But how does one characterize the relevant transaction and its essential facts? Like so many areas of law, this matter turns on the level of generality employed in characterizing the transaction at issue. We know that somewhere between "every last detail" and "something was awry" lies the requisite knowledge of an ERISA violation. The proper characterization will usually turn in part on the complexity of the underlying factual transaction, the complexity of the legal claim and the egregiousness of the alleged violation. Beyond such generalizations, however, we can only say that judges, faced with particular contexts and relying on their "situation sense," must make the determination.[96]

ERISA does not establish a statute of limitations for any cause of action other than a breach of fiduciary duty. Courts typically apply time limitations set forth in the most analogous state statute.[97] A plan can determine

---

94. *Id.* at 331–32 (citations omitted).
95. Martin v. Consultants & Adm'rs, Inc., 966 F.2d 1078, 1086 (7th Cir. 1992).
96. *Id.*
97. *See* Flanagan v. Inland Empire Elec. Workers Pension Plan & Trust, 3 F.3d 1246, 1252 (9th Cir. 1993); Hogan v. Kraft Foods, 969 F.2d 142, 145 (5th Cir. 1992); Meade v. Pension Appeals & Review Comm., 966 F.2d 190, 194–95 (6th Cir. 1992); Gluck v. Unisys Corp., 960 F.2d 1168, 1179 (3d Cir. 1992); Johnson v. State Mut. Life Assurance Co. of Am., 942 F.2d

which statute of limitations to apply. While respecting a plan's choice of law provision, the United States Court of Appeals for the Ninth Circuit observed in *Wang Laboratories, Inc. v. Kagan* that "[w]here a choice of law is made by an ERISA contract, it should be followed, if not unreasonable or fundamentally unfair."[98]

Most courts that have considered benefit denial claims under ERISA §502(a)(1)(B) have applied the state statute of limitations for a breach of contract claim.[99] At times, courts have had to choose between multiple statutes of limitations within the same state relating to contract disputes.[100] In *Heimeshoff v. Hartford Life*, the Supreme Court stated that a reasonable statute of limitations of three years in the plan could be operative even if it began to run from the due date for proof of loss.[101]

The United States Court of Appeals for the Seventh Circuit has frequently applied state statutes of limitations for retaliatory discharge claims to actions brought under ERISA § 510.[102] The Second Circuit has followed the Seventh Circuit's lead.[103] In *Musick v. Goodyear Tire & Rubber Company*, the United States Court of Appeals for the Eleventh Circuit found that statutes for wages and statutes for retaliatory discharge were the two

1260, 1261–63 (8th Cir. 1991); Lumpkin v. Envirodyne Indus., Inc., 933 F.2d 449, 465–66 (7th Cir. 1991); Wright v. Sw. Bell Tel. Co., 925 F.2d 1288, 1290–91 (10th Cir. 1991); Dameron v. Sinai Hosp. of Balt., 815 F.2d 975, 981 (4th Cir. 1987). *But see* Woods v. Qwest Info. Techs., 334 F. Supp. 2d 1187, 1195–96 (D. Neb. 2004) (citing Union Pacific R.R. Co. v. Beckham, 138 F.3d 325, 330 (8th Cir. 1998); Adamson v. Armco, Inc. 44 F.3d 650, 652 (8th Cir. 1995)) (analogizing to a state statute but applying federal common law to determine when an action accrued).

98. Wang Labs., Inc. v. Kagan, 990 F.2d 1126, 1128–29 (9th Cir. 1993).

99. *See* Harrison v. Digital Health Plan, 183 F.3d 1235, 1239–40 (11th Cir. 1999); Daill v. Sheet Metal Workers' Local 73 Pension Fund, 100 F.3d 62, 65 (7th Cir. 1996); Hogan v. Kraft Foods, 969 F.2d 142, 145 (5th Cir. 1992); Meade v. Pension Appeals and Review Comm., 966 F.2d 190, 195 (6th Cir. 1992); Held v. Mfrs. Hanover Leasing Corp., 912 F.2d 1197, 1201 (10th Cir. 1990); Dameron v. Sinai Hosp. of Balt., Inc., 815 F.2d 975, 981 (4th Cir. 1987); Pierce Cnty. Hotel Emps. and Restaurant Emps. Health Trust v. Elks Lodge, B.P.O.E. No. 1450, 827 F.2d 1324, 1328 (9th Cir. 1987).

100. *See* Syed v. Hercules, Inc., 214 F.3d 155, 158–61 (3d Cir. 2000); Adamson v. Armco, Inc., 44 F.3d 650, 652 (8th Cir. 1995).

101. Heimeshoff v. Hartford Life & Accident Ins. Co., 134 S. Ct. 604 (2013); *see also* Munro-Kienstra v. Carpenters' Health & Welfare Trust Fund of St. Louis, No. 4:12CV53 HEA, 2014 WL 562557 (E.D. Mo. Feb. 13, 2014).

102. Berger v. AXA Network LLC, 459 F.3d 804, 814–15 (7th Cir. 2006); Teumer v. Gen. Motors Corp., 34 F.3d 542, 547 (7th Cir. 1994).

103. Sandberg v. KPMG Peat Marwick, L.L.P., 111 F.3d 331, 335 (2d Cir. 1997) (citing *Teumer*, 34 F.3d at 549)).

most analogous to claims brought under § 510, but the court declined to decide which was most analogous as either would have barred the claim.[104] The Third, Seventh, Eighth, and Tenth Circuits have held that a § 510 is sufficiently developed when the employee is informed of an impending termination or denial of benefits.[105]

Both the Fifth Circuit and the Eighth Circuit have refused to apply the doctrine of equitable tolling to ERISA claims, requiring plaintiffs to bring their claims within the applicable statutes of limitations regardless of impediments to their doing so.[106] Various other courts have applied the doctrine of equitable tolling to claims brought under ERISA—particularly where claimants were required to exhaust administrative remedies prior to the filing suit.[107]

104. Musick v. Goodyear Tire & Rubber Co., Inc., 81 F.3d 136, 139 (11th Cir. 1996).
105. Jakims v. Hoffmann-La Roche, Inc., 485 F.3d 770, 778 (3d Cir. 2007); Tolle v. Carroll Touch, Inc., 977 F.2d 1129, 1140 (7th Cir. 1992); Heiderman v. PFL, Inc., 904 F.2d 1262, 1267 (8th Cir. 1990); Held v. Mfrs. Hanover Leasing Corp., 912 F.2d 1197, 1205 (10th Cir. 1990).
106. *See* Radford v. Gen. Dynamics Corp., 151 F.3d 396 (5th Cir. 1998); Mason v. Aetna Life Ins. Co., 901 F.2d 662, 664 (8th Cir. 1990).
107. *See, e.g.*, Pettaway v. Teachers Ins. & Annuity Ass'n of Am., 547 F. Supp. 2d 1, 5–6 (D. D.C. 2008); Jeffries v. Trs. of the Northrop Grumman Sav. & Inv. Plan, 169 F. Supp. 2d 1380, 1382 (M.D. Ga. 2001); Wolfe v. 3M Short-Term Disability Plan, 176 F. Supp. 2d 911, 916–19 (D. Minn. 2001).

Chapter 5

Who Has Fiduciary Liability?

Fiduciary status unlocks the remedial provisions of ERISA. In certain cases, the determination of fiduciary status is straightforward. Employee benefit plans must "provide for one or more named fiduciaries who jointly or severally shall have authority to control and manage the operation and administration of the plan."[1] Certain positions require individuals to perform fiduciary functions, including plan administrators and plan trustees.[2]

Plan trustees are not responsible or liable for the acts or omissions of the plan's investment manager, nor are they obligated to invest or otherwise manage any asset of the plan that is subject to the management of the investment manager.[3] A named fiduciary of a plan can appoint an investment manager.[4] An investment manager is a specialized fiduciary with powers to manage, acquire, or dispose of any asset of the plan, and who has accepted and acknowledged in writing that he or she is a fiduciary.[5] In addition, an investment manager is someone:

> [W]ho (i) is registered as an investment adviser under the Investment Advisers Act of 1940; (ii) is not registered as an investment adviser under such Act by reason of paragraph (1) of section 203A(a) of such Act, is registered as an investment adviser under the laws of the State

1. 29 U.S.C. § 1102(a) (2012).
2. 29 C.F.R. § 2509.75-8 (2013).
3. 29 U.S.C. § 1105(b)(1)(B) (2012).
4. 29 U.S.C. § 1102(c)(3) (2012).
5. 29 U.S.C. § 1002(38)(A) (2012).

> (referred to in such paragraph (1)) in which it maintains its principal office and place of business, and, at the time the fiduciary last filed the registration form most recently filed by the fiduciary with such State in order to maintain the fiduciary's registration under the laws of such State, also filed a copy of such form with the Secretary; (iii) is a bank, as defined in that Act; or (iv) is an insurance company qualified to perform services described in subparagraph (A) under the laws of more than one State . . . .[6]

Functional Fiduciaries

ERISA also provides for fiduciary status based on conduct or the possession of discretionary authority. Specifically, an individual is a "functional fiduciary":

> [T]o the extent (i) he exercises any discretionary authority or discretionary control respecting management of such plan or exercises any authority or control respecting management or disposition of its assets, (ii) he renders investment advice for a fee or other compensation, direct or indirect, with respect to any moneys or other property of such plan, or has any authority or responsibility to do so, or (iii) he has any discretionary authority or discretionary responsibility in the administration of such plan.[7]

Most of the litigation concerning fiduciary status involves this functional aspect of the statute, especially when applied to plans' service providers, and cases and regulations have consequently, elaborated on the statutory definition. Courts have interpreted the phrases "discretionary authority," "discretionary control," and "discretionary responsibility" to mean real decision-making power and not merely having influence over the decisions

6. 29 U.S.C. § 1002(38)(B) (2012).
7. 29 U.S.C. § 1002(21) (2012).

of a plan trustee.[8] Thus, fiduciary status does not extend to third-party service providers to the plan, such as attorneys, accountants, actuaries, and brokers, when performing functions and providing services in their usual professional capacities.[9] Someone negotiating a compensation contract for a plan but with no other relation to the plan is also outside fiduciary status.[10]

This exemption for service providers is necessary in order for these services to the plan to be accessed and provided unreservedly. However, service providers' conduct can trump the exemption when it is sufficiently invasive. The fiduciary status of accountants have generated considerable litigation. The United States Court of Appeals for the Eight Circuit held in *Martin v. Feilen* that partners of an accounting firm constituted fiduciaries when they had regularly recommended investments, structured investment deals, and provided other investment advice.[11]

Federal regulations have explained that "persons who have no power to make any decisions as to plan policy, interpretations, practices or procedure" but provide clerical and ministerial services to the plan are not fiduciaries.[12] Nonfiduciary, ministerial functions include applying rules to determine participant eligibility, calculating services and compensation to determine benefits, preparing employee communication materials, maintaining service and employment records, preparing reports to government agencies, calculating benefits, orienting participants and advising participants of their rights and options under the plan, collecting contributions,

8. *See* Pappas v. Buck Consultants, Inc., 923 F.2d 531, 535 (7th Cir. 1991); Anoka Orthopaedic Assocs. v. Lechner, 910 F.2d 514, 517 (8th Cir. 1990); Painters of Phila. Dist. Council No. 21 Welfare Fund v. Price Waterhouse, 879 F.2d 1146, 1149 (3d Cir. 1989); Nieto v. Ecker, 845 F.2d 868 (9th Cir. 1988).

9. *See generally* Merten v. Hewitt Assocs., 508 U.S. 248, 262 (1993) ("ERISA, however, defines 'fiduciary' not in terms of formal trusteeship, but in functional terms of control and authority over the plan, . . . thus expanding the universe of persons subject to fiduciary duties—and to damages—under § 409(a). Professional service providers such as actuaries become liable for damages when they cross the line from advisor to fiduciary; must disgorge assets and profits obtained through participation as parties-in-interest in transactions prohibited by § 406, and pay related civil penalties . . . or excise taxes . . . and . . . may be enjoined from participating in a fiduciary's breaches, compelled to make restitution, and subjected to other equitable decrees.").

10. *See* Renfro v. Unisys Corp., 671 F.2d 314, 324 (3d Cir. 2011) (citing F.H. Krear & Co. v. Nineteen Named Trs., 810 F.2d 1250, 1259 (2d Cir. 1987)).

11. Martin v. Feilen, 965 F.2d 660, 663–64 (8th Cir. 1992).

12. 29 C.F.R. § 2509.75-8 (2013).

preparing participant benefit statements, processing claims, and making recommendations to a person with decision-making authority.[13]

Functional Fiduciaries with Control of Management or Assets

Subsections (i) and (iii) of the definition of a functional fiduciary are the most litigated. Subsection (i) imparts fiduciary status to an individual "to the extent (i) he exercises any discretionary authority or discretionary control respecting management of such plan or exercises any authority or control respecting management or disposition of [plan] assets."[14] The United States Court of Appeals for the Eight Circuit observed in *FirsTier Bank, N.A. v. Zeller* that ERISA "imposes fiduciary duties only if one exercises discretionary authority or control over plan *management*, but imposes those duties *whenever* one deals with plan *assets*."[15] The court reasoned that "[t]his distinction is not accidental—it reflects the high standard of care trust law imposes upon those who handle money or other assets on behalf of another."[16]

Any authority or control over the disposition of plan assets is sufficient to render fiduciary status.[17] For example, writing checks on plan funds could impart fiduciary status, though probably not if a different individual than the party at issue wrote the checks in the party's name.[18] As another example, the United States Court of Appeals for the Fourth Circuit in *Phelps v. C.T. Enterprises, Inc.*, in analyzing the facts in the record and extrapolating reasonable inferences in the light most favorable to the claimants, held that representatives of an employer and plan director were fiduciaries under ERISA when they directed employees' paycheck contributions to be diverted from payment to third parties.[19]

13. *Id.*
14. 29 U.S.C. § 1002(21)(A) (2012).
15. FirsTier Bank, N.A. v. Zeller, 16 F.3d 907, 911 (8th Cir. 1994).
16. *Id.*
17. David P. Coldesina, D.D.S. v. Estate of Simper, 407 F.3d 1126, 1133 (10th Cir. 2005).
18. *See* LoPresti v. Terwiliger, 126 F.3d 34, 40 (2d Cir. 1997).
19. Phelps v. C.T. Enters., Inc., 394 F.3d 213, 221 (4th Cir. 2005).

Functional Fiduciaries Who Possess Discretionary Authority or Responsibility

Subsection (i) of ERISA's definition of a functional fiduciary requires an actual exercise of discretionary authority or an actual exercise of control over plan assets even without authority.[20] Subsection (i) creates fiduciary status based on action, whereas subsection (iii) is a passive section imparting status based on title.[21] The United States Court of Appeals for the Seventh Circuit found in its 2013 decision *Leimkuehler v. American United Life Insurance Company* that an insurance company offering investment, record keeping, and other administrative services to 401(k) plans was not a functional fiduciary under subsection (i).[22] In *Leimkuehler*, an ERISA plan trustee brought suit against the plan's insurance company claiming that its revenue-sharing practices breached the company's fiduciary duty to the plan.[23] The insurance company's contract with the plan allowed the insurance company to select a menu of mutual funds in which plan participants could invest. This was presented to the plan's trustee, who then selected which specific funds to make available to plan participants.[24] The company reserved the right to substitute or delete the trustee's selections.[25]

The company had not been a named fiduciary in the plan.[26] Thus, the company's fiduciary status could only flow from its classification as a "functional fiduciary" within ERISA's three-part definition.[27] The trustee first argued that the company acted as a fiduciary when it exercised authority

20. 29 U.S.C. § 1002(21) (2012).
21. *See* Blatt v. Marshall & Lassman, 812 F.2d 810, 812 (2d Cir. 1987) (citing Amato v. W. Union Int'l, Inc., 773 F.2d 1402, 1416-17 (2d Cir. 1985); Anderson v. Ciba-Geigy Corp., 759 F.2d 1518, 1522 (11th Cir. 1985); Donovan v. Mercer, 747 F.2d 304, 308 (5th Cir. 1984)).
22. Leimkuehler v. Am. United Life Ins. Co., 713 F.3d 905, 908 (7th Cir. 2013).
23. *Id.* at 910.
24. *Id.* at 909–10.
25. *Id.* at 910.
26. *Id.*
27. *Id.* To reiterate, a person is a fiduciary to the extent (i) he exercises any discretionary authority or discretionary control respecting management of such plan or exercises any authority or control respecting management or disposition of its assets, (ii) he renders investment advice for a fee or other compensation, direct or indirect, with respect to any moneys or other property of such plan, or has any authority or responsibility to do so, or (iii) he has any discretionary authority or discretionary responsibility in the administration of such plan. 29 U.S.C. § 1002(21) (2012).

or control over the management or disposition of the plan's assets and it selected the mutual fund share classes to make available on the plan's investment menu.[28] The court rejected this argument and confirmed its previous holding in *Hecker v. Deere & Company* that selecting funds and their share classes to present as a menu of investment options did not transform an annuity provider into a functional fiduciary.[29]

Second, the claimant asserted that the company exercised fiduciary control consistent with management and disposition of the plan's assets by establishing a separate account to track plan participants' contributions and investment directions, to invest participants' funds, and to credit returns to participants' accounts.[30] The court agreed with the other circuits that the company could still be a functional fiduciary even if it did not have discretion over how it managed and disposed of the plan's assets via the account.[31] The Supreme Court had previously held in *Pegram v. Herdrich* that fiduciary liability attaches only if an entity exercises authority or control concerning the specific action at issue in the proceeding, but this could not be said in *Leimkuehler* of the company's control over the account in relation to the company's revenue-sharing practices.[32]

Additionally, the court rejected an argument brought by the Department of Labor (DOL) as amicus curiae that the company was a fiduciary because it retained the right to delete or substitute the funds the trustee selected for the plan.[33] The DOL claimed that the company exercised its authority in a negative sense whenever it invested contributions in a mutual fund share class because the company had the power to unilaterally substitute a less expensive share class, and not doing so amounted to the exercise of authority.[34] The court responded:

28. *Leimkuehler*, 713 F.3d at 910.
29. *Id.* at 911–12 (citing Hecker v. Deere & Co., 556 F.3d 575, 583 (7th Cir. 2009)).
30. *Id.* at 912.
31. *Id.* (citing Briscoe v. Fine, 444 F.3d 478, 492–94 (6th Cir. 2006); Chao v. Day, 436 F.3d 234, 237–38 (D.C. Cir. 2006); Coldesina v. Estate of Simper, 407 F.3d 1126, 1132 (10th Cir. 2005); Bd. of Trustees of Bricklayers & Allied Craftsmen Local 6 of N.J. Welfare Fund v. Wettlin Assoc., 237 F.3d 270, 273 (3d Cir. 2001).
32. *Id.* at 913 (citing Pegram v. Herdrich, 530 U.S. 211, 226 (2000)).
33. *Id.* at 914.
34. *Id.*

> This theory is unworkable. It conflicts with a common-sense understanding of the meaning of "exercise," is unsupported by precedent, and would expand fiduciary responsibilities under Section 1002(21)(A) to entities that took no action at all with respect to a plan. In contrast to a named fiduciary, a functional fiduciary under Section 1002(21)(A) owes a duty to a plan through its actions, regardless of whether it chose to assume fiduciary responsibilities or even anticipated that such responsibilities might arise. Section 1002(21)(A)'s reach is limited to circumstances where the individual actually exercises some authority, and people may be fiduciaries when they do certain things but be entitled to act in their own interests when they do others.[35]

The *Leimkuehler* court's rejection of the DOL's argument lined up with the United States Court of Appeals for the Eighth Circuit's holding in *Trustees of the Graphic Communications International Union Upper Midwest Local 1M Health & Welfare Plan v. Bjorkedal* that an omission or failure to act is not an individual exercise of discretionary authority over plan assets.[36] In *Bjorkedal*, the Eighth Circuit put it simply:

> As noted, subsection (i) imposes fiduciary obligations on individuals who are not named as fiduciaries but nonetheless exercise actual authority over plan assets. Because this subsection imposes a fiduciary duty on those not named as a fiduciary, its reach is limited to circumstances where the individual actually exercises some authority.[37]

In *Healthcare Strategies, Inc. v. ING Life Insurance & Annuity Company*, the United States District Court for Connecticut departed from the reasoning in *Leimkuehler*.[38] Similar to *Leimkuehler*, the plan administrators in *Healthcare Strategies* brought suit against a 401(k) service provider, ING

35. *Id.* (citations and quotation marks omitted).
36. Trs. of the Graphic Commc'ns Int'l Union Upper Midwest Local 1M Health & Welfare Plan v. Bjorkedal, 516 F.3d 719, 733 (8th Cir. 2008).
37. *Id.*
38. Healthcare Strategies, Inc. v. ING Life Ins. & Annuity Co., No. 11-00282-WGY, 2013 WL 4446919, at *6 (D. Conn. Aug. 9, 2013).

Life Insurance and Annuity Company (ILIAC), claiming that the company's revenue-sharing practices violated the company's fiduciary duty to act solely for plan participants.[39] While *Healthcare Strategies* also rested on the fiduciary status of a service provider with the contractual right to substitute mutual funds in retirement plans, the court found that, unlike in *Leimkuehler*, ILIAC's authority to substitute funds constituted discretionary authority yielding fiduciary responsibility.[40] The *Healthcare Strategies* court remarked that the Seventh Circuit had failed to analyze the contractual right to substitute funds under the ERISA subsection making the possession of authority, and not only its exercise, a determinant of fiduciary status.[41] The court explained:

> The Seventh Circuit rejected this "unworkable" definition of the word "exercise," deciding that an act of omission does not constitute an exercise of discretionary authority over plan assets. Thus, the Seventh Circuit limited the service provider's fiduciary duty to those instances in which it actually changed the mutual fund selections. This reasoning is of limited value, however, because the Seventh Circuit only analyzed whether the contractual right to substitute funds implicated fiduciary status under subsection one of 29 U.S.C. section 1002(21)(A), rather than subsection three, which makes possession of authority, not its exercise, the key determinant of fiduciary status. Bound by the Second Circuit, which recognizes that subsections one and three of 29 U.S.C. section 1002(21)(A) create distinct avenues for acquiring fiduciary status, this Court cannot ignore the possibility that ILIAC's contractual authority to substitute funds is the type of "discretionary authority" that yields fiduciary responsibility under 29 U.S.C. section 1002(21)(A)(iii).[42]

39. *Id.* at *1.
40. *Id.* at *6.
41. *Id.*
42. *Id.*

Functional Fiduciaries Who Render Investment Advice

Pursuant to subsection (ii) of ERISA's definition of a functional fiduciary, a person may be classified as a functional fiduciary by rendering investment advice with respect to any assets of the plan for compensation.[43] A DOL regulation explains that a person renders "investment advice" when he or she directly "renders advice to the plan as to the value of securities or other property, or makes recommendation as to the advisability of investing in, purchasing, or selling securities or other property."[44] In addition to this requirement, a person renders investment advice only if he or she, through an affiliate or in conjunction with an affiliate, also "[h]as discretionary authority or control, whether or not pursuant to an agreement, arrangement or understanding, with respect to purchasing or selling security"; or he or she renders investment advice through or together with an affiliate:

> on a regular basis to the plan pursuant to a mutual agreement, arrangement or understanding, written or otherwise, between such person and the plan or a fiduciary with respect to the plan, that such services will serve as a primary basis for investment decisions with respect to plan assets, and that such person will render individualized investment advice to the plan based on the particular needs of the plan regarding such matters as, among other things, investment policies or strategy, overall portfolio composition, or diversification of plan investments.[45]

In its 1994 decision *Thomas, Head & Greisen Employees Trust v. Buster*, the United States Court of Appeals for the Ninth Circuit noted that all of the following five factors were required in finding that a broker named Buster was a functional fiduciary:

> (1) Buster provided individualized investment advice; (2) the advice was given pursuant to a mutual understanding; (3) the advice was provided on a regular basis; (4) the advice pertained to the value of

43. 29 U.S.C. § 1002(21)(A) (2012).
44. 29 C.F.R. § 2510.3–21 (2013).
45. *Id.*

> the property or consisted of recommendations as to the advisability of investing in certain property; and (5) the advice was rendered for a fee.[46]

District courts continue to apply the *Buster* factors.[47]

As the United States Court of Appeals for the Fifth Circuit observed in *Schloegel v. Boswell*, there is significant overlap between the requirements to satisfy subsection (ii) and subsection (i) of ERISA's definition for a functional fiduciary.[48] *Schloegel* concerned whether Laurie C. Boswell constituted a functional fiduciary in her role as a consultant to a pension and profit-sharing plan and in her role as an insurance banker.[49] The court found that Boswell was not a functional fiduciary under subsection (i) because "[m]ere influence over the trustee's investment decisions . . . is not effective control over plan assets," and Boswell did not cause the trustee "to relinquish his independent discretion in investing the plan's funds and follow the course prescribed by Boswell."[50] This conclusion, drawn in the context of a subsection (i) analysis, foreclosed one avenue for fiduciary status under subsection (ii).[51] The court observed:

> Boswell does not dispute that the first requirement of the DOL Regulation is met; he made recommendations as to the advisability of purchasing life insurance.
>
> The parties dispute whether the second requirement of the DOL Regulation is met. There are two ways to satisfy this second requirement. First, the second requirement is met if the person (Boswell) had discretionary authority or control with respect to purchasing property for the plan. Subpart (ii)(A) of the DOL Regulation appears to overlap

46. Thomas, Head & Greisen Emps. Tr. v. Buster, 24 F.3d 1114, 1117 (9th Cir. 1994).
47. *See, e.g.*, Goldenberg v. Indel, Inc., 741 F. Supp. 2d 618, 625 (D. N.J. 2010); F.W. Webb Co. v. State Street Bank & Tr. Co., No. 09 Civ. 1241(RJH), 2010 WL 3219284, at *8 (S.D. N.Y. Aug. 12, 2010); Ellis v. Rycenga Homes, Inc., 484 F. Supp. 694, 708 (W.D. Mich. 2007).
48. Schloegel v. Boswell, 994 F.2d 266, 272–73 (5th Cir. 1993).
49. *Id.* at 268.
50. *Id.* at 271–72 (citing Am. Fed'n of Unions Local 102 Health & Welfare Fund v. Equitable Life Assurance Soc'y, 841 F.2d 658, 664 (5th Cir. 1988); Sommers Drug Stores Co. Emp. Profit Sharing Trust v. Corrigan Enter., Inc., 793 F.2d 1456, 1560 (5th Cir. 1986)).
51. *Id.* at 273.

> with subsection (i) of 29 U.S.C. § 1002(21)(A), which we discussed above. If a person has discretionary authority or control with respect to purchasing or selling securities or other property for the plan, that person would satisfy subsection (i) of 29 U.S.C. § 1002(21)(A) as well as satisfy Subpart (ii)(A) of the DOL Regulation. For the reasons discussed above [in the subsection (i) analysis], we hold that Boswell did not have "discretionary authority or control" . . . .[52]

The court found that the second requirement of the DOL regulation—that investment-type advice should be rendered regularly to the plan in response to a mutual agreement, an arrangement, or some understanding between the advisor and the plan—was not met either.[53] The court observed that Boswell did not regularly give investment-type advice and that nothing in the record reflected that there was "a mutual arrangement or understanding that Boswell's advice would serve as the primary basis for the plan's investment decisions."[54]

Fiduciary Duties and Responsibilities

ERISA establishes an array of fiduciary responsibilities for the administration and management of a plan to guard the plan assets and protect the interests of plan participants and beneficiaries. Plans that do not have assets to protect are exempt from fiduciary mandates under ERISA. To that end, ERISA § 401(a)(1) exempts a top-hat plan, meaning a "plan which is unfunded and is maintained by an employer primarily for the purposes of providing deferred compensation for a select group of management or highly compensated employees," from the fiduciary standards.[55] ERISA also exempts these plans from participation, vesting, and funding requirements but not from ERISA's enforcement provisions.

52. *Id.* at 272–73 (citations omitted).
53. *Id.* at 273.
54. *Id.*
55. 29 U.S.C. § 1051 (2012).

Fiduciaries of all employee benefit plans, including welfare benefit plans and pension plans, are subject to the specific fiduciary standards of ERISA § 404(a) unless specifically exempted. ERISA requires fiduciaries to discharge their duties in the sole interest of the participants and beneficiaries and:

> (A) for the exclusive purpose of:
> (i) providing benefits to participants and their beneficiaries; and
> (ii) defraying reasonable expenses of administering the plan;
> (B) with the care, skill, prudence, and diligence under the circumstances then prevailing that a prudent man acting in a like capacity and familiar with such matters would use in the conduct of an enterprise of a like character and with like aims;
> (C) by diversifying the investments of the plan so as to minimize the risk of large losses, unless under the circumstances it is clearly prudent not to do so; and
> (D) in accordance with the documents and instruments governing the plan insofar as such documents and instruments are consistent with [ERISA].[56]

The Duty of Loyalty and the Prudent Man Standard

Most litigation on fiduciary duties arise from the requirement that fiduciaries discharge their duties for the benefit and sole interest of the participants and beneficiaries, often referred to as the duty of loyalty, as well as the requirement that fiduciaries execute their duties with the care, skill, prudence, and diligence befitting a prudent person. This mandate to operate with prudence and for the exclusive benefit of the participants and beneficiaries extends to the distribution phase and with respect to the selection of any company providing annuity services.

Concerning the duty of loyalty, the fiduciary can benefit from the fiduciary's action but only in an incidental way. The United States Court of Appeals

56. 29 U.S.C. § 1104(a)(1) (2012).

for the Second Circuit explained in *Donovan v. Bierwirth* that "officers of a corporation who are trustees of its pension plan do not violate their duties as trustees by taking action which, after careful and impartial investigation, they reasonably conclude best to promote the interests of participants and beneficiaries simply because it incidentally benefits the corporation or, indeed, themselves."[57] Still, the fiduciaries' "decisions must be made with an eye single to the interests of the participants and beneficiaries."[58]

The duty of loyalty creates disclosure requirements in addition to the extensive disclosure requirements otherwise stemming from ERISA. The United States Court of Appeals for the Eight Circuit recently observed in *Braden v. Wal-Mart Stores, Inc.*:

> It is uncontroversial that the duty of loyalty requires fiduciaries to deal fairly and honestly with all plan members, and it is a breach of this duty affirmatively to mislead a participant or beneficiary. Moreover, in some circumstances fiduciaries must on their own initiative disclose any material information that could adversely affect a participant's interests.[59]

The duty of prudence is implicated in negotiating fees, monitoring those who service the plans, making substantive investment decisions, and deciding whether to keep or dispose of stocks held in a plan's account. On the subject of investment decisions, a fiduciary's conduct is evaluated based on the circumstances existing at the time the decisions are made and not based on hindsight. The courts must objectively assess, at the time of the transaction, whether the fiduciary utilized proper tools available to investigate, evaluate, and design the investment portfolio; conducted himself or herself in a manner similar to others familiar with such issues; and exercised independent judgment when finalizing the investment decision.[60] Thus, the test of prudence relates to conduct and not necessarily to the outcome of

57. Donovan v. Bierwirth, 680 F.2d 263, 271 (2d Cir. 1982).
58. *Id.*
59. Braden v. Wal-Mart Stores, Inc., 588 F.3d 585, 598 (8th Cir. 2009) (citations and quotation marks omitted).
60. *See* Lank v. O'Higgins, 810 F. Supp. 379, 388 (N.D. N.Y. 1992) (citing Katsaros v. Cody, 744 F.2d 270, 279 (2d Cir. 1984)).

the investment decision. While the common law of trusts instructs courts to examine each investment independently, the DOL has directed courts to examine the entire investment portfolio to assess fiduciary prudence.[61]

As for the duty of prudence, a frequently litigated issue concerns whether the fiduciaries failed to prudently evaluate fees charged by various investment options in 401(k) plans. In *Hecker v. Deere & Co.*, participants claimed the fiduciary Deere & Co. violated its obligations due to the fees charged to the participants resulting from Deere & Company's plan investments.[62] The United States Court of Appeals for the Seventh Circuit rejected the participants' argument:

> We turn next to plaintiffs' contention that Deere violated its fiduciary duty by selecting investment options with excessive fees. In our view, the undisputed facts leave no room for doubt that the Deere Plans offered a sufficient mix of investments for their participants. Thus, even if, as plaintiffs urge, there is a fiduciary duty on the part of a company offering a plan to furnish an acceptable array of investment vehicles, no rational trier of fact could find, on the basis of the facts alleged in this Complaint, that Deere failed to satisfy that duty. As the district court pointed out, there was a wide range of expense ratios among the twenty Fidelity mutual funds and the 2,500 other funds available through BrokerageLink. At the low end, the expense ratio was .07%; at the high end, it was just over 1%. Importantly, all of these funds were also offered to investors in the general public, and so the expense ratios necessarily were set against the backdrop of market competition. The fact that it is possible that some other funds might have had even lower ratios is beside the point; nothing in ERISA requires every fiduciary to scour the market to find and offer the cheapest possible fund (which might, of course, be plagued by other problems).[63]

61. 29 C.F.R. § 2550.404a–1 (2013).
62. Hecker v. Deere & Co., 556 F.3d 575, 586 (7th Cir. 2009).
63. *Id.*

However, in *Braden v. Wal-Mart Stores, Inc.*, claimants survived a motion for summary judgment in the Eighth Circuit because:

> The complaint alleges that the Plan comprises a very large pool of assets, that the 401(k) marketplace is highly competitive, and that retirement plans of such size consequently have the ability to obtain institutional class shares of mutual funds. Despite this ability, according to the allegations of the complaint, each of the ten funds included in the Plan offers only retail class shares, which charge significantly higher fees than institutional shares for the same return on investment. The complaint also alleges that seven of the Plan's ten funds charge 12b–1 fees from which participants derive no benefit. The complaint states that appellees did not change the options included in the Plan despite the fact that most of them underperformed the market indices they were designed to track. Finally, it alleges that the funds included in the Plan made revenue sharing payments to the trustee, Merrill Lynch, and that these payments were not made in exchange for services rendered, but rather were a quid pro quo for inclusion in the Plan.[64]

Fully Funded Defined Benefit Plans

In evaluating the fiduciaries' conduct with respect to a defined benefit plan, the funding status of the plan can be dispositive. In *McCullough v. Aegon USA, Inc.*, plaintiffs asserted that the defendants breached their fiduciary duty but did not dispute that the defined-benefit plan was substantially overfunded at the time of suit.[65] Relying on its prior decision in *Harley v. Minnesota Mining & Manufacturing Company*, the United States Court of Appeals for the Eighth Circuit rejected the plaintiffs' argument.[66] The court in *Harley* had explained that to side with the plaintiffs would raise serious

64. *Braden*, 588 F.3d at 595–96.
65. McCullough v. Aegon USA Inc., 585 F.3d 1082, 1085 (8th Cir. 2009).
66. *Id.*

Article III issues because it would permit participants or beneficiaries who have not suffered an injury in fact to bring suit.[67]

Fiduciary Monitoring of Administrative Staff

Fiduciaries must monitor administrative staff. In *Schmidt v. Sheet Metal Workers' National Pension Fund*, the United States Court of Appeals for the Seventh Circuit considered whether trustees were liable for an administrative staff member's misstatement when an alleged breach of fiduciary duties rested on it.[68] No evidence suggested that the trustees authorized, participated in, or had knowledge of the misstatement or that they had deliberately withheld information.[69] The court concluded that the trustees were not liable for the misstatement, but the court qualified its holding:

> We hasten to add, however, that our resolution of this case depends in large measure on the fact that the Trustees provided complete and accurate information in the Plan and Plan Booklet they distributed to all participants. Although ERISA fiduciaries do not necessarily satisfy their fiduciary obligations merely by complying with the disclosure requirements imposed by the statute, we believe that the adequacy of the relevant disclosures in the written plan materials is an important consideration in a circumstance like this where a non-fiduciary agent subsequently provides erroneous information in response to a question from a single participant. If the written materials were inadequate, then the fiduciaries themselves must be held responsible for the failure to provide complete and correct material information in the event that a nonfiduciary agent provides misleading information. We are unwilling to conclude, however, that the fiduciaries also will be held responsible when their written disclosures were adequate, they had no involvement in communicating the misleading information, and there has been no showing that the fiduciaries failed to exercise

67. Harley v. Minn. Min. & Mfg. Co., 284 F.3d 901, 906 (8th Cir. 2002).
68. Schmidt v. Sheet Metal Workers' Nat'l Pension Fund, 128 F.3d 541, 547 (7th Cir. 1997).
69. *Id.*

due care in hiring, retaining, or training the non-fiduciary agent for the tasks assigned her.[70]

The Duty to Assess Available Information

Fiduciaries cannot blindly rely on available information or passively accept advice. For instance, in *Howard v. Shay*, the United States Court of Appeals for the Ninth Circuit held that conflicted fiduciaries did not take reasonable steps in reviewing the appraisal of the employer's stock before purchasing the stock with plan assets.[71] In *Howard*, even a cursory review of the valuation would have revealed that the fiduciaries acted carelessly by relying on it.[72]

On the other side of the spectrum, the employer and retirement fund manager, W.R. Grace & Company, acting as a defendant in *Bunch v. W.R. Grace & Company* adequately monitored State Street Bank, which Grace & Company had engaged for advice regarding the wisdom of retaining certain stock in its defined contribution 401(k) plan.[73] The United States Court of Appeals for the First Circuit explained:

> There can be little doubt on this record that the state of Grace's corporate health was thoroughly studied by experts who debated and considered ad nauseam the pros and cons of retaining or selling the stock held in the Plan's portfolio. The unanimous conclusion of those charged with making the decision was that divestment of this stock was the only action consistent with the prudence required of a responsible fiduciary under ERISA. Without question, State Street engaged in a substantively sound, reasonable analysis of all relevant circumstances appropriate to the decision to sell the Grace stock.[74]

70. *Id.* at 548 (citations omitted).
71. Howard v. Shay, 100 F.3d 1484, 1490 (9th Cir. 1996).
72. *Id.* at 1489.
73. Bunch v. W.R. Grace & Co., 555 F.3d 1, 3 (1st Cir. 2009).
74. *Id.* at 9–10.

The Duties to Diversify Investments and ESOP Fiduciaries

ERISA § 404(a)(1)(C) requires fiduciaries to diversify "the investments of the plan so as to minimize the risk of large losses, unless under the circumstances it is clearly prudent not to do so."[75] Under ERISA § 404(a)(2), an eligible individual account plan, such as an ESOP, a stock bonus plan, or a profit-sharing plan authorized to invest in employer securities, does not violate the diversification requirement solely based on the acquisition or holding of qualifying employer securities or qualifying employer real property.[76]

In 1995, the United States Court of Appeals for the Third Circuit made a particularly influential decision in *Moench v. Robertson*. *Moench* addressed the extent to which fiduciaries of Employee Stock Ownership Plans (ESOPs) were liable for investing solely in employer common stock when both the plan and Congress provided that the goal of such plans was to invest in employer's securities.[77] The court held that the fiduciaries could be liable in limited circumstances for following the plan's direction to invest in employer stock.[78] Before developing a standard to evaluate fiduciaries of ESOPs, the court examined the nature of ESOPs in relation to ERISA:

> ERISA contains specific provisions governing ESOPs. While fiduciaries of pension benefit plans generally must diversify investments of the plan assets so as to minimize the risk of large losses, fiduciaries of ESOPS are exempted from this duty. Specifically, the diversification requirement . . . and the prudence requirement (only to the extent that it requires diversification) . . . is not violated by acquisition or holding of . . . qualifying employer securities . . . . In other words, under normal circumstances, ESOP fiduciaries cannot be taken to task for failing to diversify investments, regardless of how prudent diversification would be under the terms of an ordinary non-ESOP pension plan. ESOPs also are exempted from ERISA's strict prohibitions against dealing with a

75. 29 U.S.C. § 1104(a)(1)(C) (2012).
76. 29 U.S.C. § 1104(a)(2) (2012).
77. Moench v. Robertson, 62 F.3d 553, 556 (3d Cir. 1995).
78. *Id.*

party in interest, and against self-dealing, that is, deal[ing] with the assets of the plan in his own interest or for his own account.

The reason for these specific rules arises out of the nature and purpose of ESOPs themselves. [E]mployee stock ownership plan[s are] designed to invest primarily in qualifying employer securities. Thus, unlike the traditional pension plan governed by ERISA, ESOP assets generally are invested in securities issued by [the plan's] sponsoring company. In keeping with this, ESOPs, unlike pension plans, are not intended to guarantee retirement benefits, and indeed, by its very nature an ESOP places employee retirement assets at much greater risk than does the typical diversified ERISA plan. The summary plan description in this case, for example, explicitly stated that the plan does not provide for a guaranteed benefit at retirement.

Rather, ESOPs serve other purposes. Under their original rationale, ESOPs were described as . . . device[s] for expanding the national capital base among employees—an effective merger of the roles of capitalist and worker. Thus, the concept of employee ownership constituted a goal in and of itself. To accomplish this end, Congress . . . enacted a number of laws designed to encourage employers to set up such plans. The Tax Reform Act of 1976 was one of those statutes, and in passing it, Congress explicitly stated its concern that courts should refrain from erecting barriers that would interfere with that goal . . . .

. . .

Notwithstanding all of this, ESOPs are covered by ERISA's stringent requirements, and except for a few select provisions . . . , ESOP fiduciaries must act in accordance with the duties of loyalty and care. In other words, Congress expressly intended that the ESOP would be both an employee retirement benefit plan and a technique of corporate finance that would encourage employee ownership. ESOP fiduciaries must, then, wear two hats, and are expected to administer ESOP investments consistent with the provisions of both a specific employee benefits plan and ERISA.

All of this makes delineating the responsibilities of ESOP trustees difficult, because they must satisfy the demands of Congressional policies that seem destined to collide.

> . . .
>
> So with the goals of ESOPs on the one hand, and ERISA's stringent fiduciary duties on the other, the courts' task in interpreting the statute is to balance these concerns so that competent fiduciaries will not be afraid to serve, but without giving unscrupulous ones a license to steal. The goals of the two statutes often serve consistent ends—ensuring that the fiduciary acts in the interest of the plan—and in those cases the nature of a plaintiff's claim will not create tension. But when the plaintiff claims that an ESOP fiduciary violated its ERISA duties by continuing to invest in employer securities, the conflict becomes particularly stark.[79]

The court then turned to trust law to formulate a standard of review, recognizing that when an ESOP is created, it is "simply a trust under which the trustee is directed to invest the assets primarily in the stock of a single company."[80] The court set forth the following standard:

> In a case such as this, in which the fiduciary is not absolutely required to invest in employer securities but is more than simply permitted to make such investments, while the fiduciary presumptively is required to invest in employer securities, there may come a time when such investments no longer serve the purpose of the trust, or the settlor's intent. Therefore fiduciaries should not be immune from judicial inquiry, as a directed trustee essentially is, but also should not be subject to the strict scrutiny that would be exercised over a trustee only authorized to make a particular investment. Thus, a court should not undertake a *de novo* review of the fiduciary's actions . . . . Rather, the most logical result is that the fiduciary's decision to continue investing in employer securities should be reviewed for an abuse of discretion.
>
> In light of the analysis detailed above, keeping in mind the purpose behind ERISA and the nature of ESOPs themselves, we hold that in the first instance, an ESOP fiduciary who invests the assets in employer

79. *Id.* at 568–69 (citations and quotation marks omitted).
80. *Id.* at 571.

> stock is entitled to a presumption that it acted consistently with ERISA by virtue of that decision. However, the plaintiff may overcome that presumption by establishing that the fiduciary abused its discretion by investing in employer securities.
>
> In attempting to rebut the presumption, the plaintiff may introduce evidence that owing to circumstances not known to the settlor and not anticipated by him [the making of such investment] would defeat or substantially impair the accomplishment of the purposes of the trust. As in all trust cases, in reviewing the fiduciary's actions, the court must be governed by the intent behind the trust—in other words, the plaintiff must show that the ERISA fiduciary could not have believed reasonably that continued adherence to the ESOP's direction was in keeping with the settlor's expectations of how a prudent trustee would operate. In determining whether the plaintiff has overcome the presumption, the courts must recognize that if the fiduciary, in what it regards as an exercise of caution, does not maintain the investment in the employer's securities, it may face liability for that caution, particularly if the employer's securities thrive.[81]

The *Moench* court created a rebuttable presumption that adherence to plan terms is not a fiduciary breach, however a claimant can overcome that presumption by asserting that the fiduciary abused its discretion.[82] The Second, Fifth, Sixth, Seventh, and Ninth Circuits adopted the *Moench* presumption.[83]

On December 13, 2013, the Supreme Court granted certiorari in *Fifth Third Bancorp v. Dudenhoeffer* in which the lower court did not apply the presumption of rational conduct during the pleading stage.[84] More particularly, the Court considered whether the Sixth Circuit erred in its holding that respondents were not required to allege in their complaint that ESOP fiduciaries abused their discretion by maintaining investments in employer

81. *Id.* at 571–72 (citations and quotation marks omitted).
82. *Id.*
83. *See In re Citigroup ERISA Litig.*, 662 F.3d 128, 138 (2d Cir. 2011); Quan v. Computer Scis. Corp., 623 F.3d 870, 874 (9th Cir. 2010); Kirschbaum v. Reliant Energy, Inc., 526 F.3d 243, 254 (5th Cir. 2008); Summers v. State Street Bank & Trust Co., 453 F.3d 404, 410 (7th Cir. 2006); Kuper v. Iovenko, 66 F.3d 1447, 1457 (6th Cir. 1995).
84. Fifth Third Bancorp v. Dudenhoeffer, 134 S. Ct. 822 (2013).

stock in order to overcome the presumption that their decision to invest was reasonable.[85] On June 25, 2014, the Court held that ESOP fiduciaries did not enjoy a presumption of prudence but, rather, possessed the same duty of prudence as all other ERISA fiduciaries except in cases where ERISA expressly provides that they need not diversify.[86] The Court explained that "[a]side from that distinction, because ESOP fiduciaries are ERISA fiduciaries and because § 1104(a)(1)(B)'s duty of prudence applies to all ERISA fiduciaries, ESOP fiduciaries are subject to the duty of prudence just as other ERISA fiduciaries are."[87]

The Court addressed the petitioners' many arguments:

> First, petitioners argue that the special purpose of an ESOP—investing participants' savings in the stock of their employer—calls for a presumption that such investments are prudent. Their argument is as follows: ERISA defines the duty of prudence in terms of what a prudent person would do in the conduct of an enterprise of a like character and with like aims. The character and aims of an ESOP differ from those of an ordinary retirement investment, such as a diversified mutual fund. An ordinary plan seeks (1) to maximize retirement savings for participants while (2) avoiding excessive risk. But an ESOP also seeks (3) to promote employee ownership of employer stock. For instance, Fifth Third's Plan requires the ESOP's assets to be invested primarily in shares of common stock of Fifth Third. In light of this additional goal, an ESOP fiduciary's decision to buy more shares of employer stock, even if it would be imprudent were it viewed solely as an attempt to secure financial retirement benefits while avoiding excessive risk, might nonetheless be prudent if understood as an attempt to promote employee ownership of employer stock, a goal that Congress views as important. Thus, a claim that an ESOP fiduciary's investment in employer stock was imprudent as a way of securing retirement savings should be viewed unfavorably because, unless the company was

85. *Id.*
86. Fifth Third Bancorp v. Dudenhoeffer, 134 S. Ct. 2459, 2467 (2014).
87. *Id.*

about to go out of business, that investment was advancing the additional goal of employee ownership of employer stock.

We cannot accept the claim that underlies this argument, namely, that the content of ERISA's duty of prudence varies depending upon the specific nonpecuniary goal set out in an ERISA plan, such as what petitioners claim is the nonpecuniary goal here. Taken in context, § 1104(a)(1)(B)'s reference to an enterprise of a like character and with like aims means an enterprise with what the immediately preceding provision calls the exclusive purpose to be pursued by all ERISA fiduciaries: providing benefits to participants and their beneficiaries while defraying reasonable expenses of administering the plan. Read in the context of ERISA as a whole, the term benefits in the provision just quoted must be understood to refer to the sort of financial benefits (such as retirement income) that trustees who manage investments typically seek to secure for the trust's beneficiaries. The term does not cover nonpecuniary benefits like those supposed to arise from employee ownership of employer stock.

Consider the statute's requirement that fiduciaries act in accordance with the documents and instruments governing the plan insofar as such documents and instruments are consistent with the provisions of this subchapter. This provision makes clear that the duty of prudence trumps the instructions of a plan document, such as an instruction to invest exclusively in employer stock even if financial goals demand the contrary. This rule would make little sense if, as petitioners argue, the duty of prudence is defined by the aims of the particular plan as set out in the plan documents, since in that case the duty of prudence could never conflict with a plan document.

Consider also § 1104(a)(2), which exempts an ESOP fiduciary from § 1104(a)(1)(B)'s duty of prudence but only to the extent that it requires diversification. What need would there be for this specific provision were the nature of § 1104(a)(1)(B)'s duty of prudence altered anyway in the case of an ESOP in light of the ESOP's aim of promoting employee ownership of employer stock?

Petitioners are right to point out that Congress, in seeking to permit and promote ESOPs, was pursuing purposes other than the financial security of plan participants. Congress pursued those purposes by promoting ESOPs with tax incentives. And it also pursued them by exempting ESOPs from ERISA's diversification requirement, which otherwise would have precluded their creation. But we are not convinced that Congress also sought to promote ESOPs by further relaxing the duty of prudence as applied to ESOPs with the sort of presumption proposed by petitioners.

Second, and relatedly, petitioners contend that the duty of prudence should be read in light of the rule under the common law of trusts that the settlor can reduce or waive the prudent man standard of care by specific language in the trust instrument. The argument is that, by commanding the ESOP fiduciary to invest primarily in Fifth Third stock, the plan documents waived the duty of prudence to the extent that it comes into conflict with investment in Fifth Third stock—at least unless extraordinary circumstances arise that so threaten the goal of employee ownership of Fifth Third stock that the fiduciaries must assume that the settlor would want them to depart from that goal under the common-law deviation doctrine. This argument fails, however, in light of this Court's holding that, by contrast to the rule at common law, trust documents cannot excuse trustees from their duties under ERISA.

Third, petitioners argue that subjecting ESOP fiduciaries to a duty of prudence without the protection of a special presumption will lead to conflicts with the legal prohibition on insider trading. The potential for conflict arises because ESOP fiduciaries often are company insiders and because suits against insider fiduciaries frequently allege, as the complaint in this case alleges, that the fiduciaries were imprudent in failing to act on inside information they had about the value of the employer's stock.

This concern is a legitimate one. But an ESOP-specific rule that a fiduciary does not act imprudently in buying or holding company stock unless the company is on the brink of collapse (or the like) is an ill-fitting means of addressing it. While ESOP fiduciaries may be more likely to have insider information about a company that the fund is investing in than are other ERISA fiduciaries, the potential for conflict with the securities laws would be the same for a non-ESOP fiduciary who had relevant inside information about a potential investment. And the potential for conflict is the same for an ESOP fiduciary whose company is on the brink of collapse as for a fiduciary who is invested in a healthier company. (Surely a fiduciary is not obligated to break the insider trading laws even if his company is about to fail.) The potential for conflict therefore does not persuade us to accept a presumption of the sort adopted by the lower courts and proposed by petitioners . . . .

Finally, petitioners argue that, without some sort of special presumption, the threat of costly duty-of-prudence lawsuits will deter companies from offering ESOPs to their employees, contrary to the stated intent of Congress. ESOP plans instruct their fiduciaries to invest in company stock, and § 1104(a)(1)(D) requires fiduciaries to follow plan documents so long as they do not conflict with ERISA. Thus, in many cases an ESOP fiduciary who fears that continuing to invest in company stock may be imprudent finds himself between a rock and a hard place: If he keeps investing and the stock goes down he may be sued for acting imprudently in violation of § 1104(a)(1)(B), but if he stops investing and the stock goes up he may be sued for disobeying the plan documents in violation of § 1104(a)(1)(D). Petitioners argue that, given the threat of such expensive litigation, ESOPs cannot thrive unless their fiduciaries are granted a defense-friendly presumption.

Petitioners are basically seeking relief from what they believe are meritless, economically burdensome lawsuits. We agree that Congress sought to encourage the creation of ESOPs. And we have recognized that ERISA represents a careful balancing between ensuring fair and prompt enforcement of rights under a plan and the encouragement of the creation of such plans.

At the same time, we do not believe that the presumption at issue here is an appropriate way to weed out meritless lawsuits or to provide the requisite balancing. The proposed presumption makes it impossible for a plaintiff to state a duty-of-prudence claim, no matter how meritorious, unless the employer is in very bad economic circumstances. Such a rule does not readily divide the plausible sheep from

> the meritless goats. That important task can be better accomplished through careful, context-sensitive scrutiny of a complaint's allegations. We consequently stand by our conclusion that the law does not create a special presumption of prudence for ESOP fiduciaries.[88]

The Court further held that, "where a stock is publicly traded, allegations that a fiduciary should have recognized from publicly available information alone that the market was over- or undervaluing the stock are implausible as a general rule."[89] The Court remarked that a fiduciary usually is not imprudent by assuming "that a major stock market . . . provides the best estimate of the value of the stocks traded on it that is available to him."[90]

In closing, the Court took up the argument that Fifth Third insiders behaved imprudently by failing to act on the basis of nonpublic information to which they had special access.[91] The Court did not resolve this argument but offered the following guidance to lower courts:

> To state a claim for breach of the duty of prudence on the basis of inside information, a plaintiff must plausibly allege an alternative action that the defendant could have taken that would have been consistent with the securities laws and that a prudent fiduciary in the same circumstances would not have viewed as more likely to harm the fund than to help it. The following three points inform the requisite analysis.
>
> First, in deciding whether the complaint states a claim upon which relief can be granted, courts must bear in mind that the duty of prudence, under ERISA as under the common law of trusts, does not require a fiduciary to break the law. Federal securities laws are violated when a corporate insider trades in the securities of his corporation on the basis of material, nonpublic information. As every Court of Appeals to address the question has held, ERISA's duty of prudence

88. *Id.* at 2467-71 (citations and quotation marks omitted).
89. *Id.* at 2471.
90. *Id.* at 2471-72 (quoting Summers v. State Street Bank & Trust Co., 453 F.3d 404, 408 (7th Cir. 2006)).
91. *Id.* at 2472.

cannot require an ESOP fiduciary to perform an action—such as divesting the fund's holdings of the employer's stock on the basis of inside information—that would violate the securities laws. To the extent that the Sixth Circuit denied dismissal based on the theory that the duty of prudence required petitioners to sell the ESOP's holdings of Fifth Third stock, its denial of dismissal was erroneous.

Second, where a complaint faults fiduciaries for failing to decide, on the basis of the inside information, to refrain from making additional stock purchases or for failing to disclose that information to the public so that the stock would no longer be overvalued, additional considerations arise. The courts should consider the extent to which an ERISA-based obligation either to refrain on the basis of inside information from making a planned trade or to disclose inside information to the public could conflict with the complex insider trading and corporate disclosure requirements imposed by the federal securities laws or with the objectives of those laws. The U.S. Securities and Exchange Commission has not advised us of its views on these matters, and we believe those views may well be relevant.

Third, lower courts faced with such claims should also consider whether the complaint has plausibly alleged that a prudent fiduciary in the defendant's position could not have concluded that stopping purchases—which the market might take as a sign that insider fiduciaries viewed the employer's stock as a bad investment—or publicly disclosing negative information would do more harm than good to the fund by causing a drop in the stock price and a concomitant drop in the value of the stock already held by the fund.[92]

The Plan Documents Rule

ERISA § 404(a)(1)(D) requires the fiduciary to carry out his or her duties in accordance with the documents that govern the plan.[93] This is known as

92. *Id.* (citations and quotation marks omitted).
93. 29 U.S.C. § 1104(a)(1)(D) (2012).

"the plan documents rule," and, in certain circumstances, it allows the plan documents to determine whether a fiduciary is in breach.[94] A common scenario under the plan documents rule involve a participant's change of intent or change of circumstances that was not represented in the plan documents. In such a situation, the plan documents prevail. Common questions in such a case have been whether the designation of a beneficiary in the plan document trumped a waiver of pension rights in a divorce decree, and whether a postdistribution lawsuit can be brought to enforce the waiver.

In *Kennedy v. Plan Administrator for DuPont Savings & Investment Plan*, the Supreme Court considered the savings and investment plan (SIP) of a decedent named William Kennedy and whether a former spouse named Liv, who was a named beneficiary, was entitled to benefits, or if only the decedent's child, Kari Kennedy and also a named beneficiary, was entitled to benefits.[95] The Court granted certiorari to resolve a split among the courts over whether a former spouse can waive pension benefits in a divorce decree.[96] The Court declared:

> The Estate's claim . . . stands or falls by the terms of the plan, a straightforward rule of hewing to the directives of the plan documents that lets employers establish a uniform administrative scheme, [with] a set of standard procedures to guide processing of claims and disbursement of benefits. The point is that by giving a plan participant a clear set of instructions for making his own instructions clear, ERISA forecloses any justification for enquiries into nice expressions of intent, in favor of the virtues of adhering to an uncomplicated rule: simple administration, avoid[ing] double liability, and ensur[ing] that beneficiaries get what's coming quickly, without the folderol essential under less-certain rules.
>
> . . .

94. *See, e.g.*, Kennedy v. Plan Adm'r for DuPont Savings & Inv. Plan, 555 U.S. 285, 303 (2009); Matschiner v. Hartford Life & Accident Ins. Co., 622 F.3d 885, 889 (8th Cir. 2010); Sun Life Assurance Co. of Can. v. Wasko, 939 F. Supp. 2d 944 (S.D. Iowa 2013).
95. *Kennedy*, 555 U.S. at 289–90.
96. *Id.* at 291.

> And this case does as well as any other in pointing out the wisdom of protecting the plan documents rule. Under the terms of the SIP Liv was William's designated beneficiary. The plan provided an easy way for William to change the designation, but for whatever reason he did not. The plan provided a way to disclaim an interest in the SIP account, but Liv did not purport to follow it. The plan administrator therefore did exactly what § 1104(a)(1)(D) required: the documents control, and those name [the ex-wife].
>
> It is no answer, as the Estate argues, that William's beneficiary-designation form should not control because it is not one of the "documents and instruments governing the plan" under § 1104(a)(1)(D) and was not treated as a plan document by the plan administrator. That is beside the point. It is uncontested that the SIP and the summary plan description are documents and instruments governing the plan. Those documents provide that the plan administrator will pay benefits to a participant's designated beneficiary, with designations and changes to be made in a particular way. William's designation of Liv as his beneficiary was made in the way required; Liv's waiver was not.[97]

The claimants in *Boyd v. Metropolitan Life Insurance Company*, the Boyds, filed suit in 2011 under circumstances extremely similar to *Kennedy* claiming eligibility for benefits and arguing that the named beneficiary had relinquished his rights to benefits under a MetLife plan.[98] The United States Court of Appeals for the Fourth Circuit rejected the Boyds' contention that *Kennedy* was not controlling. The claimants asserted that *Kennedy* did not control because the plan did not provide a clear written mechanism for beneficiaries to renounce benefits.[99] The court reasoned:

> In short, the Boyds' arguments do not provide any basis for this court to depart from the clear and evident thrust of the *Kennedy* decision. Nothing in *Kennedy* authorizes a plan administrator to disregard a validly executed beneficiary designation form where the beneficiary

97. *Id.* at 876–77 (citations and quotation marks omitted).
98. Boyd v. Metro. Life Ins. Co., 636 F.3d 138, 139 (4th Cir. 2011).
99. *Id.* at 142.

> has made no effort to disclaim his right to benefits. Rather, the Court wished to give meaning to the plain intent of Congress in 29 U.S.C. § 1104(a)(1)(D); it wished to provide beneficiaries the prospect of prompt receipt of benefits without the burdens of uncertainty; and it wished to relieve plan administrators of the need to divine obscure participant intentions and of the specter of a lengthy fight in court.
>
> MetLife represented at oral argument that it may well set forth formal disclaimer procedures in its plans going forward. But even where such procedures are absent, the beneficiary can still make his intent clear by refusing to take benefits. Moreover, to the extent the plan participant wishes to direct benefits to a different party, she can simply change the designation on file. Given the easy availability of these options—not to mention their simplicity—we see no reason to force plan administrators to scrutinize waivers extrinsic to plan documents. That approach would bring about the very same results that led the Court in *Kennedy* to adopt the plan documents rule in the first place: the difficulties of determining whether a waiver was adequate, knowing, and voluntary; the delay in the disbursement of benefits caused by increased uncertainty over how to proceed; and the increased likelihood of administrators throwing themselves squarely into the center of contentious family disputes and exposing themselves to ceaseless litigation. None of these consequences are we prepared to risk, as we would be doing if we overturned the district court.[100]

The *Kennedy* Court left open whether the decedent's estate could enforce a waiver against the plan beneficiary once the benefits were distributed by the administrator to the beneficiary named in the plan.[101] In 2013, the United States Court of Appeals for the Fourth Circuit took up this question in *Andochick v. Byrd* and held that a designated beneficiary who waived rights to the benefits in a life insurance policy may be sued for breach of

100. *Id.* at 143–44 (citations omitted).
101. *Id.* at 299 n.10 ("Nor do we express any view as to whether the Estate could have brought an action in state or federal court against Liv to obtain the benefits after they were distributed.").

contract to recover the funds after they have been paid to the designated beneficiary.[102] The Fourth Circuit observed:

> In *Kennedy*, the Court emphasized three important ERISA objectives: [1] simple administration, [2] avoid[ing] double liability [for plan administrators], and [3] ensur[ing] that beneficiaries get what's coming quickly, without the folderol essential under less-certain rules.
>
> Allowing post-distribution suits to enforce state-law waivers does nothing to interfere with any of these objectives. For in situations like that at issue here, *Kennedy* merely dictates that the plan administrator distribute plan benefits to the named beneficiary. This ensures simple administration regardless of whether post-distribution suits are permitted, because the plan administrator would have no role in any post-distribution proceedings. For the same reason, post-distribution suits do not expose the plan administrator to double liability—only the named beneficiary has any claim against the plan administrator.
>
> Finally, as the Third Circuit recently explained when addressing facts nearly identical to those at hand, the goal of ensuring that beneficiaries get what's coming quickly refers to the expeditious distribution of funds from plan administrators, not to some sort of rule providing continued shelter from contractual liability to beneficiaries who have already received plan proceeds. Permitting a post-distribution suit against a plan beneficiary based on his pre-distribution waiver does not prevent the beneficiary from get[ting] what's coming quickly. Rather, as the district court noted, it merely prevents him from keeping what he quickly received. Thus, we conclude that permitting post-distribution suits accords with the ERISA objectives discussed in *Kennedy*.[103]

In reaching the same conclusion as *Andochick*, the Third Circuit case to which *Andochick* alluded, *Estate of William E. Kensinger Jr., Appellant v. URL Pharma, Inc.*, found it persuasive that federal courts have allowed

102. Andochick v. Byrd, 709 F.3d 296, 299 (4th Cir. 2013), *cert. denied*, 134 S. Ct. 235 (U.S. 2013).
103. *Id.* at 299–300 (citations and quotation marks omitted).

creditors to sue named beneficiaries to recover plan benefits once those benefits were distributed.[104] The court explained:

> A number of circuits, including our own, have held that even though ERISA prevents a creditor from encumbering pension funds held by a plan administrator, the funds are no longer entitled to ERISA's protections against the creditor's claims once they are paid to the beneficiary. In each of these cases, the court held that once the benefits were distributed to the designated beneficiary in accordance with the plan documents, ERISA was no longer implicated. The same principle is equally applicable here. More specifically, if a creditor can enforce its rights against a beneficiary once pension funds have been distributed, we see no reason why the Estate should not be able to enforce its contractual rights . . . once [the employer] disburses the funds.[105]

Duties at Common Law

Following a review of the obligations and powers of trustees under common law, the Supreme Court concluded in *Central States, Southeast & Southwest Areas Pension Fund v. Central Transport, Inc.*:

> ERISA clearly assumes that trustees will act to ensure that a plan receives all funds to which it is entitled, so that those funds can be used on behalf of participants and beneficiaries, and that trustees will take steps to identify all participants and beneficiaries, so that the trustees can make them aware of their status and rights under the trust's terms.[106]

Courts have observed that the exclusive benefit rules require fiduciaries to take reasonable steps to collect missing payments and protect plan assets,

104. Estate of Kensinger v. URL Pharma, Inc., 674 F.3d 131, 137 (3d Cir. 2012).
105. *Id.* at 137–38 (citations omitted).
106. Cent. States, Se. & Sw. Areas Pension Fund v. Cen. Tr., Inc., 472 U.S. 559, 571–72 (1985).

and the language of the plan cannot curtail this responsibility.[107] In addition, fiduciaries must be truthful in communications with participants and in responding to inquiries. In *Varity Corporation v. Howe*, the Supreme Court held that an employer breached its fiduciary duties when it made misrepresentations to employees about the future of the plan benefits.[108]

In 2013, the United States Court of Appeals for the Sixth Circuit took up *Haviland v. Metropolitan Life Insurance Company* and allegations by participants that MetLife, which issued a group life insurance policy provided by General Motors Corporation (GM), made misrepresentations in letters to the participants in breach of its fiduciary duties.[109]

> [T]he plaintiffs allege that MetLife was a fiduciary with respect to the Plan and breached its fiduciary duty to the plaintiffs by providing written notice to each of their Plaintiffs that the amount of their continuing life insurance benefits would not be reduced for the rest of their lives, where . . . MetLife was aware that the amount of each Plaintiffs' continuing life insurance benefits was conditional upon GM's continued payment of premiums to MetLife. The plaintiffs also allege that MetLife breached its fiduciary duty by failing to inform the plaintiffs that the amount of their continuing life insurance benefits was conditioned on GM's payment of premiums to MetLife.
>
> MetLife responds by arguing that the plaintiffs failed to adequately allege that it acted in a fiduciary capacity in sending the notice letters. MetLife contends that the plaintiffs did not plausibly allege that MetLife had control over the content of the notice letters that it sent to the plaintiffs. MetLife also argues that the plaintiffs failed to state a claim for breach of fiduciary duty because they did not plausibly allege that the notice letters contained any misrepresentation. We need not decide whether the complaint adequately alleged that MetLife acted as a fiduciary because MetLife's second argument is dispositive.
>
> . . .

107. *See, e.g.*, Best v. Cyrus 310 F.3d 932, 935–36 (6th Cir. 2002)
108. Varity Corp. v. Howe, 516 U.S. 489, 506 (1996).
109. Haviland v. Metr. Life Ins. Co., 730 F.3d 563, 565 (6th Cir. 2013).

A fiduciary must discharge his duties with respect to the plan solely in the interest of the participants and beneficiaries. ERISA requires a fiduciary to act with the care, skill, prudence, and diligence under the circumstances then prevailing that a prudent man acting in a like capacity and familiar with such matters would use in the conduct of an enterprise of a like character and with like aims. [A] person may be an ERISA fiduciary for some purposes, but not for others. In *Varity Corp.*, the Supreme Court held that Varity Corporation, the employer and plan administrator, breached its fiduciary duty when it conveyed false information to the plan participants about the security of their benefits. The Court succinctly explained that [l]ying is inconsistent with the duty of loyalty owed by all fiduciaries.

In *Sprague*, we rejected the plaintiffs' claim that GM breached its fiduciary duty when it explained its retirement program to early retirees. Some of GM's [summary plans descriptions] did not explain that GM retained the right to amend or terminate the plan, but they did state that the plan participant's health care coverage would be provided by GM for his lifetime. When the plan participants explicitly asked GM representatives about future changes to health care benefits, they were told that the benefits could be changed. We held that, although GM may have acted in a fiduciary capacity in explaining its retirement program, [a]s a matter of law . . . we do not believe that GM committed a breach of any applicable fiduciary duty. . . .

We rejected the plaintiffs' fiduciary duty claim for another reason: GM was not required to disclose in its SPDs that the plan was subject to amendment or termination. It would be strange indeed if ERISA's fiduciary standards could be used to imply a duty to disclose information that ERISA's detailed disclosure provisions do not require to be disclosed.

The following year, we found that a fiduciary breached its duty and reversed the district court's grant of summary judgment to the defendant. The plaintiff, Margaret Krohn, was permanently disabled in an automobile accident. We held that Huron Memorial Hospital, her employer and plan administrator, breached its fiduciary duty by failing to respond adequately to a request by Krohn's husband for information about plan benefits and by failing to alert its long-term-disability insurer that Krohn had made an application for benefits. In doing so, we recognized that [a] fiduciary must give complete and accurate information in response to participants' questions. Furthermore, we clarified that a fiduciary breaches its duties by materially misleading plan participants, regardless of whether the fiduciary's statements or omissions were made negligently or intentionally.

In *James v. Pirelli Armstrong Tire Corp.*, we again reviewed fiduciary duty claims under ERISA. Like GM in *Sprague*, Pirelli amended its health care plan and required participants to incur greater out-of-pocket expenses. It encouraged employees to take early retirement and spoke with them about their benefits during group meetings and exit interviews. Shirley Pike, an Assistant Employee Relations Manager, testified that when employees asked her how long their benefits would last, she said during retirement. Pike also informed employees that their benefits would remain unchanged during their lifetimes. When asked about the language in the SPD allowing the company to alter or amend the plan, Pike stated that it was written for the benefit of Pirelli to enable the company to change insurance carriers.

We explained that *Sprague* explicated the contours of an ERISA fiduciary's duty to disclose information to beneficiaries. *Sprague* recognized a breach of fiduciary duty under three different conditions: (1) an early retiree asks a plan provider about the possibility of the plan changing and receives a misleading or inaccurate answer or (2) a plan provider on its own initiative provides misleading or inaccurate information about the future of the plan or (3) ERISA or its implementing regulations required the employer to forecast the future and the employer failed to do so.

In *Sprague*, none of these conditions had been met, and in *Krohn*, the first condition had been satisfied. The *James* court added the caveat that *Sprague* does not stand for the proposition that a reservation of rights provision in a SPD necessarily insulates an employer from its fiduciary duty to provide complete and accurate information when that employer on its own initiative provides inaccurate and misleading information about the future benefits of a plan. We then held that Pirelli breached its fiduciary duty in two different ways. First, some plaintiffs asked questions about the plan and received misleading and inaccurate answers. Second, Pirelli representatives provided misleading and inaccurate information on its own initiative during group meetings and exit interviews. Because Pirelli breached its fiduciary duty, we reversed the district court's partial judgment in favor of Pirelli following a bench trial.

Applying these principles to the case before us, we first note that the plaintiffs do not allege that they asked MetLife about the possibility of the plan changing and received an inaccurate or misleading answer. In addition, MetLife was not the employer and was not asked to forecast the future. We are left, therefore, with determining whether MetLife on its own initiative provided misleading information about the future of the plan. This case is distinguishable from *Sprague* because the statements that the plaintiffs allege amount to a breach of fiduciary duty were included in letters from MetLife, as opposed to SPDs promulgated by GM. Accordingly, the second reason for rejecting the plaintiffs' fiduciary duty claim in *Sprague*—that we will not imply a duty to disclose information that ERISA's detailed disclosure provisions do not require to be disclosed—does not apply here.

Nonetheless, we found that the plaintiffs' fiduciary duty claim in *Sprague* failed for another reason: GM did not make any misrepresentation. In *Sprague*, the SPDs made representations such as: (1) Your basic coverages will be provided at Corporation expense for your lifetime; (2) Your basic health care coverages will be provided at GM's expense for your lifetime; and (3) [GM] pays for full cost of any basic health care coverages that are continued for most retired employees and for eligible surviving spouses and children of deceased retirees. Not all of the SPDs put the plaintiffs on notice of GM's right to amend or terminate the plan. By comparison, the letters sent by MetLife stated: (1) This amount of Continuing Life Insurance will remain in effect for the rest of your life; (2) This fully reduced amount of your Continuing Life Insurance remains in effect, without cost to you, for the rest of your life; and (3) Metropolitan records show that you now have

> $103,400.00 of Continuing Life Insurance in effect, without cost to you, for the rest of your life.
>
> For the reasons described in *Sprague*, the representations in the letters sent by MetLife were not inaccurate or misleading. MetLife did not tell its participants that the benefits were fully paid up or vested upon retirement. Rather, MetLife told them that their benefits would be in effect for their lifetimes, which was undeniably true under the terms of GM's then-existing plan. Moreover, explanations of benefits tend to sound promissory by their very nature. While these explanations may state a company's current intentions with respect to the plan, they cannot be expected to foreclose the possibility that changing financial conditions will require a company to modify welfare benefit plan provisions at some point in the future.
>
> Without any misrepresentation or inaccurate statement, the plaintiffs' fiduciary duty claim fails as a matter of law.[110]

Another common law fiduciary duty is the duty to disclose. In determining when to disclose certain information to participants, courts are guided by the articulated goal of Congress that disclosure not only acts as a deterrent against risky behavior on the part of the fiduciary, but that it also informs participants about the administration of the plan and the financial soundness of the plan.[111]

The Supreme Court has stated that a "company does not act in a fiduciary capacity when deciding to amend or terminate a welfare benefits plan."[112] However, the sole-interest rule must be adhered to during the deliberations of any proposal to amend a plan. Courts have struggled with the proper balance between employees' right to know and employers' right not to divulge plans in their nascent stages. There is no affirmative duty to disclose any thoughts to amend a plan, but if the fiduciary decides in its discretion to disclose proposals, it must be truthful and forthcoming. The *Varity* Court

110. *Id.* at 570–73 (citations and quotation marks omitted).
111. *See generally In re Citigroup ERISA Litig.*, 662 F.3d 128, 158–59 (2d Cir. 2011).
112. Curtiss-Wright Corp. v. Schoonejongen, 514 U.S. 73, 78 (1995) (citing Adams v. Avondale Indus., Inc., 905 F.2d 943, 947 (6th Cir. 1990)).

characterized an employer's statements concerning the prognosis of the plan and prospective benefits as an exercise of discretionary authority.[113]

Severance packages and early retirement programs, typically used to effect voluntary workforce attrition, have been frequently litigated under this disclosure principle. In *Fischer II*, the United States Court of Appeals for the Third Circuit developed a test to determine when fiduciaries must disclose a proposed amendment to a severance package following an inquiry.[114] The court concluded that disclosure was required when there was serious consideration of the amendment. According to the court, a "[s]erious consideration of a change in plan benefits exists when (1) a specific proposal (2) is being discussed for purposes of implementation (3) by senior management with the authority to implement the change."[115] The court continued that "the factors themselves are not isolated criteria; the three interact and coalesce to form a composite picture of serious consideration."[116] The court's reasoning synced with the purpose of ERISA to encourage employers to establish plans and create security for employees:

> Our formulation respects the division of responsibility in corporate entities and the day-to-day realities of running a business. Even more importantly, it protects the right of employees to material information. Characterizing serious consideration in this fashion ensures that disclosures to employees about potential changes in benefits will be meaningful. Employees will learn of potential changes when the company's deliberations have reached a level where an employee should reasonably factor the potential change into an employment decision. This guarantees that employees will have the information they need, while avoiding a surfeit of meaningless disclosures. Finally, as a matter of policy, we note that imposing liability too quickly for failure to disclose a potential early retirement plan could harm employees by deterring employers from resorting to such plans.[117]

113. *Varity Corp.*, 516 U.S. at 504.
114. Fischer v. Phila. Elec. Co., 96 F.3d 1533, 1539 (3d Cir. 1996).
115. *Id.*
116. *Id.*
117. *Id.* at 1540–41 (citations omitted).

The First and Tenth Circuits have incorporated the approach in *Fischer II* into their analyses of the fiduciary duty to disclose.[118] The Second Circuit showed less reverence for the *Fischer II* approach in *Ballone v. Eastman Kodak Company* when it determined that "[w]hether a plan is under serious consideration is but one factor in the materiality inquiry" and that there was no clear requirement "that serious consideration of a future plan is a prerequisite to liability for misstatements regarding the availability of future pension benefits."[119] The Second Circuit adopted "the simple view that when a plan administrator speaks, it must speak truthfully, regardless of how seriously any changes are being considered."[120] The Second Circuit elaborated:

> Determining the materiality of false assurances like those here alleged is fact-specific and will turn on a number of factors, including . . . how significantly the statement misrepresents the present status of internal deliberations regarding future plan changes; the special relationship of trust and confidence between the plan fiduciary and beneficiary; whether the employee was aware of other information or statements from the company tending to minimize the importance of the misrepresentation or should have been so aware, taking into consideration the broad trust responsibilities owed by the plan administrator to the employee and the employee's reliance on the plan administrator for truthful information; and the specificity of the assurance. Whereas mere mispredictions are not actionable, false statements about future benefits may be material if couched as a guarantee, especially where . . . the guarantee is supported by specific statements of fact.[121]

The Ninth Circuit adopted *Fischer II* in *Bins v. Exxon* but emphasized that the test "should not be applied so rigidly as to distract attention from the

118. *See* Vartanian v. Monsanto Co., 131 F.3d 264, 268, 272 (1st Cir.1997) (employing the *Fischer II* test to define an employer's duty to disclose potential plan chances but modifying the standard and requiring that the specific proposal at issue be applicable to "a person in the position of the plaintiff"); Hockett v. Sun Co., 109 F.3d 1515, 1523 (10th Cir.1997) (finding that *Fischer II* "appropriately narrow[ed] the range of instances in which an employer must disclose, in response to employees' inquiries, its tentative intentions regarding an ERISA plan").
119. Ballone v. Eastman Kodak Co., 109 F.3d 117, 123 (2d Cir.1997).
120. *Id.* (quotation marks omitted).
121. *Id.* at 125 (citations omitted).

core inquiry, which must always be whether the employer-fiduciary has violated its fiduciary duty of loyalty to plan participants by failing to disclose material information."[122] The Ninth Circuit clarified subsequent to *Bins* in *Wayne v. Pacific Bell* that it would only apply *Fischer II* to disclosures of potential plan changes and that the Second Circuit's *Ballone* rule is more appropriate when an employer has deliberately misrepresented the availability of future plan benefits.[123]

The Fifth Circuit articulated its approach in *Martinez v. Schlumberger, Ltd.*:

> With respect to an employer's misrepresentations, we conclude, as have all of the circuits that have considered this issue, that an employer, if it chooses to communicate about the future of a participant's plan benefits, has a fiduciary duty to refrain from misrepresentations. The Supreme Court's words in *Varity* instruct that when an employer chooses, in its discretion, to communicate about future plan benefits, it does so as an ERISA fiduciary. In speaking it is exercising discretionary authority in administration of the plan, a specifically enumerated fiduciary function under ERISA. Thus, it has a duty to refrain from knowingly and significantly deceiving a plan's beneficiaries in order to save the employer money at the beneficiaries' expense, which would be inconsistent with its fiduciary responsibility to act solely in the interest of the participants and beneficiaries . . . .
>
> Although we join our sister circuits in recognizing this duty, we cannot agree that misrepresentations are actionable only after the company has seriously considered the plan change. *Varity* does not suggest that the obligation not to misrepresent materializes near the end of a progression, but rather implies that whenever an employer exercises a fiduciary function, it must speak truthfully. Nor do we find a safe harbor for predictions of the future. When an employer speaks to the future of a plan, employees are justified in concluding

122. Bins v. Exxon Co. U.S.A., 220 F.3d 1042, 1049 (9th Cir. 2000).
123. Wayne v. Pac. Bell, 238 F.3d 1048, 1055 (9th Cir. 2001).

that it is backed by the authority of a plan administrator, and should therefore be entitled to trust in those representations.

Accordingly, we reject the view that the duty to speak truthfully only arises once the employer begins seriously considering a plan. We see no reasoned justification for drawing the line at that point in time. We also decline to find, as did the *Fischer II* court, that a misrepresentation is only material, and therefore actionable, once the company has seriously considered the plan change. This view does not comport with the Supreme Court's dictates, in the related context of securities law, that materiality is a fact-specific inquiry not capable of easy line-drawing.[124]

124. Martinez v. Schlumberger, Ltd., 338 F.3d 407, 424–25 (5th Cir. 2003) (citations and quotation marks omitted).

Chapter 6

Remedies

The operation of ERISA's remedial provisions is occasionally at variance with the law's articulated purpose of enhancing pension security for employees.[1] Although the goals of creating incentives for employers to establish plans and federalizing the area of employee benefit law are also very important, the Supreme Court has found these goals "outweighed by 'Congress's desire to offer employees enhanced protection for their benefits.'"[2] Over the years, courts have recognized the perceived disconnect between the objectives of ERISA and the application of the remedial provisions and have progressively granted additional remedies by expanding their interpretation of certain aspects of ERISA.

Remedy for Denial of Benefits

ERISA § 502 (a)(1)(B) grants a participant or beneficiary the right to bring suit to recover benefits due to him or her pursuant to the terms of the plan, to enforce his or her rights under the terms of the plan, or to clarify his or her rights to future benefits.[3] Actions under this section can be brought in either federal or state court.[4]

1. 29 U.S.C. § 1001(c) (2012).
2. Metro. Life Ins. Co. v. Glenn, 554 U.S. 105, 114 (2008) (citing Varity Corp. v. Howe, 516 U.S. 489, 497 (1996)).
3. 29 U.S.C. § 1132(a)(1)(B) (2012).
4. 29 U.S.C. § 1132(e)(1) (2012).

Litigants have sought punitive and compensatory damages for claims under § 502 (a)(1)(B). However, courts have consistently reiterated that remedies under § 502(a)(1)(B) are limited to recovery of the benefits due from the plan.[5] The Supreme Court observed in *Massachusetts Mutual Life Insurance Company v. Russell*: "Significantly, the statutory provision explicitly authorizing a beneficiary to bring an action to enforce his rights under the plan—§ 502(a)(1)(B) . . . —says nothing about the recovery of extracontractual damages."[6] The only extracontractual payment allowed under § 502(a)(1)(B) is for prejudgment interest on any unjustifiably delayed payment of benefits.

A participant may bring an action under the equitable provisions of ERISA solely for the recovery of interest.[7] In *Fotta v. Trustees of the United Mine Workers of America, Health, & Retirement Fund*, plan trustees approved disability benefits for a participant but paid the participant nine years after the injury triggering the benefits.[8] When disability benefits finally commenced, the participant received a lump-sum back payment determined by adding up the monthly payments, and the trustees refused to pay interest on that amount.[9] The United States Court of Appeals for the Third Circuit determined that ERISA § 502(a)(3)(B), which permits a plan participant or beneficiary to obtain "other appropriate equitable relief," provided a vehicle for the participant to bring his claim for interest on the back payment.[10] In addition, the court ruled that the claim for benefits was not a necessary element of a claim for interest.[11] According to the court, the purpose of the interest claim was to make the participant "whole" and to prevent unjust enrichment, and the interest claim should not have been minimized

---

5. Kerr v. Charles F. Vatterott & Co., 184 F.3d 938, 942 (8th Cir. 1999); Medina v. Anthem Life Ins. Co., 983 F.2d 29, 32–33 (5th Cir. 1993); Harsch v. Eisenberg, 956 F.2d 651, 660 (7th Cir. 1992).
6. Mass. Mut. Life Ins. Co. v. Russell 473 U.S. 134, 144 (1985).
7. Dunnigan v. Metro. Life Ins. Co., 277 F.3d 223, 231 (2d Cir. 2002); Jackson v. Fortis Benefits Ins. Co., 245 F.3d 748, 749–50 (8th Cir. 2001); Clair v. Harris Trust & Sav. Bank, 190 F.3d 495, 498 (7th Cir. 1999); Fotta v. Trustees of United Mine Workers of Am., Health & Retirement Fund of 1974, 165 F.3d 209, 213 (3d Cir. 1998).
8. *Fotta*, 165 F.3d at 210–11.
9. *Id.*
10. *Id.* at 213.
11. *Id.* at 212.

or reduced simply because the plan had already paid the overdue benefits.[12] The delay in paying the benefits effectively deprived the participant of the time value of his money, regardless of whether he secured the overdue benefits through ERISA litigation.[13]

Fotta and similar holdings granting prejudgment interest on any unjustifiably delayed payment of benefits have important limitations. The United States Court of Appeals for the Eighth Circuit observed in *Kerr v. Charles F. Vatterott & Company* that relief granted under § 1132(a)(3) must be a classic equitable remedy, and the most probable way to regain lost interest is under a theory of restitution.[14] Further, the form of restitution must be equitable in nature and not compensation.[15] The court explained that "[a] restitutionary award focuses on the defendant's wrongfully obtained gain while a compensatory award focuses on the plaintiff's loss at the defendant's hands."[16] In *Kerr*, the defendant did not gain anything from the claimant's delayed receipt of earnings from a 401(k) plan, which meant that no one was unjustly enriched and that the claimant could not recover prejudgment interest.[17] The court remarked: "To the extent that *Fotta* may be read to allow recovery of interest as extracontractual or consequential damages, we respectfully disagree with that holding."[18]

Beyond *Kerr*, the United States Court of Appeals for the Eleventh Circuit observed in *Flint v. ABB, Inc.* that *Fotta* and similar decisions were decided before the Supreme Court narrowed the meaning of "appropriate equitable relief" in 2002's *Great-West Life & Annuity Insurance Company v. Knudson*, which this chapter will discuss in greater detail upon examining ERISA's "appropriate equitable relief" provision.[19] Additionally, participants

---

12. *Id.*
13. *Id.*
14. Kerr v. Charles F. Vatterott & Co., 184 F.3d 938, 943–44 (8th Cir. 1999) ("To summarize, section 1132(a)(3) provides relief for the individual harm that Kerr may have suffered from Vatterott & Co.'s breach of its fiduciary duties, but limits his recovery to 'appropriate equitable relief,' which include injunctive, restitutionary, and mandamus relief, but does not include compensatory damages.").
15. *Id.* at 944.
16. *Id.*
17. *Id.* at 945.
18. *Id.*
19. Flint v. ABB, Inc., 337 F.3d 1326, 1330 (11th Cir. 2003) (citing Great-West Life & Annuity Ins. Co. v. Knudson, 534 U.S. 204 (2002)).

who materially contribute to the delay in payment of benefits do not qualify for interest on a delayed payment. In *Rego v. Westvaco Corporation*, the United States Court of Appeals for the Fourth Circuit denied interest on delayed payments because it found that the delay was the claimant's fault due to mistakes he made in completing the distribution paperwork.[20] The plan had promptly distributed payments after the claimant had corrected his errors.[21] Elsewhere, in *Twomey v. Delta Airlines Pilots Pension Plan*, the United States Court of Appeals for the First Circuit denied a participant interest because it found that the participant had intentionally evaded receipt of pension benefits.[22]

Exhausting Administrative Remedies Before Litigation

Typically, in order to litigate the denial of benefits under § 502(a)(1)(B), the participant or beneficiary must exhaust the plan's internal administrative procedures.[23] ERISA § 503 requires all plans to have an internal appeals procedure.[24] After a claim is denied, the participant or beneficiary must access the plan's claims review process. If the claim is still denied after the internal review process, then the participant or beneficiary may proceed to independent external review or litigation. The exhaustion-of-remedies requirement reserves court action for cases that are not amenable to resolution by settlement.

Not all claims are subject to the exhaustion-of-administrative-remedies requirement. In *Communications Workers of America v. American Telephone & Telegraph Company*, the United States District Court for the District of Columbia held that a participant need not satisfy the exhaustion of remedy process by accessing an internal review if the exercise would prove futile

20. Rego v. Westvaco Corp., 319 F.3d 140, 148 (4th Cir. 2003).
21. *Id.*
22. Twomey v. Delta Airlines Pilots Pension Plan, 328 F.3d 27, 29 (1st Cir. 2003).
23. *See* Kinkhead v. Sw. Bell Corp. Sickness & Accident Disability Benefit Plan, 111 F.3d 67, 68 (8th Cir. 1997) (citing Diaz v. United Agric. Employee Welfare Benefit Plan & Trust, 50 F.3d 1478 (9th Cir. 1995); Comms. Workers of Am. v. Am. Tel. & Tel. Co., 40 F.3d 426 (D.C. Cir. 1994).
24. 29 U.S.C. § 1133 (2012).

where futility meant the participant was convinced of the certainty of an adverse decision by the fiduciary.[25] Certainty can be ascertained where the administrator has consistently ruled in a particular way on the issue, but this exception remains highly restricted.[26]

In *Conley v. Pitney Bowes*, a participant escaped the exhaustion-of-administrative-remedies requirement when the plan failed to notify him of his appeal rights, which was required by the language of the plan.[27] However, in *Kinkhead v. Southwestern Bell Corporation Sickness & Accident Disability Benefit Plan*, the United States Court of Appeals for the Eighth Circuit determined that a denial notice does not have to expressly state that administrative remedies must first be utilized before a civil action can be initiated.[28] Cases since *Kinkhead* consistently applied the exhaustion requirement when notice existed and claimants failed to show notice would be futile.[29] Pursuant to the Affordable Care Act, the participant or beneficiary of a group health plan or health insurance can access external independent review after the internal process is concluded, in lieu of pursuing court action.[30]

The exhaustion-of-remedies requirement is usually unique to claims for benefits under § 502(a)(1)(B).[31] Courts generally do not require the exhaustion of administrative remedies for discrimination claims under ERISA § 510 or for claims to enforce other statutory provisions of ERISA, such as those described in ERISA §§ 502(a)(2)–(3).[32]

---

25. Comms. Workers of Am. v. Am. Tel. & Tel. Co., 40 F.3d 426, 433 (D.C. Cir. 1994).
26. Stephens v. U.S. Airways Group, Inc., 908 F. Supp. 2d 10, 17 (D. D.C. 2012).
27. Conley v. Pitney Bowes, 34 F.3d 714, 718 (8th Cir. 1994).
28. *Kinkhead*, 111 F.3d at 69.
29. Wert v. Liberty Life Assur. Co. of Boston, Inc., 447 F.3d 1060 (8th Cir. 2006) (citing Back v. Danka Corp., 335 F.3d 790, 792 (8th Cir. 2003); Galman v. Prudential Ins. Co. of Am., 254 F.3d 768, 770 (8th Cir. 2001); Burds v. Union Pac. Corp., 223 F.3d 814, 817 (8th Cir. 2000); Schleeper v. Purina Benefits Ass'n, 170 F.3d 1157, 1157 (8th Cir. 1999); Union Pac. R.R. Co. v. Beckham, 138 F.3d 325, 332 n.4 (8th Cir. 1998)).
30. 42 U.S.C. § 300gg-19 (2012).
31. *See generally* D'Amico v. CBS Corp., 297 F.3d 287, 291 (3d Cir. 2002) (explaining that the exhaustion of plan remedies is required before claims to enforce the terms of a benefit plan may proceed but not before claims to assert rights established by ERISA) (citing Zipf v. AT&T, 799 F.2d 889, 891 (3d Cir. 1986)).
32. *Id.* (citing Harrow v. Prudential Ins. Co., 279 F.3d 244, 253 (3d Cir. 2002); Zipf, 799 F.2d at 891)). *Cf.* Shine v. Univ. of Chicago, No. 12 C 8182, 2013 WL 1290206 (N.D. Ill. Mar. 28, 2013).

Remedies for Breach of Fiduciary Duties

ERISA § 502(a)(2), which cross-references to § 409, makes a fiduciary personally liable for any breach of trust that results in losses to the plan.[33] Fiduciaries may be required to make up any losses to the plan resulting from their breach and to restore profits to the plan that the fiduciary has made through use of its assets, and a fiduciary may also face any other equitable or remedial relief that a court deems appropriate.[34] The fiduciary is personally liable for investment losses and lost-opportunity losses.[35] The Department of Labor, a participant, a beneficiary, or a fiduciary may bring an action against the fiduciary.[36] Remedies under § 502(a)(2) must benefit the plan.[37]

The fiduciary may be required to disgorge to the plan any profits earned by the fiduciary through the use of plan assets that involve a breach even if there is no loss to the plan. In *Leigh v. Engle*, the plan's investments made as a result of the breach produced a 72 percent gain, yet the breaching fiduciaries had to disgorge their personal profits to the plan.[38] The United States Court of Appeals for the Seventh Circuit observed that the claimants could recover only where there was a causal connection between the plan's assets and profits made by fiduciaries on investing the assets, and the burden was on the defendants to show they derived profits from sources other than plan assets.[39] It bears noting that, for the most part, the defendants in *Leigh* succeeded, paying out $6,704 in damages from plan-owed investments when the plaintiffs had sought millions.[40]

The fiduciary does not escape liability because the plan has terminated and benefits are paid. In such cases, courts may impose a constructive trust. In *Amalgamated Clothing & Textile Workers Union v. Murdock*, the United States Court of Appeals for the Ninth Circuit held:

33. 29 U.S.C. § 1109(a) (2012).
34. *Id.*
35. 29 U.S.C. § 1104(a) (2012).
36. 29 U.S.C. § 1132(a) (2012).
37. 29 U.S.C. § 1109(a) (2012).
38. Leigh v. Engle, 858 F.2d 361, 363, 366 (7th Cir. 1988).
39. *Id.* at 366 (citing Leigh v. Engle, 727 F.2d 113, 137 (7th Cir. 1984)).
40. *Id.*

> [W]here an ERISA fiduciary has profited by breaching his duty of loyalty to an ERISA plan, and . . . where imposing a constructive trust on the ill-gotten profits in favor of plan participants and beneficiaries is the only means available to deny the fiduciary his ill-gotten profits, a district court may impose a constructive trust on the ill-gotten profits and distribute them to plan participants and beneficiaries, even after they have received their actuarially vested plan benefits.[41]

The court noted that the purpose of an action against a fiduciary for breaching his or her duty of loyalty is not to make beneficiaries whole through compensating them for damages but rather to deter fiduciary disloyalty.[42] By allowing plaintiffs who allege that plan fiduciaries personally profited from their misuse of plan assets, to proceed in court, the *Murdock* decision carved out an exception to the *Kuntz* rule, which categorized retirees who had withdrawn their full account balance as no longer "participants" under ERISA with standing to sue.[43]

The fiduciary's liability to the plan may be offset against the benefits the fiduciary is entitled to as a participant in the plan. Persuaded by the Eleventh Circuit's permission to garnish an employee's interest fund to satisfy liabilities due to criminal misconduct, the United States Court of Appeals for the District of Columbia Circuit decided in *Crawford v. La Boucherie Bernard* to offset a fiduciary's plan interests.[44] Subsequently, the United States Court of Appeals for the Third Circuit permitted an offset in its 1993 decision *Coar v. Kazimir*.[45] Congress codified this result by amending ERISA to permit an offset for judgments, orders, and decrees issued and settlement agreements entered into on or after August 5, 1997.[46]

41. Amalgamated Clothing & Textile Workers Union, AFL-CIO v. Murdock, 861 F.2d 1406, 1408 (9th Cir. 1988).
42. *Id.* at 1411–12.
43. DeFazio v. Hollister, Inc., No. S-04-1358, 2007 WL 3231670, *3 (E.D. Cal. Nov. 1, 2007) (citing Murdock, 861 F.2d at 1418; Kuntz v. Reese, 785 F.2d 1410, 1411 (9th Cir. 1986)).
44. Crawford v. La Boucherie Bernard, Ltd., 815 F.2d 117, 121–22 (D.C. Cir. 1987) (citing St. Paul Fire & Marine Ins. Co. v. Cox, 752 F.2d 550, 552 (11th Cir. 1985)).
45. Coar v. Kazimir, 990 F.2d 1413, 1424 (3d Cir. 1993).
46. 29 U.S.C. § 1056 (2012).

Courts will broadly construe plan losses arising from fiduciary violations.[47] In *In re Schering-Plough Corporation ERISA Litigation*, the United States Court of Appeals for the Third Circuit ruled that plaintiffs seeking money damages pursuant to § 502(a)(2) for breaches of a fiduciary duty could proceed even though the alleged fiduciary violations only affected a subsection of the plan's participants.[48] The Third Circuit rejected the argument that fiduciary liability under ERISA § 409 is limited to "losses that will ultimately redound to the benefit of all participants."[49]

Breach of Fiduciary Duties That Injure Defined Contribution Plans

In *Massachusetts Mutual Life Insurance Co. v. Russell*, the Supreme Court ruled that only the plan may recover for a fiduciary breach under an action brought pursuant to ERISA § 502(a)(2) for damages to a plan with fixed-level benefits and that the provision does not provide individualized personal relief.[50] However, what if, under a defined contribution plan, the fiduciary's misconduct injured assets in an individual participant's account?

As defined contribution plans became more prevalent, courts were increasingly willing to construe relief to rectify harm to individual accounts as relief on the behalf of the plan. In *LaRue v. DeWolff, Boberg & Associates*, the Supreme Court addressed the issue in the context of a 401(k) plan.[51] The plaintiff in *LaRue* alleged that in 2001 and 2002 the fiduciaries breached their duty to him by ignoring the investment strategy and changes he had directed for his account.[52] The directions were never put into effect.[53] The

47. *See* Physicians HealthChoice, Inc. v. Trustees of Automotive Employee Ben. Trust, 988 F.2d 53, 56 (8th Cir. 1993) (explaining that the court "would not hesitate to construe 'losses to the plan' in [ERISA § 409] broadly in order to further the remedial purposes of ERISA").
48. *In re Schering-Plough Corp. ERISA Litigation*, 420 F.3d 231, 232 (3d Cir. 2005).
49. *Id.* at 235.
50. Mass. Mut. Life Ins. Co. v. Russell, 473 U.S. 134, 138 (1985).
51. LaRue v. DeWolff, Boberg & Assocs., Inc., 552 U.S. 248, 250 (2008).
52. *Id.* at 250–51.
53. *Id.*

plaintiff claimed that his account lost approximately $150,000 of value,[54] and he sought appropriate "make whole" or other equitable relief.[55]

A unanimous Court found that ERISA § 502(a)(2) permitted a participant in a defined contribution plan to sue for losses incurred on the individual's account as a result of a fiduciary breach.[56] The Court articulated the historical changes and provisions of ERISA animating its decision:

> *Russell*'s emphasis on protecting the "entire plan" from fiduciary misconduct reflects the former landscape of employee benefit plans. That landscape has changed.
>
> Defined contribution plans dominate the retirement plan scene today. . . . Unlike the defined contribution plan in this case, the disability plan at issue in *Russell* did not have individual accounts; it paid a fixed benefit based on a percentage of the employee's salary.
>
> The "entire plan" language in *Russell* speaks to the impact of § 409 on plans that pay defined benefits. Misconduct by the administrators of a defined benefit plan will not affect an individual's entitlement to a defined benefit unless it creates or enhances the risk of default by the entire plan. It was that default risk that prompted Congress to require defined benefit plans (but not defined contribution plans) to satisfy complex minimum funding requirements, and to make premium payments to the Pension Benefit Guaranty Corporation for plan termination insurance.
>
> For defined contribution plans, however, fiduciary misconduct need not threaten the solvency of the entire plan to reduce benefits below the amount that participants would otherwise receive. Whether a fiduciary breach diminishes plan assets payable to all participants and beneficiaries, or only to persons tied to particular individual accounts, it creates the kind of harms that concerned the draftsmen of § 409. Consequently, our references to the "entire plan" in *Russell*, which accurately reflect the operation of § 409 in the defined benefit context, are beside the point in the defined contribution context.

54. *Id.* at 252.
55. *Id.* at 251.
56. *Id.* at 256.

Other sections of ERISA confirm that the "entire plan" language from *Russell*, which appears nowhere in § 409 or § 502(a)(2), does not apply to defined contribution plans. Most significant is § 404(c), which exempts fiduciaries from liability for losses caused by participants' exercise of control over assets in their individual accounts. This provision would serve no real purpose if, as respondents argue, fiduciaries never had any liability for losses in an individual account.

We therefore hold that although § 502(a)(2) does not provide a remedy for individual injuries distinct from plan injuries, that provision does authorize recovery for fiduciary breaches that impair the value of plan assets in a participant's individual account.[57]

Cofiduciary Liability

ERISA § 405 makes a fiduciary liable for another fiduciary's breach if he or she "participates knowingly in, or knowingly undertakes to conceal, an act or omission of such other fiduciary, knowing such act of omission is a breach"; if he or she enables another fiduciary to commit a breach by failing to comply with his or her responsibilities; or if he or she knows of a breach by a fiduciary and does not make "reasonable efforts under the circumstances to remedy the breach."[58] "Reasonable efforts" might include notifying other plan fiduciaries or the Department of Labor.

As in a case against a fiduciary, recovery is permitted for loss resulting from the cofiduciary's breach of ERISA obligations. In a suit for damages against Principal Mutual Life Insurance Company claiming Principal's liability as a cofiduciary, the United States Court of Appeals for the Second Circuit articulated the claimant's burden as needing to show: "(i) Principal had knowledge of the trustees' embezzlement, (ii) Principal failed to make reasonable efforts to remedy the trustees' breach, and (iii) the fund's loss resulted from that failure."[59] The claimant failed to satisfy the final

57. *Id.* at 254–56 (citations omitted).
58. 29 U.S.C. § 1105(1) (2012).
59. Silverman v. Mut. Ben. Life Ins. Co., 138 F.3d 98, 104 (2d Cir. 1998).

element, and Principal avoided paying damages.[60] Subsequent cases in the Second Circuit reasserted that the burden of showing causation rests with the claimant.[61]

The Process of Spreading or Escaping Loss as a Fiduciary

Some circuits have recognized the right to contribution or indemnity, and others have not. The United States Court of Appeals for the Seventh Circuit had first mentioned that a fiduciary "may seek indemnification or contribution from co-fiduciaries" in the dicta of a 1981 case.[62] In 1984, the Seventh Circuit considered in *Free v. Briody* whether a cotrustee who was required to compensate a plan for its loss could recoup the cost of the loss from a culpable cotrustee.[63] The court found that indemnity was within ERISA's appropriate equitable relief because "the language of ERISA provides protection for cotrustees and because Congress evidenced an intent to apply general trust principles to the trustee provision of ERISA."[64] Later, in *Chemung Canal Trust Company v. Sovran Bank/Maryland*, the United States Court of Appeals for the Second Circuit determined, based on the Supreme Court's decision in *Firestone Tire & Rubber Company v. Bruch*, that ERISA authorized the development of a body of federal common law, resulting in the court's incorporation of the common law of trusts and the right of contribution among defaulting fiduciaries.[65]

The Eight Circuit and the Ninth Circuit have rejected a right to contribution and indemnity.[66] The United States Court of Appeals for the Eighth Circuit explained in 2007 that the Supreme Court had refused to recognize a federal common-law right to contribution under other federal statutes and

60. *Id.* at 105.
61. *See, e.g.*, Bd. of Trustees of AFTRA Ret. Fund v. JPMorgan Chase Bank, N.A., 860 F. Supp. 2d 251, 260–61 (S.D. N.Y. 2012).
62. Alton v. Mem'l Hosp. v. Metro. Life Ins. Co., 656 F.2d 245, 250 (7th Cir. 1981).
63. Free v. Briody, 732 F.2d 1331, 1337 (7th Cir. 1984).
64. *Id.*
65. Chemung Canal Trust Co. v. Sovran Bank/Md., 939 F.2d 12 (2d Cir. 1991) (citing Firestone Tire & Rubber Co. v. Bruch, 489 U.S. 101, 110 (1989)).
66. Travelers Cas. & Sur. Co. of Am. v. IADA Servs., Inc., 497 F.3d 862, 867 (8th Cir. 2007); Kim v. Fujikawa, 871 F.2d 1427, 1432 (9th Cir. 1989).

that "[t]o recognize a state-law cause of action that supplements the federal scheme would pose an obstacle to the purposes and objectives of Congress."[67] The United States Court of Appeals for the Ninth Circuit stressed that ERISA's equitable remedies exist for the benefit of the plan, not a fiduciary.[68] The plan may purchase insurance to cover liability or losses resulting from any commission or omission of a fiduciary, provided the insurer has recourse against the fiduciary.[69] A fiduciary may purchase liability insurance with his or her own funds, and an employer or employee organization, such as a union, may purchase liability insurance for a fiduciary.[70]

Remedies Against Nonfiduciaries

Courts have held that a nonfiduciary's knowing participation in a fiduciary's breach cannot serve as the sole basis for a suit under ERISA.[71] However, in *Harris Trust & Savings Bank v. Salomon Smith Barney, Inc.*, the Supreme Court held that a participant, beneficiary, or fiduciary may sue under ERISA § 502(a)(3) for equitable relief against a nonfiduciary party in interest for his or her participation in a prohibited transaction.[72] The Court explained at its decision's outset:

> Section 406(a) of the Employee Retirement Income Security Act of 1974 (ERISA) bars a fiduciary of an employee benefit plan from causing the plan to engage in certain transactions with a "party in interest." Section 502(a)(3) authorizes a "participant, beneficiary, or fiduciary" of a plan to bring a civil action to obtain "appropriate equitable relief" to redress violations of ERISA Title I. The question is whether

67. *Travelers*, 497 F.3d at 864, 868 (citing Nw. Airlines, Inc. v. Transp. Workers Union, 451 U.S. 77 (1981); Tex. Indus., Inc., v. Radcliff Materials, Inc., 451 U.S. 630 (1981)).
68. *Fujikawa*, 871 F.2d at 1432 (citing Mass. Mut. Life Ins. Co. v. Russell, 473 U.S. 134, 141–42 (1984)).
69. 29 U.S.C. § 1110(b)(1) (2013).
70. 29 U.S.C. § 1110(b)(2)–(3) (2012).
71. *See, e.g.*, Reich v. Cont. Casualty Co., 33 F.3d 754 (7th Cir. 1994); Reich v. Rowe, 20 F.3d 25, 26 (1st Cir. 1994).
72. Harris Trust & Savs. Bank v. Salomon Smith Barney, Inc., 520 U.S. 238, 241 (2000).

> that authorization extends to a suit against a nonfiduciary "party in interest" to a transaction barred by § 406(a). We hold that it does.[73]

In supporting its holding, the Court pointed out that the penalty provisions under ERISA § 502(1) refer to "other persons" in addition to fiduciaries who might be held liable for violations of ERISA.[74] Relief in such actions is the disgorgement of any profits earned by the nonfiduciary with respect to the transaction.[75] The Department of Labor may also bring suit pursuant to § 502(a)(5).

In *L.I. Head Start Child Development Services, Inc. v. Frank*, a New York district court allowed judgment creditors of an ERISA plan to proceed in suit against the plan's trial attorneys under the theory that the attorneys were liable as aiders and abettors of an insolvent fiduciary's breach of duty.[76] The defendant-attorneys had accepted payment by the fiduciary for attorney's fees in the underlying ERISA action with the knowledge that the payments drained reserve funds the plaintiffs claimed to own.[77] The court reasoned:

> Although the Court's research has not revealed any prior case in which a plaintiff holding a judgment against an insolvent ERISA fund has maintained an action against the fund's former counsel for restitution of previously paid legal fees paid or the imposition of a constructive trust with regard to the legal fees paid by the fund to its counsel, such an action does appear to be cognizable under ERISA. The Court agrees with the Defendants that, in the abstract, such a claim appears to effectively turn an attorney representing an ERISA fund into a guarantor of a potential judgment against that fund. However, upon further reflection, this cause of action is both wholly appropriate and consistent with ERISA's goals. Because the attorney's knowledge and participation in the fiduciary's breach of its fiduciary duty is an essential element of the claim, . . . counsel who simply provide

73. *Id.* (citations omitted).
74. *Id.* at 246–47.
75. *Id.* at 250.
76. L.I. Head Start Child Dev. Servs., Inc. v. Frank, 165 F. Supp. 2d 367, 368 (E.D. N.Y. 2011).
77. *Id.* at 369.

> representation and legal counsel to an ERISA fund will not be held liable. On the other hand, speaking hypothetically, if one assumes that an unscrupulous counsel actively participates in conduct he knows to be in violation of his client's fiduciary duties, it would be fitting and proper to require the attorney to restore the proceeds of such unlawful conduct to the fund for disbursement to participants.[78]

Typically, a plan may not indemnify its fiduciaries.[79] Plans may maintain a reserve to reimburse trustees for defending against allegations of a breach of fiduciary duties, but, subsequent to a determination of a fiduciary breach, the reserve becomes off limits.[80]

Equitable Remedies

Section 502(a)(3) authorizes a plan beneficiary, participant, or fiduciary to bring an action "(A) to enjoin any act or practice which violates any provision of [ERISA] or the terms of the plan, or (B) to obtain other appropriate equitable relief (i) to redress such violations or (ii) to enforce any provisions of [ERISA] or the terms of the plan."[81] Traditionally, plaintiffs could not obtain a monetary award pursuant to this section because monetary relief was considered to be a legal remedy and not an equitable remedy.

In the 1993 case *Mertens v. Hewitt Associates*, a class of retirement plan participants asserted claims for relief under § 502(a)(3) against the plan actuary, a nonfiduciary, alleging participation in fiduciary breaches.[82] The Court ruled that monetary relief was not available under the "other appropriate equitable relief" clause.[83] Although the Court recognized that courts of equity historically had broad powers to impose various remedies for breaches of trust, including legal remedies like compensatory damages, the Court found that interpreting the phrase "equitable relief" to include

78. *Id.* at 370–71.
79. 29 U.S.C. § 1110 (2012).
80. *See generally* Leigh v. Engle, 619 F. Supp. 154, 157-58 (N.D. Ill. 1985).
81. 29 U.S.C. § 1131(a)(3) (2012).
82. Mertens v. Hewitt Assocs., 508 U.S. 248, 249–50 (1993).
83. *Id.* at 263.

all relief that courts of equity had granted would render the "equitable" modifier superfluous.[84] Instead, the Court held that only "those categories of relief that were *typically* available in equity (such as injunction, mandamus, and restitution, but not compensatory damages)" should be available under the "other appropriate equitable relief" provision.[85] As a consequence of *Mertens*, courts denied many plaintiffs monetary relief.[86]

As previously discussed when examining ERISA's reimbursement clause, the Supreme Court later held that equitable restitution was available under § 502(a)(3) in the form of a monetary award to prevent unjust enrichment. In *Great-West Life & Annuity Insurance Company v. Knudson*, a health and welfare benefit plan required reimbursement to the insurance company for payments the company made if the beneficiary recovered the payments from a third party.[87] In this case, medical expenses covered by the plan were incurred as a result of injuries sustained in a car accident, after which the beneficiary settled liability claims with the car manufacturer.[88] Great-West, the insurance company, asserted that it should be reimbursed pursuant to the terms of the plan, invoking § 502(a)(3).[89] The United States, as amicus for the petitioners, argued that monetary relief had been awarded in courts of equity for breach of trust at common law, and so should be available as § 502(a)(3) equitable relief.[90] Relying on its decision in *Mertens*, the Court stated unequivocally that "[t]hese trust remedies are simply inapposite" and reiterated that "the term 'equitable relief' in § 502(a)(3) must refer to 'those categories of relief that were *typically* available in equity.'"[91]

84. *Id.* at 257.
85. *Id.* at 256.
86. *See, e.g.*, Fraser v. Lintas: Campbell-Ewald, 56 F.3d 722, 724 (6th Cir. 1995) ("*Mertens*' stated preference for a narrow reading of the equitable remedies available under ERISA . . . leads us to conclude that money damages are not available under § 502(a)(1)(B) for claims that are equitable in nature."); Reich v. Rowe, 20 F.3d 25, 29 (1st Cir. 1994) ("After the *Mertens* decision, the Secretary withdrew the appeal of his claim . . . because the claim only sought monetary damages."); Buckley Dement, Inc. v. Travelers Plan Adm'rs of Ill., Inc., 39 F.3d 784, 787–88 (7th Cir. 1994) (explaining that *Mertens* concerned the same sort of argument for monetary, equitable relief as the one being made and that *Mertens* precluded the claimant's recovery).
87. Great-West Life & Annuity Ins. Co. v. Knudson, 534 U.S. 204, 207 (2002).
88. *Id.* at 207–08.
89. *Id.* at 208.
90. *Id.* at 219.
91. *Id.* at 219–20 (citing Mertens v. Hewitt Assocs., 508 U.S. 248, 256 (1993)).

In the 2006 case *Sereboff v. Mid Atlantic Medical Services, Inc.*, the Supreme Court revisited the issue of what constituted equitable relief under ERISA. The plan in *Sereboff* had a reimbursement provision that was implicated by a settlement of medical expenses incurred after injuries suffered in a car accident.[92] Unlike the third-party funds in *Great-West*, however, the settlement in *Sereboff* had been set aside pending resolution of the reimbursement claim and, thus, was identifiable and traceable to the defendant's separate account.[93] This distinction led the Court to determine that the relief being sought was the traditional equitable remedy of restitution, which requires identifiable funds to be in the possession of the defendant.[94] The Court reiterated that "compensatory damages" were *not* available under § 502(a)(3).[95]

Recovery of a Surcharge as Equitable Relief

In 2011, the Supreme Court decided *CIGNA Corporation v. Amara* and expanded the monetary award available under ERISA § 502(a)(3) to include recovery of a "surcharge."[96] CIGNA's conversion of its defined benefit pension plan to a "cash balance" type of pension plan triggered this case because, during the conversion process, CIGNA provided disclosures to participants and beneficiaries that conflicted with the actual terms of the new plan.[97] Before the Court was whether the district court had applied the proper legal standard when, after finding CIGNA's notice failures had caused "likely harm," the district court found legal authority in § 501(a)(1)(B) to reform the new plan and ordered CIGNA to pay benefits in accordance with the reformed plan.[98] The Supreme Court held that § 501(a)(1)(B), permitting a participant or beneficiary to bring a civil action to recover benefits due

92. Sereboff v. Mid Atl. Med. Servs., Inc., 547 U.S. 356, 360 (2006).
93. *Id.* at 362–63.
94. *Id.*
95. *Id.* at 361–62.
96. CIGNA Corp. v. Amara, 131 S. Ct. 1866, 1880 (2011).
97. *Id.* at 1871–72.
98. *Id.* at 1870–71.

under a plan, did not allow the district court to administer the relief that it had.[99] Specifically, § 501(a)(1)(B) did not empower the district court to change or reform the terms of the plan.[100] Nevertheless, the Court recognized various forms of equitable relief that the district court could provide upon remand, including payment of a surcharge.[101] The Court reasoned:

> The case before us concerns a suit by a beneficiary against a plan fiduciary (whom ERISA typically treats as a trustee) about the terms of a plan (which ERISA typically treats as a trust). It is the kind of lawsuit that, before the merger of law and equity, respondents could have brought only in a court of equity, not a court of law.
>
> With the exception of the relief now provided by § 502(a)(1)(B), the remedies available to those courts of equity were traditionally considered equitable remedies.
>
> The District Court's affirmative and negative injunctions obviously fall within this category. And other relief ordered by the District Court resembles forms of traditional equitable relief. That is because equity chancellors developed a host of other "distinctively equitable" remedies—remedies that were "fitted to the nature of the primary right" they were intended to protect. Indeed, a maxim of equity states that "[e]quity suffers not a right to be without a remedy." And the relief entered here, insofar as it does not consist of injunctive relief, closely resembles three other traditional equitable remedies.
>
> First, what the District Court did here may be regarded as the reformation of the terms of the plan, in order to remedy the false or misleading information CIGNA provided. The power to reform contracts (as contrasted with the power to enforce contracts as written) is a traditional power of an equity court, not a court of law, and was used to prevent fraud.
>
> Second, the District Court's remedy essentially held CIGNA to what it had promised, namely, that the new plan would not take from its employees benefits they had already accrued. This aspect of the remedy

99. *Id.* at 1871.
100. *Id.* at 1876–77.
101. *Id.* at 1879–80.

> resembles estoppel, a traditional equitable remedy. And, as Justice Story long ago pointed out, equitable estoppel "forms a very essential element in . . . fair dealing, and rebuke of all fraudulent misrepresentation, which it is the boast of courts of equity constantly to promote."
>
> Third, the District Court injunctions require the plan administrator to pay to already retired beneficiaries money owed them under the plan as reformed. But the fact that this relief takes the form of a money payment does not remove it from the category of traditionally equitable relief. Equity courts possessed the power to provide relief in the form of monetary "compensation" for a loss resulting from a trustee's breach of duty, or to prevent the trustee's unjust enrichment. The surcharge remedy extended to a breach of trust committed by a fiduciary encompassing any violation of a duty imposed upon that fiduciary. Thus, insofar as an award of make-whole relief is concerned, the fact that the defendant in this case, unlike the defendant in *Mertens*, is analogous to a trustee makes a critical difference. In sum, contrary to the District Court's fears, the types of remedies the court entered here fall within the scope of the term "appropriate equitable relief" in § 502(a)(3).[102]

The Court articulated three elements that a plaintiff must show to be granted a surcharge: (1) there must be a breach of trust by a fiduciary; (2) there must be actual harm suffered by the beneficiary; and (3) the breach must have caused the harm.[103] The Court made it clear that demonstrating detrimental reliance was not necessary for equitable remedies such as the surcharge, though detrimental reliance could be an aspect of the harm analysis.[104]

The absence of unjust enrichment has not precluded the remedy of surcharge in the cases following *CIGNA*. Where the breaching trustee has caused a loss, he or she is "surcharged" to compensate for it. Surcharge is one form of what courts and commentators often call "make-whole relief." The definition of "make-whole relief" varies depending on the legal context

102. *Id.* (citations omitted).
103. *Id.* at 1881–82.
104. *Id.*

but generally refers in this context to restoring the claimant to the situation he or she would be in if the loss had not occurred.

Compensation for tax losses due to a fiduciary's erroneous information should be forthcoming post-*CIGNA*. Prior to *CIGNA*, courts have not allowed compensation for tax losses because the Internal Revenue Service (IRS) was justly enriched, and the defendant was not unjustly enriched.[105] In *Armstrong v. Jefferson Smurfit Corporation*, the First Circuit rejected a claim for compensatory damages for taxes paid on a lump-sum welfare benefit payment that the participant did not know was taxable because, relying on *Mertens*, the Court explained that the damages sought were outside "appropriate equitable relief" under ERISA.[106] In *Farr v. U.S. West Communications, Inc.*, the Ninth Circuit held that retirees could not recover for taxes incurred on lump-sum payments from an excess benefit plan merely because the fiduciary breached his or her duty in failing to adequately inform the retirees of the tax consequences on such payments.[107] The court explained: "binding precedent compels us to conclude that Plaintiffs may not recover their tax benefit losses under § 502 (a)(3), despite the fact that that conclusion leaves Plaintiffs without a remedy for an alleged breach of fiduciary duty under ERISA."[108]

Unfortunately for claimants, punitive damages continue to appear out of reach in post-*CIGNA* cases brought under § 502 (a)(3).

Equitable Defenses

In 2013, the Supreme Court held in *U.S. Airways v. McCutchen* that equitable rules limiting recovery could not overrule the terms of a plan in a suit brought pursuant to § 502(a)(3).[109] *McCutchen* concerned a health benefits

105. *See* Fraser v. Lintas: Campbell-Ewald, 56 F.3d 722 (6th Cir. 1995); Novak v. Anderson Corp., 962 F.2d 757 (8th Cir. 1992); Bouteiller v. Vulcon Iron Works, Inc., 834 F. Supp. 207 (E.D. Mich. 1993).
106. Armstrong v. Jefferson Smurfit Corp., 30 F.3d 11, 13 (1st Cir. 1994).
107. Farr v. U.S. W. Comms., Inc., 151 F.3d 908, 916 (9th Cir. 1998), *amended by* Farr v. U.S. West Comms., Inc., 179 F.3d 1252 (9th Cir. 1999).
108. *Id.*
109. U.S. Airways, Inc. v. McCutchen, 133 S. Ct. 1537, 1542-43 (2013).

plan that obliged U.S. Airways to pay an employee's medical expenses incurred as a result of a third party's actions but which entitled U.S. Airways to reimbursement if the employee later recovered against the third party.[110] The case arose after an employee had recovered against a third party, and U.S. Airways sought reimbursement under § 502(a)(3).[111]

The Court granted certiorari to resolve a circuit split regarding whether a party to an ERISA plan, such as the employee in *McCutchen*, could leverage equitable defenses to override a plan's reimbursement provision.[112] Most circuits had held that the explicit terms of the plan's reimbursement provision governed while others, including the Third Circuit in *McCutchen*, allowed those defendants who recovered funds to raise equitable defenses to avoid paying over what the plan had paid out.[113] The Supreme Court sided with the majority of circuits and held that such lawsuits were to enforce the equivalent of an equitable lien pursuant to contract terms, enforcement of which requiring the Court to hold the parties to their promises.[114] The Court explained:

> The question in this case concerns the role that equitable defenses alleging unjust enrichment can play in such a suit. As earlier noted, the Third Circuit held that "the principle of unjust enrichment" overrides U.S. Airways' reimbursement clause if and when they come into conflict. McCutchen offers a more refined version of that view, alleging that two specific equitable doctrines meant to "prevent unjust enrichment" defeat the reimbursement provision. First, he contends that in equity, an insurer in U.S. Airways' position could recoup no more than an insured's "double recovery"—the amount the insured has received from a third party to compensate for the same loss the insurance covered. That rule would limit U.S. Airways' reimbursement to the share of McCutchen's settlements paying for medical expenses; McCutchen would keep the rest (e.g., damages for loss of future earnings or pain

110. *Id.* at 1542.
111. *Id.*
112. *Id.* at 1544 (citing U.S. Airways, Inc., v. McCutchen, 663 F.3d 671 (3d Cir. 2011)).
113. *Id.* at 1546.
114. *Id.*

and suffering), even though the plan gives U.S. Airways first claim on the whole third-party recovery. Second, McCutchen claims that in equity the common-fund doctrine would have operated to reduce any award to U.S. Airways. Under that rule, "a litigant or a lawyer who recovers a common fund for the benefit of persons other than himself or his client is entitled to a reasonable attorney's fee from the fund as a whole." McCutchen urges that this doctrine, which is designed to prevent freeloading, enables him to pass on a share of his lawyer's fees to U.S. Airways, no matter what the plan provides.

We rejected a similar claim in *Sereboff*, though without altogether foreclosing McCutchen's position. The Sereboffs argued, among other things, that the lower courts erred in enforcing Mid Atlantic's reimbursement clause "without imposing various limitations" that would "apply to truly equitable relief grounded in principles of subrogation." In particular, the Sereboffs contended that a variant of the double-recovery rule, called the make-whole doctrine, trumped the plan's terms. We rebuffed that argument, explaining that the Sereboffs were improperly mixing and matching rules from different equitable boxes. The Sereboffs asserted a "parcel of equitable defenses" available when an out-of-pocket insurer brought a "freestanding action for equitable subrogation," not founded on a contract, to succeed to an insured's judgment against a third party. But Mid Atlantic's reimbursement claim was "considered equitable," we replied, because it sought to enforce a "lien based on agreement"—not a lien imposed independent of contract by virtue of equitable subrogation. In light of that fact, we viewed the Sereboffs' equitable defenses—which again, closely resemble McCutchen's—as "beside the point." And yet, we left a narrow opening for future litigants in the Sereboffs' position to make a like claim. In a footnote, we observed that the Sereboffs had forfeited a "distinct assertion" that the contract-based relief Mid Atlantic requested, although "equitable," was not "appropriate" under § 502(a)(3) because "it contravened principles like the make-whole doctrine." Enter McCutchen, to make that basic argument.

In the end, however, *Sereboff*'s logic dooms McCutchen's effort. U.S. Airways, like Mid Atlantic, is seeking to enforce the modern-day

> equivalent of an "equitable lien by agreement." And that kind of lien—as its name announces—both arises from and serves to carry out a contract's provisions. So enforcing the lien means holding the parties to their mutual promises. Conversely, it means declining to apply rules—even if they would be "equitable" in a contract's absence—at odds with the parties' expressed commitments. McCutchen therefore cannot rely on theories of unjust enrichment to defeat U.S. Airways' appeal to the plan's clear terms. Those principles, as we said in *Sereboff*, are "beside the point" when parties demand what they bargained for in a valid agreement. In those circumstances, hewing to the parties' exchange yields "appropriate" as well as "equitable" relief.[115]

The Court stated that if the plan terms are ambiguous on a particular issue, courts must use commonsense equitable understandings to decide the issue because "ignoring those rules is likely to frustrate the parties' intent and produce perverse consequences."[116] In *McCutchen*, the plan was silent on how to allocate attorney fees.[117] The Court used the common-fund doctrine, which addresses the availability of funds to obtain recovery, to allow the plaintiffs to recover attorney fees prior to reimbursing the plan.[118] Under the common-fund doctrine, a person whose recovery of funds benefits others is due reasonable attorney fees from the fund.[119]

Reimbursement clauses could explicitly state whether a participant's attorney fees will reduce the reimbursement obligation and whether the common-fund doctrine applies.

Interference with Protected Rights

ERISA § 510 provides:

115. *Id.* at 1545–47 (citations omitted).
116. *Id.* at 1549.
117. *Id.* at 1548.
118. *Id.* at 1549.
119. *Id.* at 1550 (citing Boeing Co. v. Van Gemert, 444 U.S. 472, 478 (1980)).

> It shall be unlawful for any person to discharge, fine, suspend, expel, discipline, or discriminate against a participant or beneficiary for exercising any right to which he is entitled under the provisions of an employee benefit plan, [Title I of ERISA] . . . , or for the purpose of interfering with the attainment of any right to which such participant may become entitled . . . . It shall be unlawful for any person to discharge, fine, suspend, expel, discipline, or discriminate against any person because he has given information or has testified or is about to testify in any inquiry or proceeding related to [ERISA] . . . .[120]

The participant or beneficiary can enforce § 510 by bringing suit under ERISA § 502(a)(3) to enjoin such actions that are prohibited by § 510 and also seek other equitable relief.[121] Courts are divided on the issue of whether exhaustion of administrative remedies applies to a § 510 claim.[122]

> The federal circuits have often ruled that a participant does not have to prove that his or her dismissal was for the sole reason of interfering with his or her right to benefits, but such interference must be a motivating factor.[123] The Seventh Circuit explained in *Deeming v. American Standard, Inc.*: the principle underlying § 510 "is an allegation that the employee-employer relationship . . . was changed in some discriminatory or wrongful way."[124] Courts increasingly rely on a Title VII burden-of-proof methodology in showing the specific intent underlying the discriminatory or wrongful action. This approach requires

120. 29 U.S.C. § 1140 (2012).
121. *Id.*
122. *Compare* Held v. Mfrs. Hanover Leasing Corp., 912 F.2d 1197 (10th Cir. 1990) (holding that a plaintiff is not required to exhaust administrative remedies before bringing a § 510 action), *and* Zipf v. Am. Tel. & Tel. Co., 799 F.2d 889 (distinguishing between contract-based claims requiring administrative exhaustion and statutory claims in finding exhaustion was not required in a § 510 case), *with* Lindemann v. Mobil Oil Corp., 79 F.3d 647 (refusing to distinguish between claims for benefits, which require exhaustion, and claims based upon ERISA itself and requiring exhaustion), *and* Mason v. Cont'l Group, Inc., 763 F.2d 1219 (11th Cir. 1985) (requiring exhaustion for assertion of statutory rights under ERISA).
123. Smith v. Ameritech, 129 F.3d 857, 865 (6th Cir. 1997); Kinkhead v. Sw. Bell Tel. Co., 49 F.3d 454, 457 (8th Cir. 1995); Seaman v. Arvida Realty Sales, 985 F.2d 543, 546 (11th Cir. 1993); Conkwright v. Westinghouse Elec. Corp., 933 F.2d 231, 239 (4th Cir. 1991); Gavalik v. Cont'l Can Co., 812, F.2d 834, 859 (3d Cir. 1987).
124. Deeming v. Am. Standard, Inc., 905 F.2d 1124, 1127 (7th Cir. 1990).

the claimant to present evidence of an employer's prohibited conduct, which must have been purposed to interfere with the attainment of an employee right; the employer must respond by articulating a nonpretextual, nondiscriminatory reason for the adverse employment action, with a failure to do so resulting in a presumption of discriminatory conduct; and the employee must then show by a preponderance of the evidence that the employer's proffered reasoning is a pretext for discriminatory interference.[125]

Interference with Nonvested Benefits

The Supreme Court of the United States ruled in *Inter-Modal Rail Employees Association v. Atchison* that § 510 prohibits interference with benefits even when those benefits are not vested.[126] The claimants in *Atchison* were former employees who brought suit after their subsidiary-employer lost its service agreement and the employees refused to continue employment with the potential employer who had won it, resulting in their discharge.[127] Employment with the new employer posed a substantial reduction in benefits.[128] The claimants alleged that they were discharged in order to interfere with the attainment of rights that they were entitled to under ERISA pension and welfare plans.[129] The Court of Appeals for the Ninth Circuit agreed that § 510 protected the former employees "from termination motivated by an employer's desire to prevent a pension from vesting," but the Ninth Circuit did not extend § 510's protection to welfare benefits, which "do not vest."[130] The Supreme Court unanimously disagreed with this outcome:

125. *See Gavalik*, 812 at 852–53; Dister v. Cont'l Group, Inc., 859 F.2d 1108, 1111–13 (2d Cir. 1988).
126. Inter-Modal Rail Emps. Ass'n v. Atchison, Topeka & Santa Fe Ry. Co., 520 U.S. 510, 514 (1997).
127. *Id.*
128. *Id.* at 512.
129. *Id.* at 513.
130. *Id.* (citing Inter-Modal Emps. Ass'n v. Atchison, Topeka & Santa Fe Ry. Co., 80 F.3d 348, 350–51 (1996)).

The Court of Appeals' holding that § 510 bars interference only with vested rights is contradicted by the plain language of § 510. As noted above, that section makes it unlawful to "discharge . . . a [plan] participant or beneficiary . . . for the purpose of interfering with the attainment of any right to which such participant may become entitled under the plan." ERISA defines a "plan" to include both "an employee welfare benefit plan [and] an employee pension benefit plan," and specifically exempts "employee welfare benefit plan[s]" from its stringent vesting requirements. Because a "plan" includes an "employee welfare benefit plan," and because welfare plans offer benefits that do not "vest" (at least insofar as ERISA is concerned), Congress' use of the word "plan" in § 510 all but forecloses the argument that § 510's interference clause applies only to "vested" rights. Had Congress intended to confine § 510's protection to "vested" rights, it could have easily substituted the term "pension plan" for "plan," or the term "nonforfeitable" right for "any right." But § 510 draws no distinction between those rights that "vest" under ERISA and those that do not.

The right that an employer or plan sponsor may enjoy in some circumstances to unilaterally amend or eliminate its welfare benefit plan does not, as the Court of Appeals apparently thought, justify a departure from § 510's plain language. It is true that ERISA itself "does not regulate the substantive content of welfare-benefit plans." Thus, unless an employer contractually cedes its freedom, it is "generally free under ERISA, for any reason at any time, to adopt, modify, or terminate [its] welfare pla[n]."

The flexibility an employer enjoys to amend or eliminate its welfare plan is not an accident; Congress recognized that "requir[ing] the vesting of these ancillary benefits would seriously complicate the administration and increase the cost of plans." Giving employers this flexibility also encourages them to offer more generous benefits at the outset, since they are free to reduce benefits should economic conditions sour. If employers were locked into the plans they initially offered, "they would err initially on the side of omission." Section 510 counterbalances this flexibility by ensuring that employers do not "circumvent the provision of promised benefits." In short, "§ 510

> helps to make promises credible." An employer may, of course, retain the unfettered right to alter its promises, but to do so it must follow the formal procedures set forth in the plan. Adherence to these formal procedures "increases the likelihood that proposed plan amendments, which are fairly serious events, are recognized as such and given the special consideration they deserve." The formal amendment process would be undermined if § 510 did not apply because employers could "informally" amend their plans one participant at a time. Thus, the power to amend or abolish a welfare benefit plan does not include the power to "discharge, fine, suspend, expel, discipline, or discriminate against" the plan's participants and beneficiaries "for the purpose of interfering with [their] attainment of . . . right[s] . . . under the plan." To be sure, when an employer acts without this purpose, as could be the case when making fundamental business decisions, such actions are not barred by § 510. But in the case where an employer acts with a purpose that triggers the protection of § 510, any tension that might exist between an employer's power to amend the plan and a participant's rights under § 510 is the product of a careful balance of competing interests, and is most surely not the type of "absurd or glaringly unjust" result that would warrant departure from the plain language of § 510.[131]

A § 510 claim may apply to interference with an employee's right to accrue benefits in the future and not only to his or her right to vest in benefits already accrued. In *Garratt v. Walker*, the Court of Appeals for the Tenth Circuit explained that, in light of *Inter-Modal Rail Employees*, "even though an employee may lack a present legal right to receive benefits in the future, an anticipated right to receive benefits may not be denied in a manner that would contravene § 510."[132]

---

131. *Id.* at 514–16 (citations omitted).
132. Garratt v. Walker, 164 F.3d 1249, 1252 (10th Cir. 1998); *see also* Seaman v. Arvida Realty Sales, 985 F.2d 543 (11th Cir. 1993); Conkwright v. Westinghouse Electric Corp., 933 F.2d 231 (4th Cir. 1991).

Workforce Reorganization

Without more, a change in a business's organizational structure that results in the discharge of employees is not the kind of situation that creates a cause of action under ERISA § 510.[133] In *Becker v. Mack Trucks, Inc.*, the Court of Appeals for the Third Circuit held that an employer's decision to rehire only nonvested participants was not enough to establish a viable § 510 claim.[134] The Third Circuit looked at the explicit statutory language and the purpose of § 510, concluding that neither supported the extension of § 510 to rehiring decisions.[135] The Court of Appeals for the Ninth Circuit similarly held in *West v. Greyhound Corporation* that "no violation . . . is shown where the seller of a business terminates employment under the provisions of a collective bargaining agreement and the purchaser refused to hire any of the employees because they refuse to accept a reduction of unaccrued employee benefits."[136] However, the Third Circuit affirmed the district court's holding in *McLendon v. Continental Group, Inc.*, that an employer's selection of employees for layoff to deliberately prevent them from qualifying for plan benefits violated § 510.[137] The Court of Appeals for the Tenth Circuit also held in *Maez v. Mountain States Telegraph & Telephone, Inc.* that the claimants sufficiently stated a claim to avoid dismissal when arguing that they had been constructively discharged in violation of § 510 by defendants fraudulently inducing them into quitting.[138]

In *Lessard v. Applied Risk Management*, the Ninth Circuit held that a plaintiff could retain her health benefits using § 510 when she would have otherwise lost the benefits during a corporate reorganization.[139] *Lessard* arose after an asset sale between companies that automatically transferred active employees to the new company, which covered the employees under

---

133. *See* Daughtrey v. Honeywell Inc., 3 F.3d 1488 (11th Cir 1993); Unida v. Levi Strauss & Co. 986 F.2d 970 (5th Cir. 1993); Aronson v. Servus Rubber, 730 F.2d 12 (1st Cir. 1984).
134. Becker v. Mack Trucks, Inc., 281 F.3d 372, 276 (3d Cir. 2002).
135. *Id.* at 379.
136. West v. Greyhound Corp., 813 F.2d 951, 955 (9th Cir. 987).
137. McLendon v. Continental Group, Inc., 749 F. Supp. 582, 611 (D. N.J. 1989), *aff'd*, 908 F.2s 1171 (3d Cir. 1990).
138. Maez v. Mountain States Tel. & Tel., Inc., 54 F.3d 1488, 1502 (10th Cir. 1995).
139. Lessard v. Applied Risk Mgmt., 307 F.3d 1020 (9th Cir. 2002).

its welfare benefits plan.[140] There was no interruption in coverage, however; eligibility for transfer required the employee to be actively employed on the day of the sale or on nonmedical, nonextended leave from active employment, and the agreement provided a distinct transfer schedule for employees like the claimant who were on medical or extended leave.[141] The claimant remained on extended leave without a clear return-to-work date when she brought suit under § 510.[142] The defendants argued that they could not be held liable for a termination of benefits due to a corporate reorganization.[143] The court observed that even though the purchasing company in an asset sale may determine the quality and quantity of benefits available to transferred employees, it may not exclude a group of employees without violating § 510.[144]

Section 510 Without an Employer and Employee

Most cases dealing with § 510 have focused on the employer-employee relationship, but some courts have permitted § 510 claims to succeed against other parties. In *Mattei v. Mattei*, a couple executed a prenuptial agreement under which, in the event of the husband's death, the wife surrendered all claims against his estate except for the right to live in their marital residence and to receive $300 weekly, to be increased by 6 percent at the end of the first year.[145] The husband passed away a year into the marriage, and the plan administrator of the husband's pension plan determined that the widow was entitled to the plan's death benefits, paid out in a single settlement.[146] The estate subsequently failed to increase the widow's weekly payments by 6 percent after the first year, and the estate eventually stopped the weekly payments altogether.[147] The widow brought suit under § 510 against the

140. *Id.* at 1022.
141. *Id.* at 1022–23.
142. *Id.* at 1023.
143. *Id.* at 1026.
144. *Id.* at 1026–27.
145. Mattei v. Mattei, 126 F.3d 794, 796 (6th Cir. 1997).
146. *Id.*
147. *Id.*

estate, the executor, and the will's legatee and claimed that the defendants ceased the weekly payments to deprive her of the benefits to which she was entitled under the pension plan and in retaliation against her acceptance of the death benefits.[148]

The court determined that the widow's action could be viable under § 510.[149] The court observed that Congress intended § 510 primarily—but not exclusively—to protect the employment relationship.[150] The court relied in part on the committee report's expression of the hope and desire that § 510 be available to protect pension benefits and the expectation of those receiving the benefits to be protected from economic effects arising outside the employment context.[151] Upon a review of § 510 cases, the court observed "that, rather than viewing attacks on the 'employment relationship' as sine qua non of § 510 coverage, it is more appropriate to view 'employment relationship' as an illustrative but non-exclusive description of a set of rights that are protected by § 510."[152] Thus, a § 510 claim can be brought against any party who "discharges, fines, suspends, expels, disciplines, or discriminates against a participant or beneficiary for exercising any right to which he or she is entitled under an employee benefit plan or ERISA or for the purpose of interfering with such an entitlement."[153] The court interpreted the term "discriminate" in § 510 to forbid any adverse action against an individual engaged in a protected activity, and the court determined that the defendants' actions fell within § 510's prohibitions.[154]

The Sixth Circuit also found § 510 claims reached further than the employment relationship in *Heimann v. National Elevator Industry Pension Fund* and extended to a business agent.[155] The Third Circuit, however, refused to extend either *Heimann* or *Mattei* to prospective employment relationships in *Becker v. Mack Trucks, Inc.*[156]

148. *Id.* at 796–97.
149. *Id.* at 801.
150. *Id.* at 800.
151. *Id.*
152. *Id.* at 801.
153. *Id.* at 803–04.
154. *Id.* at 804–05.
155. Heimann v. Nat'l Elevator Indus. Pension Fund, 187 F.3d 493, 507 (5th Cir. 1999), *overruled on other grounds*, Arana v. Ochsner Health Plan, 338 F.3d 433, 440 (5th Cir. 2003).
156. Becker v. Mack Trucks, Inc., 281 F.3d 372, 383 n.10 (3d Cir. 2002).

Chapter 7

Disability Benefits: A State of Denial

A "disability benefit" is a plan benefit that is conditioned on the demonstration of a "disability" as defined by the plan. Plans that provide disability benefits are covered by ERISA as one type of employee welfare benefit plan.[1] Participants in disability benefit plans may take action when their request for benefits is denied and the plan does not reverse the denial.[2] Such actions dominate litigation in this arena.

Participants in a disability plan may bring an action under ERISA § 502(a)(1)(B) to recover disability benefits.[3] ERISA has no specific statute of limitations for such actions, and courts typically require participants to first exhaust the plan's internal administrative review process prior to initiating a lawsuit.[4] ERISA and its implementing regulations govern plans' administrative remedies by requiring plans to create and maintain reasonable claims procedures,[5] and plans providing disability benefits, including pension plans that provide disability benefits, must comply with specific procedures in order for the procedures to qualify as reasonable.[6] Among these procedures are the establishment and maintenance of "reasonable procedures governing the filing of benefit claims, notification of benefit

1. 29 U.S.C. § 1002(1) (2012).
2. 29 U.S.C. § 1132(a)(1)(B) (2012).
3. *Id.*
4. Heimeshoff v. Hartford Life & Accident Ins. Co., 134 S. Ct. 604, 608 (2013).
5. 29 C.F.R. § 2560.503–1(b) (2013).
6. 29 C.F.R. § 2560.503–1(d) (2013).

determinations, and appeal of adverse benefit determinations."[7] In addition, the disability claims procedures must comply with the following:

> [1] The claims procedures do not contain any provision, and are not administered in a way, that requires a claimant to file more than two appeals of an adverse benefit determination prior to bringing a civil action under section 502(a) of the Act;
>
> [2] To the extent that a plan offers voluntary levels of appeal (except to the extent that the plan is required to do so by State law), including voluntary arbitration or any other form of dispute resolution, . . . the claims procedures provide that:
>
> (i) The plan waives any right to assert that a claimant has failed to exhaust administrative remedies because the claimant did not elect to submit a benefit dispute to any such voluntary level of appeal provided by the plan;
>
> (ii) The plan agrees that any statute of limitations or other defense based on timeliness is tolled during the time that any such voluntary appeal is pending;
>
> (iii) The claims procedures provide that a claimant may elect to submit a benefit dispute to such voluntary level of appeal only after exhaustion of the appeals permitted by . . . this section;
>
> (iv) The plan provides to any claimant, upon request, sufficient information relating to the voluntary level of appeal to enable the claimant to make an informed judgment about whether to submit a benefit dispute to the voluntary level of appeal, including a statement that the decision of a claimant as to whether or not to submit a benefit dispute to the voluntary level of appeal will have no effect on the claimant's rights to any other benefits under the plan and information about the applicable rules, the claimant's right to representation, the process for selecting the decisionmaker, and the circumstances, if any, that may affect the impartiality of the decisionmaker, such as any financial or

7. 29 C.F.R. § 2560.503–1(b) (2013).

personal interests in the result or any past or present relationship with any party to the review process; and

(v) No fees or costs are imposed on the claimant as part of the voluntary level of appeal.

[3] The claims procedures do not contain any provision for the mandatory arbitration of adverse benefit determinations, except to the extent that the plan or procedures provide that:

(i) The arbitration is conducted as one of the two appeals . . . and in accordance with the requirements applicable to such appeals; and

(ii) The claimant is not precluded from challenging the decision under section 502(a) of the Act or other applicable law.[8]

The plan administrator is required to maintain an adequate record of a decision to deny disability benefits to a claimant.[9] Administrators are typically restricted to determinations based on the administrative record,[10] although courts will consider evidence outside the administrative record when the record is deficient.[11]

Plan-Generated Time Limitations

ERISA does not provide a statute of limitation for civil actions contesting a denial of disability benefits, but a disability plan may set its own deadline for filing suit. On December 13, 2013, the Supreme Court of the United States issued its decision in *Heimeshoff v. Hartford Life & Accident Insurance Company* and enforced a disability plan's contractual limitation requiring suit within three years of the period during which a proof of loss was due under the plan.[12] The Court enforced the plan's limiting provision even

8. 29 C.F.R. § 2560.503-1(c)(2)–(4) (2013).
9. 29 U.S.C. § 1132(a)(1)(B) (2012).
10. *See* Morgan v. Contractors, Laborers, Teamsters & Eng'rs Pension Plan, 287 F.3d 716, 722–23 (8th Cir. 2002).
11. *See* Abatie v. Alta Health & Life Ins. Co., 459 F.3d 955, 973 (9th Cir. 2006); VanderKlok v. Provident Life & Accident Ins. Co., Inc., 956 F.2d 610, 617 (6th Cir. 1992).
12. Heimeshoff v. Hartford Life & Accident Ins. Co., 134 S. Ct. 604, 608 (2013).

though proof of loss was due before the completion of the plan's administrative process, which the Court recognized would, "in practice, shorten the contractual limitations period."[13] The Court concluded: "Absent a controlling statute to the contrary, a participant and a plan may agree by contract to a particular limitations period, even one that starts to run before the cause of action accrues, as long as the period is reasonable."[14]

The claimant in *Heimeshoff*, Julie Heimeshoff, was a senior public relations manager for Wal-Mart who was diagnosed with lupus and fibromyalgia.[15] Heimeshoff initially submitted a claim for long-term disability benefits to Hartford Life & Accident Insurance Company on August 22, 2005, but Hartford informed Heimeshoff in November 2005 that it could not determine her disability status because her rheumatologist did not respond to the company's request for additional information.[16] Hartford reopened the claim, and Heimeshoff submitted an evaluation by another physician stating she was disabled in July 2006.[17] In November 2006, a physician hired by Hartford reviewed Heimeshoff's medical records and contacted her rheumatologist before concluding that Heimeshoff was able to perform "her sedentary occupation."[18] Hartford denied Heimeshoff's claim later in November 2006.[19] Heimeshoff submitted her appeal of the denial on September 26, 2007, and Hartford denied the appeal on November 26, 2007.[20] On November 18, 2010, more than three years after the proof of loss was due, Heimeshoff commenced an action in district court.[21]

In enforcing the three-year limiting provision in the plan, the Court reasoned:

> The principle that contractual limitations provisions ordinarily should be enforced as written is especially appropriate when enforcing an ERISA plan. The plan, in short, is at the center of ERISA. [E]mployers

13. *Id.*
14. *Id.* at 610.
15. *Id.* at 608.
16. *Id.* at 608–09.
17. *Id.* at 609.
18. *Id.*
19. *Id.*
20. *Id.*
21. *Id.*

> have large leeway to design disability and other welfare plans as they see fit. And once a plan is established, the administrator's duty is to see that the plan is maintained pursuant to [that] written instrument. This focus on the written terms of the plan is the linchpin of a system that is [not] so complex that administrative costs, or litigation expenses, unduly discourage employers from offering [ERISA] plans in the first place.
>
> Heimeshoff's cause of action for benefits is likewise bound up with the written instrument. ERISA § 502(a)(1)(B) authorizes a plan participant to bring suit to recover benefits due to him under the terms of his plan, to enforce his rights under the terms of the plan, or to clarify his rights to future benefits under the terms of the plan. That statutory language speaks of enforc[ing] the terms of the plan, not of changing them. For that reason, we have recognized the particular importance of enforcing plan terms as written in § 502(a)(1)(B) claims. Because the rights and duties at issue in this case are no less built around reliance on the face of written plan documents, we will not presume from statutory silence that Congress intended a different approach here.[22]

Despite its deference to the plan's terms, the Supreme Court clarified that it would not give effect to the plan's limiting provision if it limited the time to bring suit to an unreasonably short period or if a controlling statute prevented the limitation from taking effect.[23] The Court found that neither exception to enforcing the terms of the plan applied in *Heimeshoff*.[24] The Court explained:

> Neither Heimeshoff nor the United States claims that the Plan's 3-year limitations provision is unreasonably short on its face. And with good reason: the United States acknowledges that the regulations governing internal review mean for mainstream claims to be resolved in about one year, leaving the participant with two years to file suit. Even in this case, where the administrative review process required more

22. *Id.* at 611–12 (citations and quotation marks omitted).
23. *Id.* at 612.
24. *Id.*

time than usual, Heimeshoff was left with approximately one year in which to file suit. Heimeshoff does not dispute that a hypothetical 1-year limitations period commencing at the conclusion of internal review would be reasonable. We cannot fault a limitations provision that would leave the same amount of time in a case with an unusually long internal review process while providing for a significantly longer period in most cases.

. . .

Heimeshoff and the United States contend that even if the Plan's limitations provision is reasonable, ERISA is a controlling statute to the contrary. But they do not contend that ERISA's statute of limitations for claims of breach of fiduciary duty controls this action to recover benefits. Nor do they claim that ERISA's text or regulations contradict the Plan's limitations provision. Rather, they assert that the limitations provision will undermine ERISA's two-tiered remedial scheme. We cannot agree.

The first tier of ERISA's remedial scheme is the internal review process required for all ERISA disability-benefit plans. After the participant files a claim for disability benefits, the plan has 45 days to make an adverse benefit determination. Two 30-day extensions are available for matters beyond the control of the plan, giving the plan a total of up to 105 days to make that determination. The plan's time for making a benefit determination may be tolled due to a claimant's failure to submit information necessary to decide a claim.

Following denial, the plan must provide the participant with at least 180 days . . . within which to appeal the determination. The plan has 45 days to resolve that appeal, with one 45-day extension available for special circumstances (such as the need to hold a hearing). The plan's time for resolving an appeal can be tolled again if the participant fails to submit necessary information. In the ordinary course, the regulations contemplate an internal review process lasting about one year. If the plan fails to meet its own deadlines under these procedures, the participant shall be deemed to have exhausted the administrative remedies. Upon exhaustion of the internal review process, the participant is entitled to proceed immediately to judicial review, the second tier of ERISA's remedial scheme.

. . .

Heimeshoff and the United States first claim that the Plan's limitations provision will undermine the foregoing internal review process. They contend that participants will shortchange their own rights during that process in order to have more time in which to seek judicial review. Their premise—that participants will sacrifice the benefits of internal review to preserve additional time for filing suit—is highly dubious in light of the consequences of that course of action.

First, to the extent participants fail to develop evidence during internal review, they risk forfeiting the use of that evidence in district court. The Courts of Appeals have generally limited the record for judicial review to the administrative record compiled during internal review. Second, participants are not likely to value judicial review of plan determinations over internal review. Many plans (including this Plan) vest discretion over benefits determinations in plan administrators. Courts ordinarily review determinations by such plans only for abuse of discretion. In short, participants have much to lose and little to gain by giving up the full measure of internal review in favor of marginal extra time to seek judicial review.

. . .

Heimeshoff and the United States next warn that it will endanger judicial review to allow plans to set limitations periods that begin to run before internal review is complete. The United States suggests that administrators may attempt to prevent judicial review by delaying the resolution of claims in bad faith. But administrators are required by the regulations governing the internal review process to take prompt action, and the penalty for failure to meet those deadlines is immediate access to judicial review for the participant. In addition, that sort of dilatory behavior may implicate one of the traditional defenses to a statute of limitations.

The United States suggests that even good-faith administration of internal review will significantly diminish the availability of judicial review if this limitations provision is enforced. Forty years of ERISA

> administration suggest otherwise. The limitations provision at issue is quite common; the vast majority of States require certain insurance policies to include 3-year limitations periods that run from the date proof of loss is due. But there is no significant evidence that limitations provisions like the one here have similarly thwarted judicial review. As explained above, ERISA regulations structure internal review to proceed in an expeditious manner. It stands to reason that the cases in which internal review leaves participants with less than one year to file suit are rare. Heimeshoff identifies only a handful of cases in which § 502(a)(1)(B) plaintiffs are actually time barred as a result of this 3-year limitations provision. Those cases suggest that this barrier falls on participants who have not diligently pursued their rights. The evidence that this 3-year limitations provision harms diligent participants is far too insubstantial to set aside the plain terms of the contract.
>
> Moreover, even in the rare cases where internal review prevents participants from bringing § 502(a)(1)(B) actions within the contractual period, courts are well equipped to apply traditional doctrines that may nevertheless allow participants to proceed. If the administrator's conduct causes a participant to miss the deadline for judicial review, waiver or estoppel may prevent the administrator from invoking the limitations provision as a defense. To the extent the participant has diligently pursued both internal review and judicial review but was prevented from filing suit by extraordinary circumstances, equitable tolling may apply. Finally, in addition to those traditional remedies, plans that offer appeals or dispute resolution beyond what is contemplated in the internal review regulations must agree to toll the limitations provision during that time. Thus, we are not persuaded that the Plan's limitations provision is inconsistent with ERISA.[25]

The Court's decision abrogated *White v. Sun Life Assurance of Company of Canada*, where the Fourth Circuit had held that an insurer could not enforce a plan provision limiting actions based on the point the claimant

25. *Id.* at 612–16 (citations and quotation marks omitted).

had filed a proof of claim,[26] as well as *Price v. Provident Life and Accident Insurance Company*, where the Ninth Circuit had held that a statute of limitations could not be triggered until the claimant had learned of a denial of benefits.[27]

Attempts to Sidestep Time Limitations

With plans' capacity to set time limitations on civil actions now clearly established, arguments that time limitations are not otherwise applicable are more important than ever. One such argument arises when claimants challenging denials of disability benefits assert that their time-limited claims should, like installment contracts, accrue starting with each improper or denied payment under the plan. On March 4, 2014, the United States Court of Appeals for the First Circuit joined the Second Circuit,[28] Third Circuit,[29] and Ninth Circuit[30] by rejecting this argument in *Riley v. Metropolitan Life Insurance Company*.[31] In *Riley*, the claimant, Robert Riley, argued that Metropolitan Life Insurance Company had underpaid his monthly disability benefits since 2005 when the company denied Riley's assertion that he was due a larger benefit payment, and the district court barred Riley's action based on a six-year limitation.[32] Riley urged the court to view each payment since 2005 as a newly accruing cause of action, but the court found that Riley's "theory of accrual is inapplicable where the alleged wrong is based on an alleged one-time miscalculation of ERISA benefits of which the plaintiff is aware."[33] The court concluded:

> Riley's entire alleged injury derives from a single action, MetLife's initial calculation of his disability benefits. Riley does not allege that the

26. White v. Sun Life Assurance Co. of Can., 488 F.3d 240, 242 (4th Cir. 2007).
27. Price v. Provident Life & Accident Ins. Co., 2 F.3d 986, 988 (9th Cir. 1993).
28. Novella v. Westchester Cnty., 661 F.3d 128, 128 (2d Cir. 2011).
29. Miller v. Fortis Benefits Ins. Co., 475 F.3d 516, 517–18 (3d Cir. 2007).
30. Pisciotta v. Teledyne Indus., Inc., 91 F.3d 1326, 1332 (9th Cir. 1996).
31. Riley v. Metro. Life Ins. Co., No. 13-2166, 2014 WL 1814742, at *4 (1st Cir. Mar. 4, 2014).
32. *Id.* at *1.
33. *Id.* at *4.

> calculation was actively confirmed at later dates, nor does he allege that there is any provision of ERISA that requires his accrual theory be accepted. Moreover, Riley has not identified any provisions of the Plan documents showing that the Plan should be interpreted as an installment contract.
>
> The policies underlying ERISA support our conclusion. One of ERISA's main purposes is the promotion of predictability, through which ERISA seeks to induc[e] employers to offer benefits by assuring a predictable set of liabilities. Allowing beneficiaries to challenge alleged miscalculations on which the statute of limitations has already run by limiting the challenge to recent and future payments would undermine that predictability interest. It could also undermine the ERISA plan's reliance on its original calculations and payments for actuarial purposes.[34]

Another argument to avert time limitations is that a defendant has waived the limitation. In a 2013 case before the United States Court of Appeals for the Sixth Circuit, *Engleson v. UNUM Life Insurance Company of America*, a claimant argued that a plan had waived its limitations period by stating in a correspondence: "If you or your physician(s) have additional information to support your request for disability benefits based upon an earlier date of disability, we will be happy to reconsider your claim."[35] Without pertinent federal common law to guide its reasoning, the court looked to the state insurance law it found most analogous to ERISA and thus to the state's insurance case law.[36] Relying on this case law, the claimant asserted that the appropriate standard for a waiver was a voluntary relinquishment of a known legal right, which the court characterized as "a clear, unequivocal, and decisive act of the party against whom the waiver is asserted."[37] The court concluded that the claimant's argument that the company had waived its time limitation failed even under the claimant's proposed standard because the letter lacked "clarity, directness, and decisiveness that the

34. *Id.* at *5 (citations and quotation marks omitted).
35. Engleson v. UNUM Life Ins. Co. of Am., 723 F.3d 611, 621 (6th Cir. 2013).
36. *Id.* at 621–22.
37. *Id.* at 622 (citing Warmack v. Arnold, 961 N.E.2d 1165, 1170 (Ohio 2011)).

general waiver rule demands"; the letter was ambiguous as to which one of the multiple claim denials it referred; the letter did not convey that the company had agreed to affirmatively take steps to reconsider; and, "perhaps more to the point, [the company's] letter sa[id] nothing about waiving the limitations period."[38]

An additional argument that claimants often make to sidestep time limitations is that the limitations period should be suspended under a theory of equitable tolling. This argument generally fails, as in *Gayle v. United Parcel Service, Inc.*, where the United States Court of Appeals for the Fourth Circuit refused to toll a limitations period after an attorney's negligence resulted in a claimant's failure to file a claim.[39] An argument for equitable tolling is more likely to succeed where the plan administrator has not fulfilled its obligations under ERISA.[40]

Conflicted Disability Determinations and the Standard of Review

As we examined in our chapter on other procedural matters, the Supreme Court held in *Firestone Tire & Rubber Company v. Bruch* that the standard of judicial review for disability claim denials is de novo unless the plan reserves discretion to the plan administrator, at which point a reviewing court should apply a more deferential standard.[41] The *Firestone* Court also emphasized an administrator's conflict of interest as an important factor when determining the proper standard of review, characterizing the significance of a conflict of interest as depending on the circumstances of each particular case.[42]

In *Metropolitan Life Insurance Company v. Glenn*, the Supreme Court returned to the standard of review in disability claim denials and held that a plan administrator that both evaluates and pays claims has a conflict of

38. *Id.* at 622–23.
39. Gayle v. United Parcel Servs., Inc., 401 F.3d 222 (4th Cir. 2005).
40. *See, e.g.*, Veltri v. Bldg. Serv., 32B-J Pension Fund, 393 F.3d 318 (2d Cir. 2004).
41. Firestone Tire & Rubber Co. v. Bruch, 489 U.S. 101, 110–11 (1989).
42. *Id.* at 115.

interest during benefit determinations.[43] Examining the weight of a conflict of interest as a factor in reviewing disability determinations, the Court explained:

> [A]ny one factor will act as a tiebreaker when the other factors are closely balanced, the degree of closeness necessary depending upon the tiebreaking factor's inherent or case-specific importance. The conflict of interest at issue here, for example, should prove more important (perhaps of great importance) where circumstances suggest a higher likelihood that it affected the benefits decision, including, but not limited to, cases where an insurance company administrator has a history of biased claims administration. It should prove less important (perhaps to the vanishing point) where the administrator has taken active steps to reduce potential bias and to promote accuracy, for example, by walling off claims administrators from those interested in firm finances, or by imposing management checks that penalize inaccurate decisionmaking irrespective of whom the inaccuracy benefits.[44]

Conflicts of interest are particularly common in disability cases.[45] However, as the Court acknowledged in *Glenn*, administrators can take steps to reduce bias and promote accuracy, and the existence of a conflict is far from dispositive.[46]

43. Metro. Life Ins. Co. v. Glenn, 554 U.S. 105, 115 (2008).
44. *Id.* at 117 (citations omitted).
45. *See, e.g.*, Schexnayder v. Hartford Life & Accident Ins. Co., 600 F.3d 465 (5th Cir. 2010); DeLisle v. Sun Life Assurance Co. of Can., 558 F.3d 440 (6th Cir. 2009); Cox v. Standard Ins. Co., 585 F.3d 295 (6th Cir. 2009); McCauley v. First UNUM Life Ins. Co., 551 F.3d 126 (2d Cir. 2008); Doyle v. Liberty Life Assurance Co. of Bos., 542 F.3d 1352 (11th Cir. 2008); Levinson v. Reliance Standard Life Ins. Co., 245 F.3d 1321 (11th Cir. 2001); Worsley v. Aetna Life Ins. Co., 780 F. Supp. 2d 397 (W.D. N.C. 2011); Mills v. Union Sec. Ins. Co., 832 F. Supp. 2d 587 (E.D. N.C. 2011); Robinson v. Hartford Life & Accident Ins. Co., 755 F. Supp. 2d 1054 (C.D. Cal. 2010); Eaton v. Metro. Life Ins. Co., 661 F. Supp. 2d 1240 (E.D. Okla. 2009); Rosby v. UNUM Life Ins. Co. of Am., 664 F. Supp. 2d 962 (E.D. Ark. 2009); Mattox v. Life Ins. Co. of N. Am., 536 F. Supp. 2d 1207 (N.A. Da. 2008).
46. *Glenn*, 554 U.S. at 117.

The Standard of Review Absent an Administrative Determination

The circuits have split on the appropriate standard of review when an administrator has not rendered a final decision on an appeal of a denial of disability benefits. Federal regulation requires administrators to review a denial of benefits within 60 days of a request for the review and within 120 days under special circumstances.[47] If no decision is forthcoming by the deadline, the claim is deemed denied.[48] In *Nichols v. Prudential Insurance Company of America*, the United States Court of Appeals for the Second Circuit addressed a deemed denied claim as well as the circuit split on the appropriate standard of review.[49] The court explained:

> A majority of circuits have held that, absent substantial compliance with the deadlines, *de novo* review applies on the grounds that inaction is not a valid exercise of discretion and leaves the court without any decision or application of expertise to which to defer. On the other hand, the Fifth Circuit has held that a deemed denied claim is still entitled to deferential review, apparently reasoning that the decision to deny is the same whether accomplished formally or by inaction. The Eighth Circuit has marked out a middle road, using deferential review unless the failure to meet the deadline raises serious doubts about the plan administrator's determination.
>
> We agree with the majority view. *Firestone* derived its holding from principles of trust law that make a deferential standard of review appropriate when a trustee exercises discretionary powers. The Supreme Court explicitly rejected the notion that the authorization of some set of discretionary powers of the plan administrator rendered all actions of the administrator discretionary. In light of this reasoning, we conclude that we may give deferential review only to actual exercises of discretion. A deemed denied claim is not denied by any exercise of discretion, but by operation of law on the 60th (or 120th)

47. 29 C.F.R. § 2560.503–1(h)(1)(i) (2013).
48. 29 C.F.R. § 2560.503–l(h)(4) (2013).
49. Nichols v. Prudential Ins. Co. of Am., 406 F.3d 98, 109 (2d Cir. 2005).

> day after the appeal is requested. We therefore hold that a deemed denied claim is entitled to *de novo* review . . . .[50]

The Sixth Circuit's holding harmonized with holdings in the Third,[51] Ninth,[52] and Tenth[53] Circuits. In contrast, the United States Court of Appeals for the Fifth Circuit held in *Southern Farm Bureau Life Insurance Company v. Moore* that the standard of review remained the same regardless of whether the administrator denied the claim outright or the claim was deemed denied.[54] The United States Court of Appeals for the Eighth Circuit held more elaborately in *Seman v. FMC Corporate Retirement Plan for Hourly Employees* that:

> When a plan administrator fails to render any decision whatsoever on a participant's application for benefits, it leaves the courts with nothing to review under any standard of review, so the matter must be sent back to the administrator for a decision. When a plan administrator denies a participant's initial application for benefits and the review panel fails to act on the participant's properly filed appeal, the administrator's decision is subject to judicial review, and the standard of review will be *de novo* rather than for abuse of discretion if the review panel's inaction raises serious doubts about the administrator's decision.[55]

Letters Denying Benefits

ERISA § 503 and accompanying regulations set specific requirements on notice of benefit denials.[56] Beyond the risks associated with violating these

50. Nichols v. Prudential Ins. Co. of Am., 406 F.3d 98, 105 (2d Cir. 2005) (citations omitted).
51. Gritzer v. CBS, Inc., 275 F.3d 291, 295 (3d Cir. 2002).
52. Jebian v. Hewlett-Packard Co. Emp. Benefits Org. Income Protection Plan, 349 F.3d 1098, 1106 (9th Cir. 2003).
53. Gilbertson v. Allied Signal, Inc., 328 F.3d 625, 634 (10th Cir. 2003).
54. S. Farm Bureau Life Ins. Co. v. Moore, 993 F.2d 98, 101 (5th Cir. 1993).
55. Seman v. FMC Corp. Ret. Plan for Hourly Emps., 334 F.3d 728, 733 (8th Cir. 2003).
56. *See generally* 29 U.S.C. § 1133 (2012); 29 C.F.R. § 2560.503–1(a) (2013).

notice requirements set forth in other chapters, missing or misleading denial letters can inform a court's review of plan administrators' determinations.

For example, in *Miller v. American Airlines, Inc.*, the United States Court of Appeals for the Third Circuit recently found that a legally deficient denial letter weighed in favor of a finding that an administrator's denial of disability benefits was arbitrary and capricious.[57] *Miller* concerned whether American Airlines impermissibly denied pilot Robert Miller's long-term disability benefits.[58] The plan communicated its denial to Miller in a letter stating "we are unable to verify . . . the existence of a continuing medical disability" and, in relevant part: "In order to receive further favorable consideration, you will need to demonstrate that you are actively pursuing obtaining your FAA medical certification. At this time, however, verification of your continued disability cannot be established and your disability benefits under the Plan will end immediately."[59]

The court found this denial letter deficient for two reasons in particular:

> First, the letter does not provide specific reasons for [the] denial, written in a manner calculated to be understood by the participant. The letter states that American is unable to verify either the existence of a continuing medical disability or [Miller's] continued substantial progress towards obtaining [his] FAA medical certification. American's inability to verify Miller's disability is a bare conclusion that does not provide a specific reason for the termination decision. Rather, this purported explanation is a general blanket assessment that Miller is ineligible for disability benefits. The letter makes no mention of Miller's specific diagnoses nor the precise information that is lacking from his file. . . . The letter's mention of FAA certification is the most specific reason given for the termination, but this reference is misleading because it was not a prerequisite under the Plan and therefore not a valid reason to deny Miller's LTD benefits. . . . Thus, we believe that the language of the termination letter is conclusory and does not

57. Miller v. Am. Airlines, Inc., 632 F.3d 837, 852–53 (3d Cir. 2011).
58. *Id.* at 841.
59. *Id.* at 843.

> provide the specific reasons as to why Miller was no longer eligible for benefits, falling short of the requirements under § 503.
>
> Second, we conclude that the termination letter does not provide the precise information necessary to advise Miller how to perfect his claim. The regulations accompanying § 503 require the termination letter to describe any additional material or information necessary for the claimant to perfect the claim and an explanation of why such material or information is necessary. Here, the letter informed Miller that [i]n order to receive further favorable consideration, you will need to demonstrate that you are actively pursuing obtaining your FAA medical certification. Obtaining this certification, however, is not a requirement under the Plan and would therefore not serve to change his disability status. Given that the letter did not set forth any additional instruction as to how Miller could achieve a favorable disability determination, it does not comply with [ERISA's accompanying regulations]. The termination letter here does not satisfy the basic procedural mandates of ERISA, as set forth in § 503 and the relevant regulations. Instead of ensuring the procedural fairness of the termination decision, this letter made it exceedingly difficult for Miller to understand, let alone challenge, the bases for American's course of action. For that reason, American's noncompliance with the statute weighs in favor of finding that their decision was arbitrary and capricious.[60]

Accordingly, the court found that Miller was entitled to retroactive reinstatement of his disability benefits.[61]

Elements of an Appeal

Courts have found that the expression of an intention to appeal a disability claim denial does not by itself constitute an appeal for purposes of

60. *Id.* at 852 (citations and quotation marks omitted).
61. *Id.* at 841.

exhausting administrative remedies before proceeding to suit.[62] The United States Court of Appeals for the Eighth Circuit's 2013 decision *Reindl v. Hartford Life and Accident Insurance Company* provides a recent illustration of this principle.[63] In *Reindl*, the claimant had received a letter of termination of her long-term disability benefits stating that she had 180 days to submit an appeal to the insurer's appeals' unit.[64] Before filing a civil action, the claimant employed an attorney to challenge the termination of her benefits, and the attorney communicated the following in a letter to the insurer's benefit management services unit:

> I have been retained to assist the above-named individual in her Long Term Disability (LTD) benefits.
>
> This letter is to request a copy of any and all medical records you may have in your file on my client. Also, copies of any other documents you might have regarding my client's medical condition would be helpful.
>
> I have enclosed a HIPPA signed by my client to enable you to release copies of these records to me.
>
> We will be reviewing the records and obtaining additional medical information for my client's appeal of the decision to terminate her Long Term Disability (LTD) benefits.
>
> Thank you for your help in this matter.[65]

The insurer responded by sending the claimant's medical record to her attorney.[66] More than 180 days after the claimant's benefits had been terminated, her attorney sent a letter to the insurer's claim appeals unit, which the insurer construed as the claimant's administrative appeal.[67] The insurer

62. *See, e.g.*, Swanson v. Hearst Corp. Long Term Disability Plan, 586 F.3d 1016, 1019 (8th Cir. 2009).
63. Reindl v. Hartford Life & Accident Ins. Co., 705 F.3d 784, 786 (8th Cir. 2013).
64. *Id.*
65. *Id.*
66. *Id.*
67. *Id.*

responded that the appeal was not received within 180 days from the claim denial and that the claimant no longer had a right to appeal.[68]

The court found that the insurer was reasonable in not characterizing the attorney's initial letter as an appeal.[69] The court explained that the letter was transmitted to a different unit than the one to which the initial notice of denial instructed the claimant to submit her appeal.[70] Moreover, the "letter's only reference to an appeal used the future tense when it stated '[w]e will be reviewing the records and obtaining additional medical information for my client's appeal.'"[71] Thus, the claimant had failed to exhaust her administrative remedies, and the suit was dismissed on summary judgment.[72]

The Stakes of Claim Denials and the UNUM/Provident Scandal

The relationship between participants seeking benefits and insurers reviewing benefit claims can become adversarial. The United States Court of Appeals for the Seventh Circuit observed in *Davis v. UNUM Life Insurance Company of America* that "plan administrators have a duty to all plan participants and beneficiaries to investigate claims and make sure to avoid paying benefits to claimants who are not entitled to receive them."[73] The Seventh Circuit also observed in *Hall v. Life Insurance Company of North America* that individuals "who know that their full income will continue after they stop working may take more risks in their daily lives and will not try as hard to return to work after injury or illness."[74]

Plan administrators are obligated to apply the terms of ERISA plans "solely in the interest of the participants and beneficiaries and . . . for the exclusive purpose of . . . providing benefits to participants and their

68. *Id.* at 787.
69. *Id.* at 788.
70. *Id.*
71. *Id.*
72. *Id.* at 786.
73. Davis v. UNUM Life Ins. Co. of Am., 444 F.3d 569, 575 (7th Cir. 2006) (citing Dougherty v. Ind. Bell Tele. Co., 440 F.3d 910, 916 (7th Cir. 2006); Barnhart v. UNUM Life Ins. Co. of Am., 179 F.3d 583, 589 (8th Cir. 1999)).
74. Hall v. Life Ins. Co. of N. Am., 317 F.3d 773, 775 (7th Cir. 2003).

beneficiaries."[75] Still, the financial incentives for plan administrators to deny claims are undeniable. The largest American disability insurer, UNUM/Provident Corporation, has repeatedly faced suit for engineering improper denials of claims, and courts have frequently found that UNUM/Provident has engaged in aggressive claim-denial practices.[76] In *Bennett v. UNUM Life Insurance Company*, a former staff physician serving as a medical advisor to UNUM/Provident alleged that the corporation had a pervasive practice of denying claims based on the corporation's current profits.[77] In *McSharry v. UNUMProvident Corporation*, a former staff physician testified that the company forced him to use certain types of language to support denials and required him to review too many claims at one time for him to review them properly.[78] In addition, the physician alleged that he was barred from ordering further tests, requesting additional information, or otherwise "help[ing] a claimant perfect a claim for disability insurance benefits."[79]

UNUM/Provident embraced ERISA preemption as a strategic advantage in litigation and even established a task force to ensure ERISA covered its policies.[80] According to an internal memorandum circulated within the corporation, the advantages of ERISA coverage included the absence of jury trials, no compensatory or punitive damages, relief being limited to the recovery of the amount of benefits claimed due, and the opportunity for administrators to receive a deferential standard of review.[81] The memorandum explained:

> In order to take advantage of ERISA protection, we need to be diligent and thorough in determining whether a policy is covered. . . . While

75. 29 U.S.C. § 1104(a)(1)(A)(i) (2012).
76. *See, e.g.*, Moon v. UNUM Provident Corp., 405 F.3d 373, 381 (6th Cir. 2005); Stup v. UNUM Life Ins. Co., 390 F.2d 301, 310 (4th Cir. 2004).
77. Bennett v. UNUM Life Ins. Co., 321 F. Supp. 2d 925, 934–35 (E.D. Tenn. 2004), *abrogated on other grounds by* Myers v. Prudential Ins. Co. of Am., 581 F. Supp. 2d 904, 907 (E.D. Tenn. 2008) (finding that internal memoranda supported "the plaintiff's claim that one of UNUMProvident's corporate goals was to terminate as many ongoing claims and deny as many new claims as possible").
78. McSharry v. UNUMProvident Corp., 237 F. Supp. 2d 875, 877 (E.D. Tenn. 2002).
79. *Id.*
80. Memorandum from Jeff McCall to IDC Management Group & Glenn Felton (Oct. 2, 1995), *available at* http://www.erisa-claims.com/library/provident%20memo.pdf.
81. *Id.*

> our objective is to pay all valid claims and deny invalid claims, there are gray areas, and ERISA applicability may influence our course of action.[82]

Nevertheless, not all of UNUM/Provident's claim denials originated in ERISA policies. When claimants have succeeded in suit against UNUM/Provident outside the ERISA context, courts have awarded sizeable punitive damages to them for the corporation's bad-faith claim denials.[83] In addition, states have forced UNUM/Provident to pay many millions of dollars in fines and to reopen claim denials from various years in the past.[84] ERISA and the Social Security Administration

The relationship between disability benefits under ERISA and those awarded by the Social Security Administration is of tremendous significance. As of December 2013, 10,988,269 individuals were receiving governmental disability benefits, which is more than ever before in history.[85] If individuals receiving governmental disability benefits formed a single state, it would be the eighth largest state in the United States.[86]

The impact of disability determinations by the Social Security Administration on ERISA litigation has evolved over time. One formerly controversial issue in ERISA benefit denials was the applicability of the "treating physician rule," which was a rule adopted by the Commissioner of Social Security giving special weight to a claimant's treating physician in determining eligibility for governmental disability benefits.[87] In *Black & Decker Disability Plan v. Nord*, the Supreme Court of the United States unanimously rejected

---

82. *Id.*
83. *See, e.g.*, Hangarter v. Paul Revere Life Ins. Co., 373 F.3d 998, 1022 (9th Cir. 2004) (sustaining a five million dollar award of punitive damages).
84. *See generally* John H. Langbein, *Trust Law as Regulatory Law: The UNUM/Provident Scandal and Judicial Review of Benefit Denials Under ERISA*, 101 Nw. U. L. Rev. 1315, 1320 (2007).
85. *See generally* Official Social Security Website, http://www.socialsecurity.gov/oact/progdata/icp.html (last visited Mar. 29, 2014).
86. Terence P. Jeffrey, *Record 10,978,040 Now on Disability; 'Disability' Would Be 8th Most Populous State*, NCSNews.com (May 29, 2013, 9:52 AM), http://cnsnews.com/news/article/record-10978040-now-disability-disability-would-be-8th-most-populous-state.
87. Black & Decker Disability Plan v. Nord, 538 U.S. 822, 825 (2003) (citing 20 C.F.R. §§ 404.1527(d)(2), 416.927(d)(2) (2002)).

the operation of the "treating physician rule" in the ERISA context.[88] The Court explained:

> ERISA was enacted to promote the interests of employees and their beneficiaries in employee benefit plans, and to protect contractually defined benefits. The Act furthers these aims in part by regulating the manner in which plans process benefits claims. Plans must provide adequate notice in writing to any participant or beneficiary whose claim for benefits under the plan has been denied, setting forth the specific reasons for such denial, written in a manner calculated to be understood by the participant. ERISA further requires that plan procedures afford a reasonable opportunity . . . for a full and fair review of dispositions adverse to the claimant. Nothing in the Act itself, however, suggests that plan administrators must accord special deference to the opinions of treating physicians. Nor does the Act impose a heightened burden of explanation on administrators when they reject a treating physician's opinion.
>
> ERISA empowers the Secretary of Labor to prescribe such regulations as he finds necessary or appropriate to carry out the statutory provisions securing employee benefit rights. The Secretary's regulations do not instruct plan administrators to accord extra respect to treating physicians' opinions. Notably, the most recent version of the Secretary's regulations, which installs no treating physician rule, issued more than nine years after the Social Security Administration codified a treating physician rule in that agency's regulations.
>
> If the Secretary of Labor found it [appropriate] to adopt a treating physician rule by regulation, courts would examine that determination with appropriate deference. The Secretary has not chosen that course, however, and an *amicus* brief reflecting the position of the Department of Labor opposes adoption of such a rule for disability determinations under plans covered by ERISA. Although Congress expect[ed] courts would develop a federal common law of rights and obligations under

88. *Id.*

> ERISA-regulated plans, the scope of permissible judicial innovation is narrower in areas where other federal actors are engaged.
>
> . . .
>
> Plan administrators, of course, may not arbitrarily refuse to credit a claimant's reliable evidence, including the opinions of a treating physician. But, we hold, courts have no warrant to require administrators automatically to accord special weight to the opinions of a claimant's physician; nor may courts impose on plan administrators a discrete burden of explanation when they credit reliable evidence that conflicts with a treating physician's evaluation.[89]

The Court's reasoning shed light on the limitations courts face when evaluating the validity of the measures used to assess disability claims:

> The question whether a treating physician rule would increas[e] the accuracy of disability determinations under ERISA plans, . . . moreover, seems to us one the Legislature or superintending administrative agency is best positioned to address. As compared to consultants retained by a plan, it may be true that treating physicians, as a rule, ha[ve] a greater opportunity to know and observe the patient as an individual. Nor do we question the Court of Appeals' concern that physicians repeatedly retained by benefits plans may have an incentive to make a finding of not disabled in order to save their employers money and to preserve their own consulting arrangements. But the assumption that the opinions of a treating physician warrant greater credit than the opinions of plan consultants may make scant sense when, for example, the relationship between the claimant and the treating physician has been of short duration, or when a specialist engaged by the plan has expertise the treating physician lacks. And if a consultant engaged by a plan may have an incentive to make a finding of not disabled, so a treating physician, in a close case, may favor a finding of disabled. Intelligent resolution of the question whether routine deference to the opinion of a claimant's treating physician

89. *Id.* at 830–34 (citations and quotation marks omitted).

would yield more accurate disability determinations, it thus appears, might be aided by empirical investigation of the kind courts are ill equipped to conduct.[90]

Vital to its rejection of the treating physician rule, the Court distinguished disability claims brought under the Social Security Act from those brought under ERISA plans:

> Finally, and of prime importance, critical differences between the Social Security disability program and ERISA benefit plans caution against importing a treating physician rule from the former area into the latter. The Social Security Act creates a nationwide benefits program funded by Federal Insurance Contributions Act payments and superintended by the Commissioner of Social Security. To cope with the more than 2.5 million claims for disability benefits [filed] each year, the Commissioner has published detailed regulations governing benefits adjudications. Presumptions employed in the Commissioner's regulations grow out of the need to administer a large benefits system efficiently. By accepting and codifying a treating physician rule, the Commissioner sought to serve that need. Along with other regulations, the treating physician rule works to foster uniformity and regularity in Social Security benefits determinations made in the first instance by a corps of administrative law judges.
>
> In contrast to the obligatory, nationwide Social Security program, [n]othing in ERISA requires employers to establish employee benefits plans. Nor does ERISA mandate what kind of benefits employers must provide if they choose to have such a plan. Rather, employers have large leeway to design disability and other welfare plans as they see fit. In determining entitlement to Social Security benefits, the adjudicator measures the claimant's condition against a uniform set of federal criteria. [T]he validity of a claim to benefits under an ERISA plan, on the other hand, is likely to turn, in large part, on the interpretation of terms in the plan at issue. It is the Secretary of Labor's view that

90. *Id.* at 832 (citations and quotation marks omitted).

> ERISA is best served by preserv[ing] the greatest flexibility possible for . . . operating claims processing systems consistent with the prudent administration of a plan. Deference is due that view.[91]

Despite the Supreme Court's forceful expounding of the differences between Social Security and ERISA disability claims, courts have found Social Security disability determinations to be probative when making ERISA disability benefit determinations.[92] In *Metropolitan Life Insurance Company v. Glenn*, the Supreme Court found "nothing improper" in its review of an administrator who had considered proceedings before the Social Security Administration in determining benefit eligibility.[93] In its 2014 decision *Melech v. Life Insurance Company of North America*, the United States Court of Appeals for the Eleventh Circuit held that, during the appeal of a disability benefit denial, an insurer had the responsibility to consider the evidence presented to the Social Security Administration even though the Social Security Administration had not issued its final determination until after the insurer's benefit denial.[94] In the 2013 case *Govrik v. UNUM Life Insurance Company of America*, the United States Court of Appeals for the Eighth Circuit concluded that it was not an abuse of discretion for a disability insurer to rely on a claimant's statement to the Social Security Administration that had contradicted his statement to the plan administrator.[95]

Evidence from Third Parties

Courts will consider evidence from third parties even outside the context of Social Security Administration disability determinations. In its 2013 decision

91. *Id.* at 832–34 (citations and quotation marks omitted).
92. For example, the United States Court of Appeals for the First Circuit has observed: "Although the SSA's determination of a claimant's entitlement to social security disability benefits is not binding on disability insurers, it can be relevant to an insurer's determination whether that claimant is eligible for disability benefits." Gannon v. Metro. Life Ins. Co., 360 F.3d 211, 215 (1st Cir. 2004) (citing Leahy v. Raytheon Co., 315 F.3d 11, 19 (1st Cir. 2002); Pari-Fasano v. ITT Hartford Life & Accident Ins. Co, 230 F.3d 415, 420 (1st Cir. 2000)).
93. Metro. Life Ins. Co. v. Glenn, 554 U.S. 105, 118 (2008).
94. Melech v. Life Ins. Co. of N. Am., 739 F.3d 663, 666 (11th Cir. 2014).
95. Govrik v. UNUM Life Ins. Co. of Am., 702 F.3d 1103, 1109 (8th Cir. 2013).

Truitt v. UNUM Life Insurance Company of America, the United States Court of Appeals for the Fifth Circuit held that the UNUM Life Insurance Company of America rightfully considered emails provided to the company by a claimant's former companion and that the company was not obligated to investigate the source of the evidence.[96] *Truitt* concerned a claimant, Terri Truitt, who had received long-term disability benefits from UNUM until her former companion came forward with more than 600 pages of e-mails revealing that Truitt had engaged in activities that did not comport with her alleged disability.[97] The court placed the burden on Truitt to discredit the evidence relied on by the plan administrator.[98] The court explained:

> We reiterate that, in the context of ERISA, evidence is tested through a probing administrative process, and that, in that process, issues of inauthenticity, contradiction, unreliability, and bias all may be pertinent. This probing process contemplates that the plan administrator must first identify evidence to support its decision to deny benefits. Then the claimant may attempt to discredit that evidence by, among other things, attacking its source. And, finally, the plan administrator will consider whether, given its asserted deficiencies, the evidence in question continues to support its decision to deny benefits. . . . [T]herefore, [t]here is no justifiable basis for placing the burden solely on the administrator to generate evidence relevant to deciding the claim, which may or may not be available to it, or which may be more readily available to the claimant.[99]

Subjective Evidence

Beyond the objective evidence of a disability offered by professional evaluations and medical testing,[100] a court must also consider subjective evidence of

96. Truitt v. UNUM Life Ins. Co. of Am., 729 F.3d 497, 500 (5th Cir. 2013).
97. *Id.*
98. *Id.*
99. *Id.* at 511–12 (citations and quotation marks omitted).
100. In addition, claimants may request during discovery and courts may consider the number of claimants seeking long-term disability benefits for certain diagnoses and the approval

a disability. In the 2013 case *Miles v. Principal Life Insurance Company*, the United States Court of Appeals for the Second Circuit held that a disability plan administrator did not give adequate weight to a claimant's subjective complaints and that the administrator's demand for objective evidence was unreasonable.[101] *Miles* concerned a commercial real estate attorney, Miles, who stopped working as the result of a high-frequency noise in both of his ears known as tinnitus, intractable ear and head pain, and a feeling of disorientation.[102] When Miles filed for long-term disability benefits, his physician, Dr. Etra, indicated that Miles was diagnosed with tinnitus, hearing loss, and headache and also complained "of a pounding in his head [that is] synchronous with his heartbeat."[103] Dr. Etra further opined:

> I believe at this time he appears to be with significant tinnitus, hearing loss and intractable head pain. Etiology at this point is undetermined. He seems to be very foggy and unable to concentrate and it seems that he will at the present time be unable to carry on his job.[104]

Miles himself provided an in-depth description of his symptoms and the work duties he would be unable to fulfill in his application for benefits.[105] In addition, Miles engaged in a phone interview with Principal Life Insurance Company's claims examiner, during which he continued to elaborate on his symptoms and how the symptoms prevented him from carrying out his work responsibilities.[106] Miles offered to undergo examination during the initial determination stage, but Principal explained that it "relied on the information from treating physicians and exercised its discretion to schedule an examination only if that information proved inadequate."[107]

---

rate of such claims as well as the compensation agreement between insurers and other medical professionals. *See, e.g.*, Zewdu v. Citigroup Long Term Disability Plan, 264 F.R.D. 622, 628 (N.D. Cal. 2010); Santos v. Quebcor World Long Term Disability Plan, 254 F.R.D. 643, 649 (E.D. Cal. 2009).

101. Miles v. Principal Life Ins. Co., 720 F.3d 472, 487–88 (2d Cir. 2013).
102. *Id.* at 475–76.
103. *Id.* at 476.
104. *Id.*
105. *Id.* at 476–77.
106. *Id.* at 477–78.
107. *Id.* at 478.

Months after Miles applied for benefits, Principal sent Miles a letter stating that it had received medical records from his physicians but that it lacked information "regarding specific restrictions and limitations" his symptoms placed on him preventing him from performing his job.[108] The company eventually engaged two specialists to conduct a peer review of Miles' file and discuss with Miles' treating neurologist what impeded Miles' work.[109] One of the reviewers, who did not discuss the case with Miles' treating neurologist, concluded that "[t]here are no objective findings to support impairment from a neurological perspective" and that Miles was "capable of full time work."[110] The other specialist concluded:

> While the claimant has a history of hearing loss, vertigo and ear pain, with the exception of the hearing loss there is no clinical documentation . . . from the treating provider that clearly details any significant or severe positive objective findings or significant severe functional limitations occurring that would have prevented his return back to his regular job. The observeable [sic] information provided does not clearly support severity of impairment with significant limitations of functioning.[111]

The company denied Miles' claim.[112] The denial summarized its reasoning:

> While you have a history of hearing loss, vertigo and ear pain, with the exception of the hearing loss there is no clinical documentation available for review from the treating providers that clearly states . . . any significant severe functional limitations . . . that would have prevented you from returning back to your regular job. The observable information provided does not clearly support the severity of impairment with significant limitations of functioning. Therefore, we are declining your claim for Long Term Disability Benefits as the information

108. *Id.*
109. *Id.* at 479.
110. *Id.*
111. *Id.*
112. *Id.* at 479–80.

> we have received does not support the severity of symptoms related to a condition/conditions that would prevent you from performing your Own Occupation.[113]

The company reaffirmed its decision after Miles appealed, stating that the "description of his symptoms . . . does not match any recognizable pattern of any primary or secondary headaches syndrome known to neurologists."[114] Miles brought suit and argued that he had "met all his obligations under the terms of the Policy and the Plan" and that the company had "arbitrarily and capriciously denied [his] claim for benefits and then arbitrarily and capriciously failed to provide a full and fair review of that denial."[115]

In siding with Miles, the court found that the company had failed to adequately consider Miles' subjective complaints:

> Looking to the record before us, we conclude that Principal did not give adequate attention to Miles's subjective complaints, as it failed to either assign any weight to them or to provide specific reasons for its decision to discount them. Instead, in its initial denial, Principal cited Dr. Etra's statement that the tinnitus was subjective as a reason for denying Miles's claims. Pointing out that evidence is subjective is not, by itself, a proper basis to reject evidence. Moreover, Principal failed to mention that Dr. Etra himself had found these subjective complaints credible, concluding that Miles appears to be with significant tinnitus, hearing loss, and intractable head pain. As Principal cites to no reason to discount the evidence (other than its subjective nature), we conclude that Principal arbitrarily rejected Miles's subjective evidence of disability.
>
> In its final determination, Principal continued to point to the subjective nature of Miles's complaints as the only basis for disregarding the evidence. For example, Principal stated that Miles's self-reported loss of orientation and concentration was never verified by objective testing and remained self-reported only, and pointed out that [m]any

113. *Id.* at 480.
114. *Id.* at 484.
115. *Id.* at 484–85.

> of the claimant's complaints . . . [were] never observed by his neurologist and [were] never confirmed by exams. However, as discussed above, pointing out that evidence is subjective is not, standing alone, a reasonable basis on which to accord that evidence limited weight. Since subjective evidence is more than ample to establish [Miles's] disability, if believed, Principal must do more than simply point to the subjective nature of the evidence when denying his claim. It must either assign some weight to the evidence or provide a reason for its decision not to do so.
>
> Principal has identified nothing in the present record that would support a rejection of Miles's subjective complaints. Though there is no objective evidence of tinnitus, multiple specialists have said there is no objective test for it. Tinnitus is consistent with hearing loss, for which there are objective tests, and the record indicates that there is undisputed objective evidence of such hearing loss in Miles's case. Finally, as the Commissioner of Social Security observed in crediting Miles's account of his symptoms, Miles's long history of hard work supports his credibility on this issue. We do not mean to suggest that Principal is required on remand to credit Miles's statements regarding the nature and severity of his subjective symptoms. However, considering the present record as a whole, we conclude that Principal acted arbitrarily and capriciously by disregarding Miles's subjective complaints without providing any reason for this decision.[116]

As a final note, the use of subjective evidence is particularly important for denials of disability benefits relating to mental health issues, as these issues may not be readily discernible using quantitative measures. The extent to which mental health issues are covered and thus the validity of administrators' claim denials are plan-specific inquiries, with the language of the plan generally functioning as the focal point of a court's analysis alongside subjective and other evidence of the claimant's disability.[117]

116. *Id.* at 487–88 (citations and quotation marks omitted).

117. *See, e.g.*, Mattox v. Life Ins. Co. of N. Am., 536 F. Supp. 2d 1307 (N.D. Ga. 2009), *aff'd*, 395 F. App'x 669 (11th Cir. 2010).

Chapter 8

ERISA Disclosure

Reporting and disclosure requirements apply to all ERISA plans.[1] The statutory notice and disclosure rules are designed to apprise the participants of their position with respect to the plan benefits and to ensure that they understand their rights under the plan, who to contact for information regarding the plan, and how to file claims for benefits.[2]

A fiduciary is responsible for complying with the statutory disclosure rules. Fiduciary's compliance has two fundamental forms. One is an affirmative compliance where the fiduciary must automatically disclose information; ERISA § 104(b)(1) mandates that plan administrators furnish certain documents to participants and beneficiaries who are receiving benefits under the plan, whether or not they request such documents.[3] The other form of compliance is disclosure upon request for information by the participant or beneficiary, such as requests to view the agreements establishing the plan.[4]

The Summary Plan Description

One of the most important documents that an administrator must prepare and provide to participants and beneficiaries pursuant to the statutory

1. 29 U.S.C. §§ 1021–31 (2012).
2. H.R. Rep. No. 93-533, at 11 (1973); *see also* Firestone Tire & Rubber Co. v. Bruch, 489 U.S. 101, 117 (1989) (holding that plan participants are entitled to disclosure of benefit plan information under ERISA).
3. 29 U.S.C. § 1024(b)(1) (2012).
4. 29 U.S.C. § 1024(b)(2), (4) (2012).

disclosure rules is the summary plan description (SPD). ERISA requires that plan administrators provide beneficiaries with an SPD explaining the features of the plan.[5] The administrator, who typically drafts this document, must include specific information, including identifying information about any administrators and trustees, written in an easily understandable manner.[6]

ERISA grants the plan administrator some latitude with respect to the timing of the distribution of the SPD. A copy of the SPD must be given to each participant within 90 days of becoming a participant, 90 days after first receiving a benefit, or 120 days after the plan comes into legal existence.[7] In addition, a summary of any non-health-care material modification in the terms of the plan and any change in the information includable in the SPD must be furnished to participants and beneficiaries no later than 210 days after the close of the plan year in which the modification or change was adopted.[8]

If a plan is amended many times during the course of an employee's participation, receipt of every modification would be unwieldy and therefore counterproductive to the goal of apprising the participant of critical information. Accordingly, § 104(b)(1) requires the plan administrator to prepare and furnish participants and beneficiaries with an updated SPD every five years, and the updated SPD must incorporate all plan amendments made during that five-year interval.[9] If there are no plan amendments during that time, § 104(b)(1) requires the distribution of updated SPDs only at ten-year intervals.[10] Both the five-year and ten-year intervals are measured beginning from the date the plan became subject to ERISA's reporting and disclosure requirements.[11]

Administrators must also make the SPD and other documents available for examination. Specifically, § 104(b)(2) provides:

---

5. 29 U.S.C. § 1024(b)(4) (2012).
6. 29 U.S.C. §1022(a)(1) (2012).
7. 29 U.S.C. § 1024(b)(1) (2012).
8. *Id.*
9. *Id.*
10. *Id.*
11. *Id.*

> The administrator shall make copies of the latest updated summary plan description and the latest annual report and the bargaining agreement, trust agreement, contract, or other instruments under which the plan was established or is operated available for examination by any plan participant or beneficiary in the principal office of the administrator and in such other places as may be necessary to make available all pertinent information to all participants (including such places as the Secretary may prescribe by regulations).[12]

The SPD must contain:

> The name and type of administration of the plan; in the case of a group health plan . . . , whether a health insurance issuer . . . is responsible for the financing or administration (including payment of claims) of the plan and (if so) the name and address of such issuer; the name and address of the person designated as agent for the service of legal process, if such person is not the administrator; the name and address of the administrator; names, titles, and addresses of any trustee or trustees (if they are persons different from the administrator); a description of the relevant provisions of any applicable collective bargaining agreement; the plan's requirements respecting eligibility for participation and benefits; a description of the provisions providing for nonforfeitable pension benefits; circumstances which may result in disqualification, ineligibility, or denial or loss of benefits; the source of financing of the plan and the identity of any organization through which benefits are provided; the date of the end of the plan year and whether the records of the plan are kept on a calendar, policy, or fiscal year basis; the procedures to be followed in presenting claims for benefits under the plan including the office at the Department of Labor through which participants and beneficiaries may seek assistance or information regarding their rights under this chapter and the Health Insurance Portability and Accountability Act of 1996 with respect to health benefits that are offered through a group health plan . . . , the

12. 29 U.S.C. § 1024(b)(2) (2012).

> remedies available under the plan for the redress of claims which are denied in whole or in part . . . , and if the employer so elects . . . , the model notice applicable to the State in which the participants and beneficiaries reside.[13]

Litigation under ERISA's statutory disclosure rules typically concern the SPD and, in particular, issues pertaining to conflicts between the plan and the SPD, inadequacies in the SPD, and delay or failure to provide the SPD or modifications to it. Failures to timely respond to document requests are also especially likely to result in litigation.

Conflicts Between the SPD and the Plan

When there is a discrepancy between the SPD and plan, the Supreme Court has refused to equate the SPD with the plan or to enforce the SPD as if it were the terms of a plan.[14] In *CIGNA Corporation v. Amara*, the Supreme Court stated:

> [W]e cannot agree that the terms of statutorily required plan summaries (or summaries of plan modifications) necessarily may be enforced (under §502(a)(1)(B)) as the terms of the plan itself. . . . The syntax of that provision, requiring that participants and beneficiaries be advised of their rights and obligations "under the plan," suggests that the information *about* the plan provided by those disclosures is not itself *part* of the plan.[15]

The Court further explained:

> The SPD is not part of the ERISA plan, and it is not written by plan's sponsor. Although in this case CIGNA wrote both the plan and the SPD, it did so in different capacities: as sponsor when writing the

13. 29 U.S.C. § 1022(b) (2012).
14. CIGNA Corp. v. Amara, 131 S. Ct. 1866, 1877 (2011).
15. *Id.*

plan, and as administrator when preparing the SPD. ERISA carefully distinguishes these roles.[16]

The Court pointed out that if SPD terms were enforceable, plan administrators might use more complex language in SPDs and thereby thwart their purpose, which is to provide "clear, simple communication."[17] Courts after *Amara* have recognized that the SPD is neither a plan document nor legally binding.[18] Consequently, where the SPD and the plan terms conflict, the plan controls.[19]

Inadequacies in the SPD

Participants often challenge the SPD on the grounds that they were not adequately apprised, as required by federal regulation, of the "circumstances which may result in disqualification, ineligibility, or denial, loss, forfeiture, suspension, offset, reduction, or recovery . . . of any benefits that a participant or beneficiary might otherwise reasonably expect the plan to provide" or the remedies under the plan to redress claim denials.[20]

The SPD does not need to include specific formulas used to grant or deny benefits. Where a vested employee opts for early retirement, there is typically an actuarial reduction in benefits to reflect the fact that the payout will span a longer period. In *McCarthy v. Dun & Bradstreet Corporation*, the United States Court of Appeals for the Second Circuit found it adequate that an SPD contained the circumstances under which benefits would be reduced even though it did not articulate the specific method of actuarial reduction.[21] Similarly, in *Morse v. Stanley*, the Second Circuit rejected the argument that trustees had violated their duties by failing to disclose a

16. *Id.* at 1884–85 (citations and quotation marks omitted).
17. *Id.* at 1877.
18. *See* Engleson v. UNUM Life Ins. Co. of Am., 723 F.3d 611, 620 (6th Cir. 2013) (citing Moore v. Menasha Corp., 690 F.3d 444, 455–56 (6th Cir. 2012)); Eugene S. v. Horizon Blue Cross Blue Shield of N.J., 663 F.3d 1124, 1131 (10th Cir. 2011); Skinner v. Northrop Grumman Ret. Plan B, 673 F.3d 1162, 1167 (9th Cir. 2012).
19. *Amara*, 131 S. Ct. at 1884.
20. 29 C.F.R. § 2520.102–03 (2013).
21. McCarthy v. Dun & Bradstreet Corp, 482 F.3d 184, 196 (2d Cir. 2007).

specific policy of denying acceleration of profit-sharing benefits in an ERISA plan or its SPD.[22] The *Morse* court explained:

> [H]ere there is no denial of benefits required under the Plan to any of these plaintiffs, and they ultimately will receive all of their benefits, with interest, upon reaching age 65. Under the Plan's terms, payment of benefits is mandated only upon participant's reaching his normal or early retirement date or on account of his death or disability. Payment of benefits under other circumstances is expressly left to the Trustees' sole discretion. Were we to require the Trustees to spell out those circumstances in which accelerated distribution would be granted or denied, we would read out of the Plan the discretionary powers expressly granted to the Trustees to act as varying circumstances arise.[23]

Although the SPD need not provide specific formulas, the SPD may not be misleading. Federal regulation provides:

> The format of the summary plan description must not have the effect to [sic] misleading, misinforming or failing to inform participants and beneficiaries. Any description of exception, limitations, reductions, and other restrictions of plan benefits shall not be minimized, rendered obscure or otherwise made to appear unimportant. Such exceptions, limitations, reductions, or restrictions of plan benefits shall be described or summarized in a manner not less prominent than the style, captions, printing type, and prominence used to describe or summarize plan benefits. The advantages and disadvantages of the plan shall be presented without either exaggerating the benefits or minimizing the limitations. The description or summary of restrictive plan provisions need not be disclosed in the summary plan description in close conjunction with the description or summary of benefits, provided that adjacent to the benefit description the page on which the restrictions are described is noted.[24]

---

22. Morse v. Stanley, 732 F.2d 1139, 1147 (2d Cir. 1984).
23. *Id.*
24. 29 C.F.R. § 2520.102-2 (2013).

Even if the SPD itself is not misleading, it could be considered misleading if it incorporates misleading documents by reference. In *Harris v. Amgen, Inc.*, the United States Court of Appeals for the Ninth Circuit found that an employer's SEC filings were incorporated by reference in the SPDs of employer-sponsored plans and that certain statements in the SEC filings "were materially false and misleading."[25] The employer had explicitly incorporated by reference its filings in the SPDs it distributed to participants.[26] The court agreed with a Sixth Circuit decision, *Dudenhoefer v. Fifth Third Bancorp*, that this incorporation by reference constituted an act performed in a fiduciary capacity:

> Defendants exercised discretion in choosing to incorporate the [SEC] filings into the Plan's SPD as a direct source of information for Plan participants about the financial health of [the company] and the value of its stock, an investment option under the plan. The SPD is a fiduciary communication to plan participants and selecting the information to convey through the SPD is a fiduciary activity. Moreover, whether the fiduciary states information in the SPD itself or incorporates by reference another document containing that information is of no moment. To hold otherwise would authorize fiduciaries to convey misleading or patently untrue information through documents incorporated by reference, all while safely insulated from ERISA's governing reach. Such a result is inconsistent with the intent and stated purposes of ERISA . . . and would create a loophole in ERISA large enough to devour all its protections.[27]

In *Amgen*, the Ninth Circuit concluded that the filings could therefore be used to show that the defendants were aware or should have been aware that shares affecting the profit-sharing plans were inflated and that the plaintiffs detrimentally relied on the defendants' statements.[28] The Supreme

25. Harris v. Amgen, Inc., 738 F.3d 1026, 1044 (9th Cir. 2013), *vacated*, 134 S.Ct. 2870, 2871 (2014).
26. *Id.* at 1043.
27. *Id.* at 1044 (citing Dudenhoefer v. Fifth Third Bancorp, 692 F.3d 410, 423 (6th Cir. 2012)).
28. *Id.* at 1044.

Court has since vacated the Sixth Circuit decision *Dudenhoeffer v. Fifth Third Bancorp* on which the *Amgen* court relied.[29] The final outcome of the controversy at issue in *Amgen* is not settled at the time of this writing, as the Supreme Court recently vacated and remanded the Ninth Circuit's decision for reconsideration in light of the Court's decision in *Fifth Third Bancorp v. Dudenhoeffer*.[30]

Failure to Timely Furnish SPD Modifications

Modifications to the SPD must be furnished in a timely fashion to the participant or beneficiary personally,[31] and making the modifications available for inspection is not enough. Under federal regulation, the summary of the modification provided to participants must be "written in a manner calculated to be understood by the average plan participant."[32] Pursuant to the Affordable Care Act, modifications to health-care benefits must be given 60 days in advance.[33] Plan modifications like changes to fiduciaries' addresses or identities and changes to the address of the plan's agent for service of process must be communicated but do not constitute "plan amendments" triggering the distribution of an updated SPD.[34] Amendments can be rendered ineffective if the disclosure requirements for modifications are not followed and claimants show bad faith, active concealment, detrimental reliance, and sufficient harm from the failure to disclose.[35]

There are other documents that administrators must affirmatively furnish to participants or beneficiaries. The plan administrator must furnish a summary annual report (SAR) to all participants and to all beneficiaries actually receiving benefits under the plan.[36] This is the SAR required for

29. Fifth Third Bancorp v. Dudenhoeffer, 134 S.Ct. 2459, 2473 (2014).
30. Amgen v. Harris, 134 S.Ct. 2870, 2871 (2014).
31. 29 U.S.C. § 1024(b)(1) (2012).
32. 29 C.F.R. § 2520.104b-3 (2013).
33. 29 U.S.C. § 1024(b)(1) (2012).
34. 29 C.F.R. § 2520.104b-2 (2013).
35. Murphy v. Keystone Steel & Wire Co., 61 F.3d 560, 569 (7th Cir. 1995); Godwin v. Sun Life Assurance Co. of Can., 980 F.2d 323, 328 (5th Cir. 1992); Veilleux v. Atochem N. Am., Inc., 929 F.2d 74, 76 (2d Cir. 1991).
36. 29 U.S.C. § 1024(b)(3) (2012).

annual filing with the IRS. The SAR must be furnished to participants and beneficiaries within 210 days after the close of each plan year.[37] Administrators of defined benefit plans must furnish funding notices.

Document Requests

ERISA requires the administrator to furnish benefit statements upon written request.[38] Upon a written request from a beneficiary or participant, administrators must make available "the latest updated summary plan description, and the latest annual report, any terminal report, the bargaining agreement, trust agreement, contract, or other instruments under which the plan is established or operated."[39]

The request must be in writing.[40] Courts have found that a letter, even when not artfully drafted, could suffice[41] but that a scribbled note at the bottom of a social security card did not.[42] In *Haberern v. Kaupp Vascular Surgeons*, the United States Court of Appeals for the Third Circuit rejected the argument that a letter requesting a meeting and complaining that certain materials had not been supplied was not a written request.[43] At no point did the letter request that the missing materials be supplied.[44]

Upon request, administrators must provide "other instruments under which the plan is established or operated."[45] When participants or beneficiaries request documents that are not specifically enumerated in the statute, the challenge for the court is to determine whether the documents requested fall within this general category. In this context, issues that commonly arise concern whether the documents requested are governing documents within

37. 29 U.S.C. § 1024(a)(1) (2012).
38. 29 U.S.C. § 1025 (2012).
39. 29 U.S.C. § 1024(b)(4) (2012).
40. *See* Boone v. Leavenworth Anesthesia, Inc., 20 F.3d 1108, 1110 (10th Cir. 1994) (citing Tracey v. Heublein, Inc., 772 F. Supp. 726, 727 (D. Conn. 1991)).
41. *Id.* at 1111.
42. Fisher v. Metro. Life Ins. Co., 895 F.2d 1073, 1077 (5th Cir. 1990).
43. Haberern v. Kaupp Vascular Surgeons Ltd. Defined Ben. Pension Plan, 24 F.3d 1491, 1505 (3d Cir. 1994).
44. *Id.*
45. 29 U.S.C. § 1024(b)(4) (2012).

the meaning of the statute and whether the request for these documents was clear.

Most courts interpret the phrase "other instruments under which the plan is established" narrowly to refer only to formal documents that pertain to the establishment and operation of the plan.[46] A typical request for "other instruments" asks for internal guidelines or memoranda upon which a claim's benefit denial was decided. Since these are not specifically listed in the disclosure statute, many courts have concluded that internal documents or memoranda that claims administrators may use to decide whether or not to grant a claim for benefits does not fall into "other instruments." They are used internally and informally, are not necessarily binding on the claims administrator, and therefore cannot be considered a formal document governing the operation of the plan.[47]

In its 2013 unpublished decision *Fox v. Blue Cross & Blue Shield of Florida, Inc.*, the United States Court of Appeals for the Eleventh Circuit rejected the appeal of a claimant, Brian Fox, arguing that Blue Cross's failure to disclose what it relied on to calculate and verify an allowed benefit amount violated ERISA.[48] The court explained why documents used to calculate a benefit amount are not subject to disclosure:

> Blue Cross responds that . . . the documents Fox requested in his complaint—those that Blue Cross relied on to calculate and verify the Allowed Amount—are not subject to disclosure under § 1024(b)(4). We agree. Fox argues only that these documents qualify as other instruments under which the plan is established or operated and must therefore be disclosed. But that provision encompasses formal or legal documents under which a plan is set up or managed. Because the documents Blue Cross used to calculate and verify the Allowed Amount are not such documents, Blue Cross's failure to disclose them

46. *See* Mondry v. Am. Family Mut. Ins. Co., 557 F.3d 781, 797 (7th Cir. 2009); Faircloth v. Lundy Packing Co., 91 F.3d 648, 653 (4th Cir. 1996); Gabrenya v. Managed Disability Plan, No. 2:12-CV-1217, 2013 WL 6154573, at *3 (S.D. Ohio Nov. 20, 2013).
47. *See e.g.*, Doe v. Travelers Ins. Co., 167 F.3d 53, 60 (1st Cir. 1999).
48. Fox v. Blue Cross & Blue Shield of Fla. Inc., 517 F. App'x 754, 757 (11th Cir. 2013), *cert. denied*, 134 S. Ct. 902 (2014).

> did not violate § 1024(b)(4), and the district court correctly dismissed Fox's claim.[49]

A few courts as well as the Department of Labor, in an opinion letter, have disagreed and would consider such documents "instruments under which the plan is established."[50]

Claim forms, enrollment forms, and e-mails do not fall under the disclosure requirements because they do not provide information on how the plan is operated.[51] In *Jordan v. Tyson Foods, Inc.*, the court held that items like enrollment forms, envelopes, and e-mail are not covered within § 1024(b)(4).[52] The court reasoned:

> It is undisputed that the three documents at issue do not constitute a summary plan description, annual report, terminal report, bargaining agreement, trust agreement, or contract. The only contention that remains . . . is that these documents constitute other instruments under which the plan is established or operated. But any contention in that regard lacks merit. This court has held that the term other instruments in § 1024(b)(4) is . . . properly limited to those class of documents which provide a plan participant with information concerning how the plan is operated.[53]

In *Faircloth v. Lundy Packing Company*, the United States Court of Appeals for the Fourth Circuit held that documents containing the funding and investment policies of the plan are considered instruments upon which a plan is established or operated and therefore must be provided upon request.[54]

49. *Id.* (citations and quotation marks omitted).
50. Hernandez ex rel. Hernandez v. Prudential Ins. Co. of Am., No. 2:99-CV-898B, 2001 WL 1152835, at *6 (D. Utah Mar. 28, 2001); Teen Help, Inc. v. Operating Eng'rs Health & Welfare Trust Fund, No. C 98-2084 VRW, 1999 WL 1069756, at *1 (N.D. Cal. Aug. 24, 1999); Lee v. Dayton Power & Light Co., 604 F. Supp. 987, 1002 (S.D. Ohio 1985); Dep't of Labor Adv. Op. Letter 96-14a (July 31, 1996).
51. *See* Jordan v. Tyson Foods, Inc., 312 F. App'x 726, 733–34 (6th Cir. 2008); Allinder v. Inter-City Prods. Corp. (USA), 152 F.3d 544, 549 (6th Cir. 1998); Arsenault, 724 F. Supp. 1064, 1065–67 (D. Mass. 1989); Wesley v. Monsanto Co., 554 F. Supp. 93, 98 (E.D. Mo. 1982).
52. *Jordan*, 312 F. App'x at 734.
53. *Id.* (citations and quotation marks omitted).
54. Faircloth v. Lundy Packing Co., 91 F.3d 648, 655 (4th Cir. 1996).

Likewise, in *Bartling v. Fruehauf Corporation*, the United States Court of Appeals for the Sixth Circuit held that actuarial valuation reports that were "indispensable to the operation of the plan" and a written protocol detailing the procedures followed to determine benefits under the plan must be disclosed upon request.[55]

In requesting documents, the participant or beneficiary must be specific. In *Kollman v. Hewitt Associates*, the United States Court of Appeals for the Third Circuit held that a request for "[a]ll documents of any nature which relate, reflect or refer" to an adjustment in benefits was not specific enough to trigger the disclosure requirement.[56] The court explained:

> Each decision depended upon the circumstances of that case and no general rule can be formulated. We should look to whether either the request or the response indicates that [defendant] knew or should have known that [plaintiff] had requested a copy of any document relating to the . . . [p]lan.[57]

Penalties

The statutory penalties for the unjustified failure to comply with the notice and disclosure requirements can be exorbitant. The principal sanctions for violating the reporting and disclosure requirements are a fine of $5,000 or less, imprisonment for one year or less, or both, "except that in the case of such violation by a person not an individual," in which case the fine cannot exceed $100,000.[58] In addition, 18 U.S.C. § 1027 provides:

> Whoever, in any document required by title I of the Employee Retirement Income Security Act of 1974 . . . to be published, or kept as part of the records of any employee welfare benefit plan or employee pension benefit plan, or certified to the administrator of any such plan,

55. Bartling v. Fruehauf Corp., 29 F.3d 1062, 1070 (6th Cir. 1994).
56. Kollman v. Hewitt Assocs., 487 F.3d 139, 146–47 (3d Cir. 2007).
57. *Id.* at 145 (citations and quotation marks omitted).
58. 29 U.S.C. § 1131 (2012).

> makes any false statement or representation of fact, knowing it to be false, or knowingly conceals, covers up, or fails to disclose any fact the disclosure of which is required by such title or is necessary to verify, explain, clarify or check for accuracy and completeness any report required by such title to be published or any information required by such title to be certified, shall be fined under this title, or imprisoned not more than five years, or both.[59]

Civil fines are the most frequently applied type of penalty. The Secretary of Labor, participants, and beneficiaries are authorized by § 502(a)(4) to bring a civil action in federal district court for relief under § 502(c), which provides:

> Any administrator (A) who fails to meet the requirements of . . . this title with respect to a participant or beneficiary, or (B) who fails or refuses to comply with a request for any information which such administrator is required . . . to furnish to a participant or beneficiary (unless such failure or refusal results from matters reasonably beyond the control of the administrator) by mailing the material requested to the last known address of the requesting participant or beneficiary within 30 days after such request may in the court's discretion be personally liable to such participant or beneficiary in the amount of up to $100 a day from the date of such failure or refusal, and the court may in its discretion order such other relief as it deems proper. For purposes of this paragraph, each violation described in subparagraph (A) with respect to any single participant, and each violation described in subparagraph (B) with respect to any single participant or beneficiary, shall be treated as a separate violation.[60]

For example, in *Daniels v. Thomas Betts Corporation*, a plaintiff requested "the instruments under which [an ERISA] plan is established or operated."[61] The United States Court of Appeals for the Third Circuit imposed penalties because no excuses were forthcoming for an extraordinary delay of

59. 18 U.S.C. § 1027 (2012).
60. 29 U.S.C. § 1132(c) (2012).
61. Daniels v. Thomas Betts Corp., 263 F.3d 66, 72 (3d Cir. 2001).

291 days.[62] Penalties were imposed for 261 days because the first 30 days were excluded, and the court also held that the plaintiff maintained "beneficiary" status to bring the action even though she had received all the insurance benefits to which she was entitled before the time of the appeal.[63]

The statutory penalty provisions are designed to be punitive and not compensatory.[64] Prejudice to the participant or beneficiary who failed to receive a requested document and the administrator's bad faith when refusing to submit the requested documents are factors to be considered when determining the amount of the statutory penalty.[65] Equitable remedies like surcharge are available under § 502(a)(3) for discrepancies between the SPD and the plan upon a showing of actual harm.[66]

62. Id. at 79–80.
63. Id. at 72–73, 78.
64. Daughtrey v. Honeywell, Inc., 3 F.3d 1488, 1494–95 (11th Cir. 1993).
65. Crosby v. Rohm & Haas Co., 480 F.3d 423, 432 (6th Cir. 2007); Moothart v. Bell, 21 F.3d 1499, 1506 (10th Cir. 1994); Rodriguez-Abreu v. Chase Manhattan Bank, N.A., 986 F.2d 580, 588 (1st Cir. 1993).
66. CIGNA Corp. v. Amara, 131 S. Ct. 1866, 1881 (2011).

Chapter 9

Spousal Protections

Participants in ERISA pension plans may not assign or alienate their interests in plan benefits.[1] This is popularly known as the spendthrift rule, and it prevents joint ownership of a pension plan and limits encumbrances on pension plan benefits.[2] Prior to the Retirement Equity Act's amendments to ERISA, the spendthrift rule greatly limited a participant's spouse's plan interests, which was particularly harmful for unemployed women caring for their children and home when ERISA passed in 1974.

Spousal Survivorship Rights

The Retirement Equity Act of 1984 amended ERISA to require pension plans to provide automatic surviving spouse benefits and thus a flow of income to surviving spouses. Under the Retirement Equity Act, a married participant who survives to retirement age has the right to receive pension benefits in the form of a qualified joint and survivor annuity (QJSA), ensuring that payments will continue throughout the lives of both the spouse and the participant.[3] Moreover, if a vested participant dies before an annuity start date, then a surviving spouse to whom the participant had been married for at least one year, if the plan so provides, will receive a qualified

1. 26 U.S.C. § 401(a)(13)(A) (2012).
2. 26 U.S.C. § 401(a)(13)(B) (2012).
3. 29 U.S.C. § 1055(a)(1) (2012).

preretirement survivor annuity (QPSA).[4] These rights can be waived under specific circumstances.[5] A QPSA is an annuity that must be at least 50 percent of the annuity in which the participant had a vested right.[6] Federal regulation explicitly states that the automatic survivor annuity requirements of ERISA do not apply to individual retirement accounts (IRAs), which exist beyond ERISA's reach.[7] In *Charles Schwab and Company, Inc. v. Debickero*, the United States Court of Appeals for the Ninth Circuit observed that this exclusion included funds that were rolled into an IRA from an ERISA-governed plan.[8]

---

4. 29 U.S.C. § 1055(a)(2) (2012); *see also* Dorn v. Int'l Broth. of Elec. Workers, 211 F.3d 938, 946–47 (5th Cir. 2000) (explaining that a claimant should not qualify as a surviving spouse when she was not married to the participant during the applicable election period, on the annuity starting date, or at the time of the participant's death).

5. Section 1055(c) allows the protective joint and survivor annuity and preretirement survivor annuity to be waived. The statute states:

> (1) A plan meets the requirements of this section only if—
>
> (A) under the plan, each participant—
>
> (i) may elect at any time during the applicable election period to waive the qualified joint and survivor annuity form of benefit or the qualified preretirement survivor annuity form of benefit (or both),
>
> (ii) if the participant elects a waiver under clause (i), may elect the qualified optional survivor annuity at any time during the applicable election period, and
>
> (iii) may revoke any such election at any time during the applicable election period, and
>
> (B) the plan meets the requirements of paragraphs (2), (3), and (4).
>
> (2) Each plan shall provide that an election under paragraph (1)(A)(i) shall not take effect unless—
>
> (A) (i) the spouse of the participant consents in writing to such election, (ii) such election designates a beneficiary (or a form of benefits) which may not be changed without spousal consent (or the consent of the spouse expressly permits designations by the participant without any requirement of further consent by the spouse), and (iii) the spouse's consent acknowledges the effect of such election and is witnessed by a plan representative or a notary public, or
>
> (B) it is established to the satisfaction of a plan representative that the consent required under subparagraph (A) may not be obtained because there is no spouse, because the spouse cannot be located, or because of such other circumstances as the Secretary of the Treasury may by regulations prescribe.
>
> Any consent by a spouse (or establishment that the consent of a spouse may not be obtained) under the preceding sentence shall be effective only with respect to such spouse. 29 U.S.C. § 1055(c) (2012).

6. 29 U.S.C. § 1055(e)(2) (2012). The QPSA of a defined benefit plan is calculated under § 1055(e)(1).

7. 26 C.F.R. § 1.401(a)-20(A-3)(d) (2013).

8. Charles Schwab & Co., Inc. v Debickero, 593 F. 3d 916, 922 (9th Cir. 2010).

These rules also do not apply to individual accounts under certain circumstances. An "individual account plan" is a "defined contribution plan," which ERISA defines as "a pension plan which provides for an individual account for each participant and for benefits based solely upon the amount contributed to the participant's account, and any income, expenses, gains and losses, and any forfeitures of accounts of other participants which may be allocated to such participant's account."[9]

The determination of who is a lawful spouse, after successive marriages, for purposes of ERISA survivorship rights, is a state-law issue that is not preempted by ERISA. Identification in a plan document of an individual as a spouse does not constitute a de facto waiver and is not dispositive in the face of a credible allegation that a previous marriage was not dissolved. In *IBEW Pacific Coast Pension Fund v. Lee*, the United States Court of Appeals for the Sixth Circuit reversed a lower court's determination that there was no material factual dispute where a spouse was a named pension beneficiary, because the district court did not properly evaluate whether the participant had divorced a former spouse in accordance with state law.[10] The participant, Wayne, had identified his spouse Lois as the beneficiary of a pension plan, but Wayne had previously married Cleta.[11] According to the Sixth Circuit, Cleta and Wayne had never appeared to divorce, which presented a major barrier to the lower court's finding that Lois's interest

9. 29 U.S.C. § 1002(34). Plans meeting the certain conditions are exempt from the requirement:

(i) such plan provides that the participant's nonforfeitable accrued benefit (reduced by any security interest held by the plan by reason of a loan outstanding to such participant) is payable in full, on the death of the participant, to the participant's surviving spouse (or, if there is no surviving spouse or the surviving spouse consents in the manner required under subsection (c)(2) of this section, to a designated beneficiary),

(ii) such participant does not elect the payment of benefits in the form of a life annuity, and

(iii) with respect to such participant, such plan is not a direct or indirect transferee (in a transfer after December 31, 1984) of a plan which is described in subparagraph (A) or (B) or to which this clause applied with respect to the participant. 29 U.S.C. § 1055(b)(i)(C) (2012).

"Transfer" in section (ii) refers to involuntary transfers. *See* Leckey v. Stefano, 501 F.3d 212 (3d Cir. 2007).

10. IBEW Pacific Coast Pension Fund v. Lee, 462 F. App'x 546, 548 (6th Cir. 2012).

11. *Id.* at 549.

in the benefits should prevail over Cleta's interest as a matter of law.[12] The court reasoned:

> Wayne identified Lois as his spouse, but the validity of that designation appears to be incorrect. Mississippi, the state in which Wayne and Lois married, observes a presumption in favor of the validity of a successive marriage, but that presumption may be overcome with evidence that the first marriage was not dissolved by divorce or annulment. Washington and Tennessee maintain the same rule. Relying on Wayne's designation of Lois as his spousal beneficiary, the district court did not determine whether the marriage between Wayne and Cleta was dissolved by divorce. From the record it appears likely that their marriage was not, though we leave that question for the district court to answer after appropriate inquiry. If it was not dissolved by divorce or annulment, then Cleta would be Wayne's surviving spouse. And Cleta's status as Wayne's surviving spouse would take precedence over Wayne's express selection of Lois as his spouse and beneficiary, because Cleta has not waived receipt of the benefits as required by 29 U.S.C. § 1055(c)(2)(A).
>
> Reliance on state law for determining Wayne's marital status does not run afoul of ERISA's preemptive effect on state laws that relate to an ERISA plan. Plan administrators and federal courts routinely rely on state law to identify a participant's spouse in determining the proper recipient of spousal benefits. In fact, the failure to rely on the state-law determination of the identity of Wayne's lawful spouse would conflict with the plan documents' definition of spouse, which in turn would represent a failure to honor the primacy of the written plan governing Wayne's benefits. And if Cleta is Wayne's surviving spouse, then both § 1055(c)(2)(A) and the implementing provision of Wayne's plan documents prohibited him from naming a beneficiary other than Cleta without her permission by notarized writing.
>
> The terms of § 1055(c)(2)(A) have been appropriately described as clear and unambiguous, and the courts have applied it as such. . . . The

12. *Id.* at 549–50.

> provision's application to this case appears clear and unambiguous . . . : simply selecting Lois as his beneficiary could not overcome the stringent requirements of § 1055(c)(2)(A), which condition Wayne's selection of Lois on Cleta's permission.[13]

With respect to waiver of survivorship benefits, litigation often surrounds whether the waiver was flawed in some way. Even if a waiver facially conforms to the statutory requirements, if the plan fiduciary has actual knowledge of its possible invalidity or if there is coercion or fraud, the waiver will not be respected. Therefore, a fiduciary's conduct may render a waiver inoperable. In the unpublished opinion *Canestri v. NYSA-ILA Pension Trust Fund & Plan*, the United States District Court for the District of New Jersey explained:

> ERISA requires that a fiduciary shall discharge his duties with respect to a plan solely in the interest of the participants and beneficiaries . . . with the care, skill, prudence, and diligence under the circumstances then prevailing that a prudent man acting in a like capacity and familiar with such matters would use in the conduct of an enterprise of a like character and with like aims. This duty does not require an oral explanation of the effect of waiver of Joint and Survivor Annuity Benefits. But, a fiduciary has a legal duty to disclose to the beneficiary those material facts, known to the fiduciary but unknown to the beneficiary, which the beneficiary must know for its own protection. Additionally, the duty to inform also entails . . . a negative duty not to misinform. Thus, to prove breach of fiduciary duty under ERISA, a plaintiff must demonstrate that: (1) the defendant was acting in a fiduciary capacity; (2) the defendant made affirmative misrepresentations or failed to adequately inform plan participants and beneficiaries; (3) the misrepresentation or inadequate disclosure was material; and (4) the plaintiff detrimentally relied on the misrepresentation or inadequate disclosure.[14]

13. *Id.* (citations and quotation marks omitted).
14. Canestri v. NYSA-ILA Pension Trust Fund and Plan, No. 07-1603, 2010 WL 4291489, at *8 (D. N.J. Oct. 22, 2010) (citations and quotation marks omitted). For example, it is

Substantial compliance is not enough for a waiver of spousal survivorship rights. Courts' strict adherence to the statutory requirements for waiver of spousal survivorship rights is protective of the surviving spouse's rights. Another condition for waiver of QJSA and QPSA survivorship benefits requires proper notarization of the written waiver.[15] The waiving spouse must also specifically designate a substitute beneficiary for the survivor benefits.[16] In *Hagwood v. Newton*, the United States Court of Appeals for the Fourth Circuit elucidated the reason for requiring this designation of a substitute:

> In order to ensure that a surviving spouse clearly understand that he or she will not be the beneficiary designated by ERISA, ERISA requires that the surviving spouse actually designate another beneficiary who will receive the benefits in lieu of the surviving spouse. Not only does this requirement ensure voluntariness, but it gives the surviving spouse control over who would receive the benefits in lieu of the surviving spouse.[17]

Under certain circumstances, spousal consent is not required to alter the statutory survivorship beneficiary designation. Specifically, no consent is required when "it is established to the satisfaction of a plan representative that the consent required . . . may not be obtained because there is no spouse, because the spouse cannot be located, or because of such other circumstances as the Secretary of the Treasury may by regulations prescribe."[18] Federal regulation provides that if "the participant is legally separated or the participant has been abandoned (within the meaning of local law) and the participant has a court order to such effect," the participant does not need consent from the beneficiary spouse to alter the designated beneficiary.[19]

breach of a fiduciary duty for an administrator to ignore signs that may indicate that a consent signature for a waiver was forged. See Rice v. Rochester Laborers' Annuity Fund, 888 F. Supp. 494 (1995).

15. *See generally* Alfieri v. Guild Times Pension Plan, 446 F. Supp. 2d 99 (E.D. N.Y. 2006).
16. 29 U.S.C. § 1055(c)(2) (2012).
17. Hagwood v. Newton, 282 F.3d 285, 291 (4th Cir. 2002).
18. 29 U.S.C. § 1005(c)(2)(B) (2012).
19. 26 C.F.R. § 1.401(a)-20, A-27 (1991).

Rights at Marital Dissolution

The Retirement Equity Act of 1984 amended ERISA to formalize an important exception to ERISA's spendthrift rule for qualified domestic relations orders (QDRO), which are typically domestic relations orders that create or recognize an alternate payee's right to receive benefits payable under a participant's plan.[20] QDROs cover decrees and orders relating to child support, alimony, and marital property rights.[21] Plans are primarily responsible for deciding whether a domestic relations order qualifies as a QDRO under ERISA.[22]

For the purposes of the QDRO exception to the spendthrift rule, a surviving spouse includes a former spouse to whom the deceased participant was married for at least one year.[23] The Supreme Court of the United States remarked in *Boggs v. Boggs* that this and other characteristics of the QDRO were essential to one of the Retirement Equity Act's central purposes: "to give enhanced protection to the spouse and dependent children in the event of divorce or separation, or in the event of death."[24] In *Boggs*, the Court held that a nonparticipant could not transfer an interest in pension benefits, which was not yet distributed, to her sons in her will.[25] The Court observed that "ERISA's solicitude for the economic security of surviving spouses would be undermined by allowing a predeceasing spouse's heirs and legatees to have a community property interest in the survivor's annuity."[26]

The circuits have divided as to whether a former spouse is entitled to a deceased participant's pension benefits if the participant passes away before the former spouse applies for the benefits granted under a divorce decree. The Third Circuit and Fourth Circuit have recognized the death of the

20. 29 U.S.C. § 1056(d)(3) (2012).
21. *Id.*
22. 29 U.S.C. § 1056(d)(3)(G) (2012); *see also* Trs. of Dirs. Guild of Am.-Producer Pension Benefits Plans v. Tisa, 234 F.3d 415, 420 (9th Cir. 2000) ("Upon obtaining a domestic relations order in a state court proceeding, an alternate payee who seeks to establish a right to payment pursuant to that order from an ERISA-covered benefit plan must present the order to the pension plan administrator for a determination of whether it is a QDRO.").
23. 29 U.S.C. § 1056(d)(3)(F)(i) (2012).
24. Boggs v. Boggs, 520 U.S. 833, 847 (1997).
25. *Id.* at 844.
26. *Id.* at 843.

participant as the endpoint for a former spouse's opportunity to apply for pension benefits.[27] Courts in these circuits have reasoned that "defined benefit plans are based on actuarial calculations that would be rendered invalid if participants were allowed to change the operative facts retroactively."[28] In comparison, the Eighth, Ninth, and Tenth Circuits have each held that there is no deadline associated with the application process when a participant dies before the application for benefits of a former spouse pursuant to a divorce decree.[29] These circuits have typically found that even if a participant has died before entry of an order, the entry is qualified if it occurred within the statutorily required 18-month period.[30]

QDROs' Specificity Requirements

A domestic relations order must meet specificity requirements for courts to consider it a QDRO.[31] The order must contain "the name and the last known mailing address (if any) of the participant and the name and mailing address of each alternate payee covered by the order," the percentage or amount "of the participant's benefits to be paid by the plan to each such alternate payee" or at least how to determine the amount or percentage, the number of payments or the period covered by the order, and "each plan to which such order applies."[32] The order cannot "require a plan to provide any type or form of benefits, or any option, not otherwise provided under the plan"; require the plan to increase benefits; or make "the payment of benefits to an alternate payee which are required to be paid to another alternate payee under another order previously determined to be a qualified domestic relations order."[33]

27. *See* Samaroo v. Samaroo, 193 F.3d 185 (3d Cir. 1999); Hopkins v. AT&T Global Info. Solutions Co., 105 F.3d 153 (4th Cir. 1997).
28. *Samaroo*, 193 F.3d at 190 (citing *Hopkins*, 105 F.3d at 155–57).
29. *See* Patton v. Denver Post Corp., 326 F.3d 1148 (10th Cir. 2003); Hogan v. Raytheon, Co., 302 F.3d 854 (8th Cir. 2002); Trs. of Dirs. Guild of Am-Producer Pension Benefits Plans v. Tise, 234 F.3d 415 (9th Cir. 2000).
30. *Patton*, 326 F.3d at 1152-52 (citing *Hogan*, 302 F.3d at 857).
31. 29 U.S.C. § 1056(d)(3)(C) (2012).
32. *Id.*
33. 29 U.S.C. § 1056(d)(3)(D) (2012).

Courts have not demanded that domestic relations orders rigidly adhere to every specificity requirement that ERISA places on QDROs. For instance, courts have often overlooked the address requirement, such as when the administrator already has independent reasons to be aware of the address of the alternate payee.[34] This accords with the Retirement Equity Act's legislative history; a more exacting standard might disturb the law's underlying purpose to protect the property interests of former spouses.[35] Similarly, courts have classified orders as QDROs for the purposes of one type of a participant's employee benefits and not another, such as for a participant's pension benefits but not the same participant's life insurance benefits.[36]

Courts have classified domestic relation orders as QDROs when they substantially comply with the specificity requirements. An example of the substantial-compliance doctrine arose in *Hamilton v. Washington State Plumbing & Pipefitting Industry Pension Plan*, where the United States Court of Appeals for the Ninth Circuit contemplated "the intersection between a surviving spouse's statutorily-guaranteed survivor annuity, a QPSA, and a marriage dissolution order, a QDRO, that is silent with respect to surviving spouse rights."[37] In *Hamilton*, a pension plan participant named Michael passed away before retirement, and his children from a prior marriage claimed a right to his survivor benefits in competition with his new wife's alleged right.[38] The Ninth Circuit considered whether the marital dissolution decree requiring the participant to name his children from the prior marriage as beneficiaries qualified as a QDRO under ERISA, and thereby supplanted his new wife's right to a QPSA.[39] The court held that that there existed significant obstacles to classifying the order as a QDRO:

34. *See* Stewart v. Thorpe Holding Co. Profit Sharing Plan, 207 F.3d 1143, 1151 (9th Cir. 2000) (citing Tolstad v. Tolstad, 527 N.W. 2d 668, 673 (N.D. 1995); Stinner v. Stinner, 554 A.2d 49 (Pa. 1989)).

35. *Id.* at 1151–53.

36. *See, e.g.*, Metro. Life Ins. Co. v. McCray, No. 4:11-CV-1488CDP, 2013 WL 398791, at *6 (E.D. Miss. Feb. 6, 2013) (recognizing an order as a QDRO as it pertained to pension benefits but not life insurance benefits due to a lack of specificity about its application to the life insurance benefits).

37. Hamilton v. Wash. State Plumbing & Pipefitting Indus. Pension Plan, 433 F.3d 1091, 1094 (9th Cir. 2006).

38. *Id.*

39. *Id.*

A domestic relations order qualifies as a QDRO only if it meets the specificity requirements set forth in § 1056(d)(3)(c): (1) the order must specify the name and mailing address of the alternate payee and the affected plan participant, (2) the amount or percentage of the participant's benefits to be paid or the means by which that amount will be determined, (3) the number of payments or time period to which the order applies, and (4) each plan to which the order applies. In addition, under § 1056(d)(3)(D), a QDRO must not (1) require the plan to provide any type of benefit not otherwise provided, (2) require the plan to provide increased benefits, or (3) require benefits to be paid to an alternate payee which must be paid to another alternate payee under another QDRO.

We require substantial compliance with these requirements, and have rejected an unduly narrow reading of these requirements. We have, however, also echoed the Tenth Circuit's concerns that an overly expansive interpretation may render the specificity requirements toothless. The pivotal question is whether the dissolution order clearly contains the information specified in the statute that a plan administrator would need to make an informed decision. Here, the paucity of relevant information in the dissolution order compels a negative answer.

Exhibit A to the Decree of Dissolution is a list of property to be distributed to the husband. The only mention of the children and the pension is the cryptic reference with respect to each pension plan that the husband shall name the children of the marriage, David and Sarah, as the beneficiaries under the pension in lieu of life insurance which he is presently unable to obtain, which obligation shall terminate when the youngest child reaches 18 years of age.

As the Plans pointed out in rejecting the Children's claim, the order requires the husband to designate the Children as beneficiaries but does not require any action by the Plans, does not assign death benefits to the Children, and does not specify when payments begin or the amount, calculation, or form of the payments. Nor does the order deal with the issue of the surviving spouse annuity.

> The required details are not hypothetical hurdles. Under the Plans, before the Children reached maturity, Michael or his qualified beneficiary was potentially eligible for a variety of pension benefits, such as a disability pension, an early retirement pension, death benefits and survivor benefits. The dissolution order neither lays out what pension benefits are at issue nor allocates payment of the benefits.[40]

The Ninth Circuit did not deem the domestic relations order to be a QDRO.[41] But even assuming the order was a QDRO, the court reasoned that the QDRO would not supplant the surviving spouse's interest in pension benefits in the absence of an explicit assignment to the former spouse:

> Relying on the plain language of the statute, we hold that the purported assignment of pension rights did not meet the strict requirements of a QDRO. Even if the dissolution order is liberally construed as a QDRO, under the statutory language coupled with a complementary interpretation of the plans, the surviving spouse benefit must be explicitly assigned to a former spouse in a QDRO in order to overcome the surviving spouse's right to an annuity under ERISA. Consequently, Mary, the surviving spouse, prevails over the Children . . . .[42]

Waiver of Pension Benefits in Orders That Are Not QDROs

As the Ninth Circuit stated in *Hamilton*, to overcome a surviving spouse's right to an annuity, the surviving spouse's statutory benefit must be explicitly and clearly assigned to a former spouse in a QDRO.[43] In its 2009 decision *Kennedy v. Plan Administrator for DuPont Savings and Investment Plan*, the

40. *Id.* at 1097–98 (citations and quotation marks omitted).
41. *Id.* at 1098.
42. *Id.*
43. *Id.*; *see also* Burns v. Orthotek, Inc. Emps. Pension Plan & Trust, 657 F.3d 571, 575 (7th Cir. 2011) (explaining that ERISA "requires written spousal consent, witnessed by a notary or plan representative, for a pension-plan participant to validly waive a survivor annuity and designate a new beneficiary" and, as a result, "the doctrine of substantial compliance cannot cure an unwitnessed spousal consent").

Supreme Court took up the related question of whether a divorced spouse could waive pension benefits via a divorce decree that did not amount to a QDRO.[44] The Court held that such a waiver could survive ERISA's antialienation provision but that, in the case at bar, the administrator nonetheless correctly disregarded the waiver based on its conflict with plan documents.[45]

Kennedy concerned a savings and investment plan (SIP) that qualified as a pension plan under ERISA and that granted each participant the power "to designate any beneficiary or beneficiaries . . . to receive all or part" of the plan's funds at the participant's death as well as the ability to revoke or replace the designation.[46] Before their divorce, William, who was a participant in the plan, designated his wife Liv to take his benefits under the SIP.[47] The couple divorced pursuant to a decree purporting to divest Liv "of all right, title, interest, and claim in and to . . . [a]ny and all sums . . . the proceeds [from], and any other rights related to any . . . pension plan . . . existing by reason of [William's] past or present or future employment."[48] William did not execute the necessary documents to remove Liv as his SIP beneficiary, however, and the plan, administered by DuPont, paid the balance of the SIP to Liv.[49] The estate responded by filing suit, asserting that the divorce decree represented Liv's waiver of the SIP benefits.[50]

With respect to the intersection of the divorce decree and the antialienation rule, the court relied on the law of trusts and reasoned that ERISA's antialienation provision alone would not trump the divorce decree:

> We explained before that § 1056(d)(1) is much like a spendthrift trust provision barring assignment or alienation of a benefit, and the cognate trust law is highly suggestive here. Although the beneficiary of a spendthrift trust traditionally lacked the means to transfer his beneficial interest to anyone else, he did have the power to disclaim

44. Kennedy v. Plan Adm'r for DuPont Savs. and Inv. Plan, 555 U.S. 285, 291 (2009).
45. *Id.* at 288.
46. *Id.*
47. *Id.* at 289.
48. *Id.*
49. *Id.*
50. *Id.* at 290.

prior to accepting it, so long as the disclaimer made no attempt to direct the interest to a beneficiary in his stead.

We do not mean that the whole law of spendthrift trusts and disclaimers turns up in § 1056(d)(1), but the general principle that a designated spendthrift can disclaim his trust interest magnifies the improbability that a statute written with an eye on the old law would effectively force a beneficiary to take an interest willy-nilly. Common sense and common law both say that [t]he law certainly is not so absurd as to force a man to take an estate against his will.

The Treasury is certainly comfortable with the state of the old law, for the way it reads its own regulation no party acquires from a beneficiary a right or interest enforceable against the plan pursuant to a beneficiary's waiver of rights where the beneficiary does not attempt to direct her interest in pension benefits to another person. And, being neither plainly erroneous [n]or inconsistent with the regulation, the Treasury Department's interpretation of its regulation is controlling.

The Fifth Circuit found significant support for its contrary holding in the QDRO subsections, reasoning that [i]n the marital-dissolution context, the QDRO provisions supply the sole exception to the anti-alienation provision . . . . But the negative implication of the QDRO language is not that simple. If a QDRO provided a way for a former spouse like Liv merely to waive benefits, this would be powerful evidence that the antialienation provision was meant to deny any effect to a waiver within a divorce decree but not a QDRO, else there would have been no need for the QDRO exception. But this is not so . . . . In fact, a beneficiary seeking only to relinquish her right to benefits cannot do this by a QDRO, for a QDRO by definition requires that it be the creat[ion] or recogni[tion of] the existence of an alternate payee's right to, or assign[ment] to an alternate payee [of] the right to, receive all or a portion of the benefits payable with respect to a participant under a plan. There is no QDRO for a simple waiver; there must be some succeeding designation of an alternate payee. Not being a mechanism for simply renouncing a claim to benefits, then, the QDRO provisions shed no light on whether a beneficiary may waive by a non-QDRO.

> In sum, Liv did not attempt to direct her interest in the SIP benefits to the Estate or any other potential beneficiary, and accordingly we think that the better view is that her waiver did not constitute an assignment or alienation rendered void under the terms of § 1056(d)(1).[51]

Nonetheless, the Court rejected the decree as a waiver of the SIP benefits based on the rationale that recognizing the waiver would conflict with the language of the plan.[52] The Court explained:

> [T]he question remains whether the plan administrator was required to honor Liv's waiver with the consequence of distributing the SIP balance to the Estate. We hold that it was not, and that the plan administrator did its statutory ERISA duty by paying the benefits to Liv in conformity with the plan documents.
>
> ERISA requires [e]very employee benefit plan [to] be established and maintained pursuant to a written instrument specify[ing] the basis on which payments are made to and from the plan. The plan administrator is obliged to act in accordance with the documents and instruments governing the plan insofar as such documents and instruments are consistent with the provisions of [Title I] and [Title IV] of [ERISA], and ERISA provides no exemption from this duty when it comes time to pay benefits. On the contrary, § 1132(a)(1)(B) . . . reinforces the directive, with its provision that a participant or beneficiary may bring a cause of action to recover benefits due to him under the terms of his plan, to enforce his rights under the terms of the plan, or to clarify his rights to future benefits under the terms of the plan.
>
> The Estate's claim therefore stands or falls by the terms of the plan, a straightforward rule of hewing to the directives of the plan documents that lets employers establish a uniform administrative scheme, [with] a set of standard procedures to guide processing of claims and disbursement of benefits. The point is that by giving a plan participant

51. *Id.* at 294–97 (citations and quotation marks omitted).
52. *Id.* at 304.

a clear set of instructions for making his own instructions clear, ERISA forecloses any justification for enquiries into nice expressions of intent, in favor of the virtues of adhering to an uncomplicated rule: simple administration, avoid[ing] double liability, and ensur[ing] that beneficiaries get what's coming quickly, without the folderol essential under less-certain rules.

And the cost of less certain rules would be too plain. Plan administrators would be forced to examine a multitude of external documents that might purport to affect the dispensation of benefits and be drawn into litigation like this over the meaning and enforceability of purported waivers. The Estate's suggestion that a plan administrator could resolve these sorts of disputes through interpleader actions merely restates the problem with the Estate's position: it would destroy a plan administrator's ability to look at the plan documents and records conforming to them to get clear distribution instructions, without going into court.

The Estate of course is right that this guarantee of simplicity is not absolute. The very enforceability of QDROs means that sometimes a plan administrator must look for the beneficiaries outside plan documents notwithstanding § 1104(a)(1)(D); § 1056(d)(3)(J) provides that a person who is an alternate payee under a [QDRO] shall be considered for purposes of any provision of [ERISA] a beneficiary under the plan. But this in effect means that a plan administrator who enforces a QDRO must be said to enforce plan documents, not ignore them. In any case, a QDRO enquiry is relatively discrete, given the specific and objective criteria for a domestic relations order that qualifies as a QDRO, requirements that amount to a statutory checklist working to spare [an administrator] from litigation-fomenting ambiguities. This is a far cry from asking a plan administrator to figure out whether a claimed federal common law waiver was knowing and voluntary, whether its language addressed the particular benefits at issue, and so forth, on into factually complex and subjective determinations.

These are good and sufficient reasons for holding the line, just as we have done in cases of state laws that might blur the bright-line requirement to follow plan documents in distributing benefits. Two recent preemption cases are instructive here. *Boggs v. Boggs* held that ERISA preempted a state law permitting the testamentary transfer of a nonparticipant spouse's community property interest in undistributed pension plan benefits. We rejected the entreaty to create through case law . . . a new class of persons for whom plan assets are to be held and administered, explaining that [t]he statute is not amenable to this sweeping extratextual extension. And in *Egelhoff* we held that ERISA preempted a state law providing that the designation of a spouse as the beneficiary of a nonprobate asset is revoked automatically upon divorce. We said the law was at fault for standing in the way of making payments simply by identifying the beneficiary specified by the plan documents and thus for purporting to undermine the congressional goal of minimiz[ing] the administrative and financial burden[s] on plan administrators.

What goes for inconsistent state law goes for a federal common law of waiver that might obscure a plan administrator's duty to act in accordance with the documents and instruments. And this case does as well as any other in pointing out the wisdom of protecting the plan documents rule. Under the terms of the SIP Liv was William's designated beneficiary. The plan provided an easy way for William to change the designation, but for whatever reason he did not. The plan provided a way to disclaim an interest in the SIP account, but Liv did not purport to follow it. The plan administrator therefore did exactly what § 1104(a)(1)(D) required: the documents control, and those name [the ex-wife].[53]

Recovery in the Absence of Waiver

Kennedy communicated to lower courts that plans are beholden under the plan documents rule to pay out to former spouses named as beneficiaries in the plan document despite waivers in divorce decrees when deceased participants fail to update their beneficiary designations. In *Estate of Kensinger*

53. *Id.* at 299–304 (citations and quotation marks omitted).

v. URL Pharma, Inc., the United States Court of Appeals for the Third Circuit took up the question left open by the *Kennedy* Court as to whether an estate could recover benefits from the former spouse after distribution.[54] The Third Circuit held that it could.[55]

Kensinger came to the Third Circuit on a set of facts nearly identical to those in *Kennedy*.[56] William, a participant in his employer's 401(k) plan, designated his wife Adele as his primary beneficiary.[57] The couple subsequently divorced and entered into a property settlement agreement providing:

> [T]he parties mutually agree to waive, release, and relinquish any and all right, title and interest either may have in and to the other's IRA account(s), or any other such retirement benefit and deferred savings plan of like kind and character, and neither shall make any claim to possession of such property as it is presently titled.[58]

After William died intestate, the estate filed an action against Adele and the plan administrator, URL, and requested a determination that the estate was entitled to the 401(k).[59] The Third Circuit ultimately obliged, finding that the concerns implicated in *Kennedy*—"the need for the straightforward administration of plans and the avoidance of potential double liability"—were not at stake in *Kensinger*.[60] Rather, "a post-distribution suit against Adele would neither destroy a plan administrator's ability . . . to get clear distribution instructions, without going to court nor subject URL to litigation-fomenting ambiguities."[61] According to the United States Court of Appeals for the Third Circuit:

> In this case, when URL pays the benefits to Adele, as it must, she will get what's coming under the plan. If, after distribution, her right to

54. Estate of Kensinger v. URL Pharma, Inc., 674 F.3d 131, 134 (3d Cir. 2012).
55. *Id.* at 132.
56. *Id.* at 134.
57. *Id.* at 132.
58. *Id.* at 132–33.
59. *Id.* at 133.
60. *Id.* at 136.
61. *Id.* (citations and quotation marks omitted).

> these funds is challenged because of her common law waiver, that challenge will be litigated as an ordinary contract dispute. Accordingly, to the extent that ERISA is concerned with the expeditious payment of plan proceeds to beneficiaries, permitting suits against beneficiaries after benefits have been paid does not implicate any concern of expeditious payment or undermine any core objective of ERISA.[62]

The Third Circuit further noted that the Michigan Supreme Court, the Oklahoma Court of Civil Appeals, and the Court of Appeals of Georgia had each held that an estate could enforce a common-law waiver against a named beneficiary after the distribution of pension funds.[63]

Waiver in Antenuptial Agreements

Regarding waiver, federal regulation states: "An agreement entered into prior to marriage does not satisfy the applicable consent requirements, even if the agreement is executed within the applicable election period."[64] Accordingly, various courts have found such agreements unenforceable for purposes of waiver.[65] In *Hagwood v. Newtown*, the United States Court of Appeals for the Fourth Circuit observed that at the time of executing an antenuptial agreement, a signatory cannot satisfy the requirement of § 1055(c) that "the spouse of the participant consent [ ] in writing to such election [to waive]" because he or she does not yet possess spousal rights.[66]

Some other courts, such as the District of Columbia Court of Appeals in *Critchell v. Critchell*, have enforced a waiver in an antenuptial agreement.[67] Vital to the court's analysis in *Critchell* was the Supreme Court's contemporaneous narrowing of preemption in areas that are traditionally left to

62. *Id.* at 136–37 (citations and quotation marks omitted).
63. *Id.* at 137 (citing Sweebe v. Sweebe, 712 N.W.2d 708 (Mich. 2006); Alcorn v. Appleton, 708 S.E.2d 390 (Ga. App. 2011); Pardee v. Pardee, 112 P.3d 308 (Okla. Civ. App. 2004)).
64. 26 C.F.R. § 1.401(a)-20 (2006).
65. *See, e.g.*, Manning v. Hayes, 212 F.3d 866 (4th Cir. 2000); Manning v. Hayes, 212 F.3d 866 (5th Cir. 2000).
66. Hagwood v. Newtown, Jr., 282 F.3d 285, 289 (4th Cir. 2002).
67. Critchell v. Critchell, 746 A.2d 282, 288 (D.C. 2000).

state regulation, the fact that "[d]omestic relations is an area of law usually governed by state law," and "ERISA expressly defers to state domestic relations law to define a spouse's property rights in the event of divorce."[68] The District of Columbia's marital property law recognized the waiver of a spouse's potential property interest pursuant to an antenuptial agreement, and the waiver of pension benefits in *Critchell* survived preemption.[69]

Moving beyond the timing of waiver and questions of preemption, a 2013 case before the United States Court of Appeals for the Eighth Circuit, *MidAmerican Pension and Employee Benefits Plans Administrative Committee v. Cox*, underscored the importance of acknowledgment in antenuptial waivers. *Cox* concerned an antenuptial agreement Michael and Kathy signed both before and after their wedding that stated:

> To the extent that either party is entitled to benefits receivable under a retirement plan or individual retirement account, subject to the terms of the Employee Retirement Income Security Act (ERISA) as now existing or hereafter amended, 29 USCS §§ 1001–1461, which require joint and survivor annuities, preretirement survivor annuities, or any other similar benefit, the other party hereby irrevocably consents to the participant employee's change in beneficiary or change in the form of payment of benefits without further consent by the non-participant spouse.[70]

Before executing the antenuptial agreement with Kathy, Michael had designated his parents as the beneficiaries of his MidAmerican Energy Corporation (MEC) 401(k) plan.[71] Michael passed away while the couple was in the process of divorce, and Michael's parents disputed whether Kathy should receive the funds in Michael's MEC 401(k) plan based on the couple's agreement.[72] The Eighth Circuit found that the agreement was insufficient to waive Kathy's rights:

68. *Id.* at 284 (citing 29 U.S.C. § 1056(d)(3)(B)(i)(1)).
69. *Id.* at 288.
70. MidAmerican Pension and Emp. Benefits Plan Admin. Comm. v. Cox, 720 F.3d 715, 716–17 (8th Cir. 2013).
71. *Id.* at 716.
72. *Id.* at 717.

To be sure, the antenuptial agreement contains several broad waiver provisions regarding retirement accounts, both generally and the MEC 401(k) Plan specifically, by incorporation of an attached exhibit. Section B(8)(a), for example, expressly disclaims, "[t]o the extent that either party is entitled" to them, the right to benefits receivable under a retirement plan governed by ERISA requiring a preretirement survivor annuity.

As a whole, however, the antenuptial agreement is equivocal whether Kathy waived her rights at all. Sections B(8)(b) and (c) of the antenuptial agreement contemplate the future execution of a waiver or consent to change in beneficiary. The inclusion of these sections suggests that Kathy did not waive her spousal rights in the antenuptial agreement because, as the district court recognized, were the antenuptial agreement itself a sufficient waiver, "then Subparagraphs (b) and (c) should not have been included in the agreement." In light of this promise to execute a waiver and in the absence of the fulfillment of this promise, Kathy could not have meaningfully acknowledged the effect of any waiver of her spousal rights in the antenuptial agreement.

Moreover, and as the district court noted, notwithstanding its lengthy above-recounted provisions, the antenuptial agreement failed to inform Kathy—in clear and express terms—that she both had a spousal right to receive the funds in the MEC 401(k) Plan and that she was waiving this right. Section B(8)(a), for example, is couched by the equivocal language, "[t]o the extent that either party is entitled to benefits receivable under a retirement plan[,]" and fails to make clear that, by executing the waiver, Kathy would not receive the funds to which she would otherwise be entitled in the MEC 401(k) Plan.

. . . Given ERISA's strict compliance requirements, we conclude that the antenuptial agreement did not contain an acknowledgment by Kathy sufficient to satisfy § 1055(c)(2)(A)(iii). Accordingly, Michael's designation of his Parents as beneficiaries of the MEC 401(k) Plan must yield to Kathy's rights as surviving spouse.[73]

73. *Id.* at 719–20 (citations omitted).

QDROs in Quasi-Marriage Relationships

Courts have validated QDROs even in the absence of formal marriages. *Owens v. Automotive Machinists Pension Trust* is an example which was decided by the United States Court of Appeals for the Ninth Circuit in 2009.[74] *Owens* concerned a 30-year relationship between Phillip, a decedent whose pension benefits precipitated the case, and Norma, who devoted much of her relationship with Phillip to caring for him and their children.[75] Phillip and Norma never married but publicly represented themselves as married and acquired various joint assets while, at times, holding joint bank accounts.[76] After Phillip's death, the Superior Court of King County, Washington, issued a court order allotting Norma an interest in 50 percent of Phillip's pension benefits, which the plan, Automotive Machinist Pension Trust, appealed.[77]

The Ninth Circuit observed that a QDRO "creates or recognizes the existence of an alternate payee's right to [receive] benefits payable with respect to a participant under a plan."[78] A domestic relations order includes an order that "relates to the provision of child support, alimony payments, or marital property rights to a spouse, former spouse, child, or other dependent of a participant" when the order was issued "pursuant to a domestic relations law."[79] Thus, for the Washington state order in *Owens* to qualify as a QDRO, it had to "recognize . . . the right of an alternate payee to receive all or a portion of the benefits payable with respect to a participant under the plan . . . and it must [have related] to 'marital property rights.'"[80]

Automotive contended that the Washington state court order did not relate to marital property rights and that Norma did not qualify as an alternate payee under ERISA because she was not an "other dependent."[81] The Ninth Circuit rejected both of Automotive's contentions:

74. Owens v. Automotive Machinists Pension Trusts, 551 F.3d 1138, 1147 (9th Cir. 2009).
75. *Id.*
76. *Id.* at 1140.
77. *Id.* at 1139.
78. *Id.* at 1142 (citing 29 U.S.C. § 1056(d)(3)(B)(i)(I)).
79. *Id.* at 1143 (citing 29 U.S.C. § 1056(d)(3)(B)(ii)(I)).
80. *Id.* (citing Hamilton v. Wash. State Plumbing & Pipefitting Indus. Pension Plan, 433 F.3d 1091, 1096 (9th Cir. 2006)).
81. *Id.* at 1139–40.

The state of Washington recognizes quasi-marital relationships for purposes of property division. Wholly unrelated to either kind of marriage, [Washington] courts have recognized the existence of [quasi-marital] relationships, which this court has determined to be stable, cohabiting relationships. Norma and Phillip enjoyed just such a stable, marital-like relationship[,] where both parties cohabit[ed] with the knowledge that a lawful marriage between them [did] not exist. In *Connell*, the court concluded that Washington state limit[s] the distribution of property following a [quasi-marital] relationship to property that would have been characterized as community property had the parties been married.

Norma and Phillip lived together in a quasi-marital relationship for more than thirty years. During that time, they jointly accumulated various forms of community property. In addition to purchasing a home together, the Owens obtained numerous joint assets including real property, furniture, furnishings, and vehicles. The couple's community property also included jointly acquired funds, some of which were held in joint bank accounts, as well as the interest that Phillip acquired in various retirement accounts, including the Automotive Trust pension plan at issue here.

As the U.S. District Court stated, *Connell* is instructive on the question of property division pursuant to State community property laws, and . . . [on] the limits of a quasi-marital relationship under Washington law. *Connell* held:

> Until the Legislature, as a matter of public policy, concludes [quasi-marital] relationships are the legal equivalent to marriages, we limit the distribution of property following a [quasi-marital] relationship to property that would have been characterized as community property had the parties been married. This will allow the trial court to justly divide property the couple has earned during the relationship through their efforts without creating a common law marriage or making a decision for a couple which they have declined to make for themselves.

Furthermore, *Connell* recognized that Washington state does not permit common law marriages. But Norma does not argue on common law grounds. Instead, she seeks an equitable distribution of community property pursuant to a valid quasi-marital relationship. Importantly, *Connell* concluded that the limits that Washington state has placed on quasi-marital relationships do not extend to the division of property: property that would have been characterized as community property had the couple been married is before the trial court for a just and equitable distribution.

Reading the relevant statutory provisions [of ERISA] as a whole, which requires that a QDRO be made pursuant to a [s]tate domestic relations law (including a community property law), compels us to apply Washington state domestic relations law here. Applying *Connell*, it is clear that the Superior Court's Order did relate to marital property rights because Phillip's pension benefits comprise property that would have been characterized as community property had the parties been married. Assigning Norma a fifty-percent interest in Phillip's pension benefits was consistent with Washington law regarding the distribution of property following a [quasi-marital] relationship. Relying on Washington state domestic relations law, we hold that the Superior Court's Order did relate to marital property rights.

. . .

The Superior Court's Order fulfilled the first requirement for a valid Qualified Domestic Relations Order—that the order relate to marital property rights. The second requirement is whether Norma qualifies as an Alternate Payee under 29 U.S.C. § 1056(d)(3)(K). ERISA defines the term Alternate Payee as follows:

> The term [A]lternate [P]ayee means any spouse, former spouse, child, or other dependent of a participant who is recognized by a domestic relations order as having a right to receive all, or a portion of, the benefits payable under a plan with respect to such participant.

Automotive Trust contends that Norma does not qualify as an Alternate Payee because she was not a spouse, former spouse, child, or other dependent of Phillip. Norma, on the other hand, posits that she is an Alternate Payee because she qualified as Phillip's dependent. In support of her argument, Norma cites to (1) her designation as

Phillip's wife on the couple's joint tax returns; (2) her designation as wife and beneficiary on Phillip's life insurance application; and (3) her undisputed financial dependence on Phillip during their thirty-year long quasi-marital relationship. The U.S. District Court held that, because Norma's dependent status is undisputed for the [thirty]-year term of her quasi-marital relationship with Phillip, and that no facts in the record indicate otherwise, Norma was an Alternate Payee under the statute. We agree.

To determine whether Norma qualifies as Phillip's dependent, we look to the Internal Revenue Code, I.R.C. § 152(d)(2)(H). Section 152(d)(2)(H) defines the term dependent as [a]n individual (other than . . . the spouse . . . of the taxpayer) who, for the taxable year of the taxpayer, has the same principal place of abode as the taxpayer and is a member of the taxpayer's household.

It is undisputed that, for more than thirty years, Norma and Phillip shared the same principal place of abode in Seattle, Washington. In fact, the Owens purchased the home together, lived there together, and even jointly used the proceeds from the sale of the home to pay off the mortgage and other debts. Phillip was the primary wage-earner while Norma devoted her time to caring for her husband's and children's needs and tending to the couple's home. As the couple's joint tax returns indicate, Norma was a member of Phillip's household; she is listed on the couple's tax returns as Phillip's wife. Because Norma qualifies as an other dependent under I.R.C. § 152(d)(2)(H), we find that she was properly designated as an Alternate Payee under 29 U.S.C. § 1056(d)(3)(K), thereby fulfilling the second requirement for a valid QDRO.[82]

Same-Sex Marriages

Recent expansions in governmental recognitions of same-sex marriages have transformed employee benefit law for many sexual minorities in the

82. *Id.* at 1145-47 (citations and quotation marks omitted).

United States. On June 26, 2013, the Supreme Court ruled in *United States v. Windsor* that Section 3 of the Defense of Marriage Act (DOMA), which excluded a same-sex partner from qualifying as a "spouse" in federal statutes, was an unconstitutional deprivation and violation of the Fifth Amendment's guarantee of equal liberty.[83] The Court recognized the absence of certain federally mediated spousal and other familial benefits as a significant harm that DOMA visited on same-sex couples married under state but not federal law:

> DOMA's principal effect is to identify a subset of state-sanctioned marriages and make them unequal. The principal purpose is to impose inequality, not for other reasons like governmental efficiency. Responsibilities, as well as rights, enhance the dignity and integrity of the person. And DOMA contrives to deprive some couples married under the laws of their State, but not other couples, of both rights and responsibilities. By creating two contradictory marriage regimes within the same State, DOMA forces same-sex couples to live as married for the purpose of state law but unmarried for the purpose of federal law, thus diminishing the stability and predictability of basic personal relations the State has found it proper to acknowledge and protect. By this dynamic DOMA undermines both the public and private significance of state-sanctioned same-sex marriages; for it tells those couples, and all the world, that their otherwise valid marriages are unworthy of federal recognition. This places same-sex couples in an unstable position of being in a second-tier marriage. The differentiation demeans the couple, whose moral and sexual choices the Constitution protects, and whose relationship the State has sought to dignify. And it humiliates tens of thousands of children now being raised by same-sex couples. The law in question makes it even more difficult for the children to understand the integrity and closeness of their own family and its concord with other families in their community and in their daily lives.
>
> Under DOMA, same-sex married couples have their lives burdened, by reason of government decree, in visible and public ways. By its

83. United States v. Windsor, 133 S. Ct. 2675, 2695–96 (2013).

> great reach, DOMA touches many aspects of married and family life, from the mundane to the profound. It prevents same-sex married couples from obtaining government healthcare benefits they would otherwise receive. It deprives them of the Bankruptcy Code's special protections for domestic-support obligations. It forces them to follow a complicated procedure to file their state and federal taxes jointly. It prohibits them from being buried together in veterans' cemeteries.
>
> . . .
>
> DOMA also brings financial harm to children of same-sex couples. It raises the cost of health care for families by taxing health benefits provided by employers to their workers' same-sex spouses. And it denies or reduces benefits allowed to families upon the loss of a spouse and parent, benefits that are an integral part of family security.[84]

Currently, 19 states and the District of Columbia allow marriage between spouses of the same sex: California, Connecticut, Delaware, Hawaii, Illinois, Iowa, Maine, Maryland, Massachusetts, Minnesota, New Hampshire, New Jersey, New Mexico, New York, Oregon, Pennsylvania, Rhode Island, Vermont, and Washington. After *Windsor*, married same-sex couples in these states enjoy all of the same protections as opposite-sex married couples that are set forth in this chapter as well as other federal protections and benefits to which spouses and former spouses are entitled.[85] The Department of Labor has provided post-*Windsor* guidance stating that "spouse" and "marriage" in Title I of ERISA and related regulations should extend to married same-sex couples.[86] On August 29, 2013, the IRS announced: "same sex couples legally married in jurisdictions that recognize their marriages, will be treated as married for federal tax purposes . . . regardless of

84. *Id.* at 2694–95 (citations and quotation marks omitted).
85. *See* Cozen O'Connor, P.C. v. Tobits, No. 11-0045, 2013 WL 3878688, at *4 (E.D. Pa. July 29, 2013) ("Post-*Windsor*, where a state recognizes a party as a 'Surviving Spouse,' the federal government must do the same with respect to ERISA benefits—at least pursuant to the express language of the ERISA-qualified Plan at issue . . . .").
86. United States Department of Labor, Technical Release No. 2013-04, Guidance to Employee Benefit Plans on the Definition of "Spouse" and "Marriage" under ERISA and the Supreme Court's Decision in United States v. Windsor (Sept. 18, 2013), *available at* http://www.dol.gov/ebsa/newsroom/tr13-04.html.

whether the couple lives in a jurisdiction that recognizes same-sex marriage or a jurisdiction that does not recognize same-sex marriage."[87]

Marriage is especially relevant to the extension of ERISA benefits to same-sex couples because courts have not recognized protection from employment discrimination on the basis of sexual orientation, including denials of ERISA benefits based on the sex of a couple. An interesting example is the United States District Court for the District of Massachusetts's decision *Partners Healthcare System, Inc. v. Sullivan*. In *Sullivan*, a plaintiff brought suit against an ERISA plan that extended benefits to same-sex domestic partners and argued that the plan must extend the same benefits to his opposite-sex domestic partner.[88] The claimant relied on Massachusetts's sexual orientation and "associational sex" antidiscrimination laws that prohibited employment discrimination based on sexual orientation, but the court deemed these laws preempted.[89] Couples who are unmarried are without recourse for denials of ERISA benefits based on the same-sex or opposite-sex configuration of their relationship because ERISA preempts state law and because federal law, specifically Title VII, allows employment discrimination on the basis of sexual orientation.[90]

Air Transport Association of America v. City and County of San Francisco, involving domestic partnership benefits in San Francisco, mirrored the outcome in *Sullivan*. In 1996, the city of San Francisco sought to compel private employers to offer domestic partnership benefits by amending its administrative code and barring the city from contracting with companies that did not provide domestic partnership benefits. In a decision affirmed by the Ninth Circuit in 2001, the United States District Court for the Northern District of California found that ERISA preempted the ordinance insofar as it affected ERISA plans providing ERISA-covered benefits.[91]

The long-gestating bill known as the Employment Non-discrimination Act, which would prohibit employment discrimination based on perceived or actual sexual orientation or gender identity, could provide a new remedy

---

87. *Rev. Rul.* 2013-17, 2013-38 I.R.B. 201.
88. Partners Healthcare Sys., Inc. v. Sullvan, 497 F. Supp. 2d 42, 44 (D. Mass. 2007).
89. *Id.* at 44.
90. *Id.* at 44 n.3.
91. Air Transport Ass'n of Am. v. City and County of San Francisco, 992 F. Supp. 1149, 1155 (N.D. Cal. 1998), *aff'd*, 266 F.3d 1064 (9th Cir. 2001).

for same-sex couples in this arena. For now, where state law does not recognize same-sex marriage either in its own jurisdiction or originating from the jurisdiction of another state, same-sex couples do not have legally mandated access to ERISA benefits. However, the United States Department of Labor has proposed a rule to change the definition of spouse for purposes of the Family Medical Leave Act (FMLA) from whether a couple qualifies as married in the state of residence to whether the couple has entered into a marriage in any state recognizing the marriage.

Windsor did not guarantee the recognition of same-sex marriage across every state, nor did it in itself invalidate state constitutional bans on same-sex marriage. However, in the wake of *Windsor*, same-sex couples have flooded courts with dozens of cases across the country asking for courts to extend the benefits of marriage, often challenging "mini DOMAs" in states banning same-sex marriage. At the time of this writing, nine of those cases have reached federal appeals courts in five circuits, and nine states—Arkansas, Idaho, Indiana, Michigan, Oklahoma, Oregon, Pennsylvania, Utah, and Virginia—have struck down same-sex marriage bans. Courts in Kentucky, Ohio, and Tennessee have ordered authorities to recognize same-sex marriages performed in other states. No mini DOMA has survived a federal court ruling since *Windsor*. Welfare and pension benefits remain an articulated interest of same-sex couples in these post-*Windsor* cases.[92]

92. *See, e.g.*, Obergefell v. Wymslo, 962 F. Supp. 2d 968, 980 (S.D. Ohio 2013) (identifying the injuries resulting from the deprivation of state-sanctioned marriage and explaining that same-sex couples are denied access to entitlement programs, including welfare benefits, available to heterosexual couples).

Chapter 10

Additional Protections

The Internal Revenue Code (IRC) offers tax incentives to encourage the establishment of plans and places restrictions on employee benefit plans to protect employees' rights to pension benefits.[1] Provisions in the IRC for tax-qualified plans are also designed to reduce the tax subsidy from tax incentives and to ensure that plans are administered to the benefit of a fair cross section of the employers' workforce.[2] The quid pro quo for receiving tax-favored status is that employees must be treated in a fair manner. The threat of losing tax-qualified status provides the paramount remedial mechanism for the protections in this chapter, although litigation under ERISA is available where the provisions in the IRC have counterparts in ERISA.[3] At times, tax disqualification of a plan may be a swifter, more potent remedy than litigation.

1. *See, e.g.*, 29 U.S.C. §§ 1201–1204 (2012) (providing tax benefits to pension and welfare benefit plans).
2. *See* 26 U.S.C. § 404 (2012); 26 U.S.C. § 401(a)(17) (2012); 26 U.S.C. § 415 (2012); 26 U.S.C 410(b) (2012).
3. These counterparts include requirements for a written plan, the holding of assets in trusts, operating a plan for the exclusive benefit of employees, participation, accrual, vesting, benefit commencement, spousal annuities, plan mergers, assignment, and alienation. *See generally* Langbein et al., Pension and Employee Benefit Law 344–46 (4th ed. 2006). Tax-qualification requirements without ERISA counterparts include the IRS expectation that a plan be permanent rather than temporary, what constitutes incidental benefits, minimum coverage requirements for non-highly compensated employees, the prohibition against discriminating in favor of highly compensated employees, vesting of accrued benefits upon termination, distribution rules, limitations on benefits and deferrals, a ceiling on allowable compensation for covered employees, specifications for top-heavy plans, defined benefit plan forfeitures, and the transfer of rollover distributions. *See generally id.* at 346–47.

Many of the requirements imposed by ERISA appear in both ERISA and the IRC. The Treasury Department's rulings and regulations guide the protections in this chapter. ERISA specifically authorizes the Treasury Department to prescribe the regulations relating to minimum participation,[4] vesting,[5] and funding standards.[6] In 1978, the responsibilities of the Department of Labor (DOL) and the Treasury were reorganized in Reorganization Plan No. 4, which granted the regulatory authority for virtually all of Parts 2 and 3 of Subtitle B of Title I of ERISA to the Treasury.[7] The DOL may still enforce these requirements, but the DOL will be informed by regulations and rulings of the Treasury.

The provisions under Title 1 of ERISA prohibiting amendments that reduce or eliminate accrued benefits generate more litigation than the other areas over which the IRS has primary enforcement activity. ERISA does not bar amendments relating to prospective accruals provided plans give adequate notice of such material modifications. Vesting rules require plans to grant employees a nonforfeitable right to their accrued benefits after completion of a statutorily delineated maximum number of years of service.[8] Employee welfare benefit plans do not vest.[9] Relatedly, ERISA limits an employer's ability to impose unreasonable eligibility requirements concerning age or service as a condition of plan participation.[10] In order to give meaning to the vesting rules, ERISA and the IRC have specific rules relating to the rate at which benefits are accrued.[11]

4. 26 U.S.C. § 410 (2012).
5. 26 U.S.C. § 411 (2012).
6. 26 U.S.C. § 412 (2012).
7. Reorganization Plan No. 4 of 1978, § 101, 43 Fed. Reg. 47713 (Aug. 10, 1978). *See generally* Cent. Laborers Pension Fund v. Heinz, 541 U.S. 739, 746–48 (2004).
8. 26 U.S.C. § 411 (2012).
9. 29 U.S.C. § 1051 (a)(1) (2012); H H Music v. McGann, 946 F. 2d 401 (5th Cir. 1991).
10. 26 U.S.C. § 410 (2012).
11. 26 U.S.C. § 411(b) (2012).

The Anti-Cutback Rule and the Protection of Accrued Benefits

The anti-cutback rule prohibits a decrease of an accrued benefit by a plan amendment.[12] The rule also prevents eliminating or reducing an early retirement benefit or subsidy or an optional form of a benefit.[13] The termination of a plan qualifies as a plan amendment.[14] An accrued benefit is an individual benefit "expressed in the form of an annual benefit commencing at normal retirement age" in the case of a defined benefit plan or, in the case of an individual account plan, "the balance of the individual's account."[15] Claimants have tried and failed to convince courts to classify disability benefits as retirement subsidies.[16]

Cases concerning the anti-cutback rule often center on whether a participant has satisfied the requirements to attain an accrued benefit. *Fallin v. Commonwealth Industries, Inc.* was a recent example before the United States Court of Appeals for the Sixth Circuit in which a retiree, Donald Corley, alleged that a pension plan, administered by a Benefits Committee, underpaid him by failing to include a subsidy for early retirement when calculating benefits.[17] The case hinged on whether Corley's benefits had accrued under the plan:

> Corley . . . argues that the Committee's calculation of his lump-sum payment violated an ERISA provision known as the anti-cutback rule. With exceptions not applicable here, that rule provides that a plan amendment shall not decrease a participant's accrued benefit. Corley contends that the Committee paid him an early-retirement benefit that was less than he would have received under the pre-amendment Plan,

12. 29 U.S.C. § 1054(g)(1) (2012).
13. 29 U.S.C. § 1054(g)(2) (2012).
14. *See* Shaver v. Siemens Corp., 670 F.3d 462, 472 (3d Cir. 2012) (citing Gillis v. Hoechst Celanese Corp., 4 F.3d 1137, 1145 (3d Cir. 1993)).
15. 29 U.S.C. § 1002(23)(A) (2012).
16. *See, e.g.*, Arndt v. Security Bank S.S.B. Emps. Pension Plan, 182 F.3d 538, 544 (7th Cir. 1999).
17. Fallin v. Commonwealth Indus., Inc., 695 F.3d 512, 514 (6th Cir. 2012).

> thereby reducing his accrued benefit. The district court disagreed. We review its reading of § 1054(g) *de novo.*
>
> The district court reasoned that a benefit accrues only after a participant has met all of the plan's criteria for that benefit. Here, before the Plan amendment, Corley satisfied one criterion for the early-retirement benefit—that he have five years of credited service. But he did not meet the other—that he reach age 55—until after the amendment (although he did satisfy this condition before he retired). He argues that his early-retirement benefit was accrued nonetheless under § 1054(g).[18]

The court found that Corley's benefits had accrued and that the plan could not reduce the benefits under the anti-cutback rule:

> Here, Corley had more than five years of service before the Plan was amended in 1998. The subsidy he seeks was therefore attributable to his service before the amendment. And though Corley had not satisfied the age requirement by that time, the statute allows him to do so either before or after the amendment[.] Thus, in summary, early-retirement benefits attributable to pre-[amendment] service remain inviolate whether the age condition be satisfied before or after the amendment . . . .
>
> . . . That Corley satisfied the service condition before the plan was amended, and the age condition afterward, was enough for his subsidy to be accrued. Under the anti-cutback rule, therefore, the Plan could not reduce that benefit.
>
> As a factual matter, however, it is not clear that the Plan actually reduced Corley's benefits. Neither party has explained to us the calculations the Plan was supposed to perform or those it did perform. Indeed, in rejecting Plaintiffs' administrative claims, the Benefits Committee told Plaintiffs that they did not provide sufficient detail for the Benefits Committee to fully understand their assertion that the early retirement factors are incorrect.

18. *Id.* at 516–17 (citations and quotation marks omitted).

On remand, the district court should consider whether the benefits payable to Corley under the relevant versions of the Plan constituted an early retirement benefit or a retirement-type subsidy which would be protected from elimination or reduction, or an optional form of benefit which would only be protected from elimination. To the extent that Corley may be seeking separately calculated benefits under former versions of the Plan in addition to the benefits payable under the Plan in effect at the time of his retirement, the district court should be mindful of the risk of double counting his early-retirement benefits.[19]

The Anti-Cutback Rule and Postretirement Employment

In *Central Laborers' Pension Fund v. Heinz*, the Supreme Court held that the anti-cutback rule extends to amendments that change the types of post-retirement employment that can trigger the suspension of benefits.[20] The plan in *Heinz* suspended benefits when participants engaged in certain "disqualifying employment."[21] In 1998, administrators amended the plan to classify any employment involving construction as disqualifying after a participant named Heinz had already retired and taken on supervisory work in construction.[22] The Court agreed with Heinz's contention that the anti-cutback rule prohibited the amendment's deprivation of his benefits:

> ERISA's anti-cutback rule is crucial to this object, and (with two exceptions of no concern here) provides that [t]he accrued benefit of a participant under a plan may not be decreased by an amendment of the plan . . . . After some initial question about whether the provision addressed early retirement benefits, a 1984 amendment made it clear that it does. Now § 204(g) provides that a plan amendment which has the effect of . . . eliminating or reducing an early retirement

19. *Id.* (citations and quotation marks omitted).
20. Cent. Laborers Pension Fund v. Heinz, 541 U.S. 739, 741 (2004).
21. *Id.* at 742.
22. *Id.*

> benefit . . . with respect to benefits attributable to service before the amendment shall be treated as reducing accrued benefits.
>
> Hence the question here: did the 1998 amendment to the Plan have the effect of eliminating or reducing an early retirement benefit that was earned by service before the amendment was passed? The statute, admittedly, is not as helpful as it might be in answering this question; it does not explicitly define early retirement benefit, and it rather circularly defines accrued benefit as the individual's accrued benefit determined under the plan . . . . Still, it certainly looks as though a benefit has suffered under the amendment here, for we agree with the Seventh Circuit that, as a matter of common sense, [a] participant's benefits cannot be understood without reference to the conditions imposed on receiving those benefits, and an amendment placing materially greater restrictions on the receipt of the benefit reduces the benefit just as surely as a decrease in the size of the monthly benefit payment. Heinz worked and accrued retirement benefits under a plan with terms allowing him to supplement retirement income by certain employment, and he was being reasonable if he relied on those terms in planning his retirement. The 1998 amendment undercut any such reliance, paying retirement income only if he accepted a substantial curtailment of his opportunity to do the kind of work he knew. We simply do not see how, in any practical sense, this change of terms could not be viewed as shrinking the value of Heinz's pension rights and reducing his promised benefits.[23]

In determining that the anti-cutback rule prohibited the plan from disqualifying Heinz, the Court found strong support in the position of the Internal Revenue Service:

> Our conclusion is confirmed by a regulation of the Internal Revenue Service (IRS) that adopts just this reading of § 204(g). When Title I of ERISA was enacted to impose substantive legal requirements on employee pension plans (including the anti-cutback rule), Title II of

23. *Id.* at 744–45 (citations and quotation marks omitted).

ERISA amended the Internal Revenue Code to condition the eligibility of pension plans for preferential tax treatment on compliance with many of the Title I requirements. The result was a curious duplicate structure with nearly verbatim replication in the Internal Revenue Code of whole sections of text from Title I of ERISA. The anti-cutback rule of ERISA § 204(g) is one such section, showing up in substantially identical form as 26 U.S.C. § 411(d)(6). This duplication explains the provision of the Reorganization Plan No. 4 of 1978, giving the Secretary of the Treasury the ultimate authority to interpret these overlapping anti-cutback provisions. Although the pertinent regulations refer only to the Internal Revenue Code version of the anti-cutback rule, they apply with equal force to ERISA § 204(g).

The IRS has formally taken the position that the anti-cutback rule does not keep employers from specifying in advance of accrual that [t]he availability of a section 411(d)(6) protected benefit [is] limited to employees who satisfy certain objective conditions . . . . Without running afoul of the rule, for example, plans may say from the outset that a single sum distribution of benefits is conditioned on the execution of a covenant not to compete. And employers are perfectly free to modify the deal they are offering their employees, as long as the change goes to the terms of compensation for continued, future employment: a plan may be amended to eliminate or reduce section 411(d)(6) protected benefits with respect to benefits not yet accrued . . . . The IRS regulations treat such conditions very differently, however, when they turn up as part of an amendment adding new conditions to the receipt of benefits already accrued. The rule in that case is categorical: [t]he addition of . . . objective conditions with respect to a section 411(d)(6) protected benefit that has already accrued violates section 411(d)(6). Also, the addition of conditions (whether or not objective) or any change to existing conditions with respect to section 411(d)(6) protected benefits that results in any further restriction violates section 411(d)(6). So far as the IRS regulations are concerned, then, the anti-cutback provision flatly prohibits plans from attaching new conditions to benefits that an employee has already earned.

> The IRS has, however, told two stories. The Plan points to a provision of the Internal Revenue Manual that supports its position: [a]n amendment that reduces IRC 411(d)(6) protected benefits on account of [a plan's disqualifying employment provision] does not violate IRC 411(d)(6). And the United States as amicus curiae says that the IRS has routinely approved amendments to plan definitions of disqualifying employment, even when they apply retroactively to accrued benefits. But neither an unreasoned statement in the manual nor allegedly longstanding agency practice can trump a formal regulation with the procedural history necessary to take on the force of law. Speaking in its most authoritative voice, the IRS has long since approved the interpretation of § 204(g) that we adopt today.[24]

The Anti-Cutback Rule and Discount Rates

The Pension Protection Act of 2006 empowered plan sponsors to amend a plan's lump-sum discount rate and increase the rate retroactively without implicating the anti-cutback rule.[25] The United States Court of Appeals for the Seventh Circuit confronted this relatively new law in the 2013 case *Dennison v. MONY Life Retirement Income Security Plan for Employees*, and denied a pension plan participant's request for a higher lump-sum benefit calculated using the discount rate that was in effect when he terminated employment.[26] The court held that an amendment retroactively increasing the discount rate did not violate the anti-cutback rule, thereby validating the increase in the discount rate that resulted in decreasing the participant's benefit value.[27]

Even after the Pension Protection Act of 2006, the plan's terms remained vital to the *Dennison* court's analysis of the retroactive discount rate:

---

24. *Id.* at 746–48 (citations and quotation marks omitted).
25. 29 U.S.C. § 1054 (2012).
26. Dennison v. MONY Life Ret. Income Sec. Plan for Emps., 710 F.3d 741, 743 (7th Cir. 2012).
27. *Id.* at 743–44.

In 2009, three years after the Pension Protection Act was passed and shortly before the plaintiff turned 55 and thus became entitled to begin receiving his retirement benefits, MONY raised the [Retirement Income Security Plan] discount rate to the segment rate. The rate that MONY used to compute the plaintiff's benefits under the Excess Plan remained at 7.5 percent.

MONY could lawfully change the RISPE discount rate retroactively only if the plan authorized such an amendment. A plan is not required to do that, and it can if it wants promise not to, thereby creating a contractual anti-cutback rule that is enforceable like any other plan provision. The Pension Protection Act provides an out only with respect to the statutory anti-cutback rule.

The RISPE plan in force when the plaintiff left MONY states that the pension rights of an employee who left on or before the effective date of a particular amendment to the plan shall be determined solely under the terms of the Plan as in effect on the date of his or her termination of employment or retirement . . . unless [the amendment is] made applicable to former Employees. So the plan did allow MONY to amend it to change the discount rate retroactively. But the plan also provides that no amendment shall . . . reduce the Accrued Benefit of any Participant. The plaintiff was a plan participant and his benefit had accrued back in 1996, when he left the company. But Accrued Benefit is a defined term in the plan—defined as the value of a Participant's Retirement Benefit expressed as a Straight-Life Annuity determined according to the terms of the Plan. Retirement Benefit is another defined term: it means a benefit payable on the dates, in the forms specified in a section of the plan that under the heading Optional Forms allows the participant to choose a lump sum in lieu of the Normal Form, which is the straight-life annuity.

We interpret these provisions to mean that the Accrued Benefit—that which cannot be reduced retroactively by amendment—is the annuity, and that the lump sum, while a Retirement Benefit, is not the Accrued Benefit and therefore can be reduced retroactively. The term Retirement Benefit encompasses all forms of benefits payment that a participant can choose, including the lump sum option that the plaintiff chose in lieu of the annuity. Nothing in the plan forbids retroactively amending the discount rate used to calculate the lump sum benefit if the participant chooses the lump sum in preference to the annuity.[28]

The Anti-Cutback Rule and Optional Forms of Benefits

A plan amendment that removes a plan's subsidy for early retirement benefits or that eliminates optional forms of benefits violates the anti-cutback rule because such an amendment constitutes a reduction in accrued benefits.[29] The Treasury has explained that an amendment does not eliminate an optional form of a benefit or reduce a retirement subsidy "if, effective after the plan amendment, there is another optional form of benefit available to the participant under the plan that is of inherently equal or greater value."[30]

In *Wetzler v. Illinois CPA Society & Foundation Retirement Income Plan*, the United States Court of Appeals for the Seventh Circuit considered whether an amendment to a plan to allow the plan to conform to the requirements of the IRC, could violate the anti-cutback rule.[31] The claimant in *Wetzler*, Thomas Wetzler, contested a postretirement amendment to the plan that brought the plan into compliance with Treasury regulations.[32] Prior to the amendment, highly compensated employees (HCEs), including Wetzler, could take a lump-sum payout of his or her benefits without providing any security to the underfunded plan.[33] Once the plan determined that this lump-sum distribution violated Treasury regulations and compromised the plan's tax-qualified status, administrators adopted Amendment One, which ensured that all plan distributions complied with federal regulation.[34] After

28. *Id.* at 744 (citations and quotation marks omitted).
29. 29 U.S.C. § 1054(g)(1) (2012).
30. 26 C.F.R. § 1.411(d)-3 (2013).
31. Wetzler v. Ill. CPA & Soc. & Found. Ret. Income Plan, 586 F.3d 1053, 1060 (7th Cir. 2009).
32. *Id.* at 1055.
33. *Id.* at 1056.
34. *Id.*

the plan denied a lump-sum distribution to Wetzler, he filed suit, asserting that Amendment One violated the anti-cutback rule.[35]

The court held that an amendment to bring a plan into legal compliance was outside the purview of the anti-cutback rule:

> ERISA's anti-cutback provision states that the accrued benefit of a participant under a plan may not be decreased by an amendment of the plan. The purpose of this provision is to protect employees' justified expectations. For example, in *Heinz*, the plan at issue suspended payments to retired beneficiaries if they engaged in disqualifying employment and after Heinz's retirement, amended the definition of disqualifying employment to include working as a supervisor. In finding that this amendment violated ERISA's anti-cutback provision, the Court determined that Heinz had accrued benefits under the plan allowing him to supplement his retirement income by working as a supervisor and those benefits were curtailed by the amendment.
>
> As set forth in ERISA's anti-cutback provision, an accrued benefit is separate and distinct from an optional form of benefit despite the fact that the statute treats a plan amendment which reduces or eliminates an optional form of benefit as reducing accrued benefits. Title 29 United States Code Section 1002(23)(A) defines accrued benefit as the individual's accrued benefit determined under the plan . . . expressed in the form of an annual benefit commencing at the normal retirement age. An optional form of benefit is not defined in ERISA, and while its meaning is obscure, it is generally a benefit that involves the right of a plan participant to choose the way in which his payments under a plan will be made or applied. A plan participant's ability to take a lump-sum distribution of benefits is an optional form of benefit as defined by the anti-cutback provision of ERISA. Therefore, for purposes of the statutory anti-cutback provision, a plan amendment may not eliminate one's entitlement to take his pension benefits as a lump sum at normal retirement age.

35. *Id.*

> Here, Wetzler asserts that the implementation of Amendment One violated ERISA's anti-cutback provision because Amendment One eliminated a pre-existing optional form of benefit, namely the ability to receive a lump-sum distribution. . . . [H]owever, due to underfunding, HCEs never had the option of collecting lump-sum distributions prior to Amendment One, which makes this case distinct from *Heinz* where the amendment altered a pre-existing benefit. While the anti-cutback provision in Section 204(g)(2)(B) of ERISA states that eliminating an optional form of benefit shall be treated as reducing accrued benefits, Section 204(g)(2) only applies if the benefit—a lump-sum distribution—qualifies as an optional form of benefit and is therefore attributable to service before the amendment . . . . As the Plan rightly argues, Amendment One did not eliminate or affect any lump-sum option that was previously available to plan members. Instead, the Amendment gave the Plan a way of correcting a distribution that was not allowed under the Treasury Regulations at the time it was made. Because plan participants were not entitled, under the Plan, to a lump-sum distribution, Amendment One did not eliminate an optional form of benefit and does not violate ERISA's anti-cutback provision.
>
> Furthermore, even if the right to receive lump-sum distributions had been an optional form of benefit that was attributable to service prior to Amendment One, Amendment One brought the Plan into compliance with the Internal Revenue Code and accompanying Treasury Regulations, bringing it outside the ambit of ERISA's anti-cutback statute.[36]

The Anti-Cutback Rule Following Employment

The anti-cutback rule extends protections to participants facing amendments made after they have already left employment. In *Alcantara v. Bakery and Confectionary Union and Industry International Pension Fund Pension Plan*, decided May 1, 2014, the United States Court of Appeals for

36. *Id.* at 1058–60 (citations and quotation marks omitted).

the Second Circuit took up the question of whether the anti-cutback rule precluded a plan amendment from reducing a retirement-type subsidy for those participants who had ceased employment before satisfying the pre-amendment conditions of the subsidy.[37] *Alcantara* concerned a plan offering a range of benefits:

> The standard benefit, payable at age 65—the "normal retirement age" under the Plan—was labeled Plan A. Participants could elect to receive their Plan A pension benefits as early as age 55, but at an actuarially reduced level that reflected the earlier (and longer) expected stream of payments. Certain employers elected to offer additional subsidized early retirement benefits that were not actuarially reduced. Two of these plans, Plan G (the "Golden 80 Plan"), and Plan C (the "Golden 90 Plan"), are at issue here. Under those Plans, a participant who had completed at least ten years of service with a participating employer, and whose combination of his age and years of service totaled 80 or 90 years, respectively, could retire and receive full pension benefits.[38]

The case arose after the plan eliminated the option for former employees to age into the Golden 80 or 90 benefits even after failing to reach the benefits' requirements before leaving employment.[39] The court held that the anti-cutback rule preserved a subsidy for former employees who could have satisfied preamendment conditions for the subsidy:

> In our view, it is clear that the Golden 80 and 90 Plans are retirement-type subsid[ies] that qualify for protection under § 204(g)(2). The term retirement-type subsidy is defined in IRS regulations interpreting a parallel provision of the Internal Revenue Code. A retirement-type subsidy is:
>
> > the excess, if any, of the actuarial present value of a retirement-type benefit over the actuarial present value of the accrued

37. Alcantara v. Bakery and Confectionery Union and Indus. Int'l Pension Fund Pension Plan, No. 12-4834-CV, 2014 WL 1705015, at *1 (2d Cir. May 1, 2014).
38. *Id.*
39. *Id.*

benefit commencing at normal retirement age or at actual commencement date, if later, with both such actuarial present values determined as of the date the retirement-type benefit commences. Examples of retirement-type subsidies include a subsidized early retirement benefit . . .

The Golden 80 and 90 Plans fall within this definition. The Plans provide a retirement-type benefit because they provide a benefit under a defined benefit plan . . . that . . . continues after retirement, and is not an ancillary benefit. It is undisputed that the actuarial value of the Golden 80 and 90 Plans at the time they begin distributing benefits is in excess of the actuarial present value of the accrued benefit commencing at normal retirement age. Accordingly, for the purposes of the anti-cutback rule, the Golden 80 and 90 Plans are retirement-type subsidies.

The evolution of § 204(g) reinforces this conclusion. Prior to the passage of the Retirement Equity Act of 1984 (REA), the anti-cutback rule was limited to the text now included in § 204(g)(1) and thus applied only to accrued benefits. Whether early retirement benefits, retirement-type subsidies, and optional forms of benefits were protected was unclear because the statute did not specifically address those types of benefits.

Congress recognized that these benefits could be important components of retirement packages and passed the REA in part to limit the circumstances under which these benefits could be reduced or eliminated through plan amendments. To do so, Congress added § 204(g)(2) which did not disturb the existing protection for accrued benefits, but went on to provide that reductions to early retirement benefits, retirement-type subsidies, and optional forms of benefits were to be treated as reductions of accrued benefits. Accordingly, where a benefit qualifies as a retirement-type subsidy, it is subject to § 204(g)(2) of the anti-cutback rule.

Section 204(g)(2) contains an additional provision, the meaning of which is the primary point of disagreement on this appeal. Under that provision, the anti-cutback rule applies to retirement-type subsidies, only with respect to a participant who satisfies (either before or after the amendment) the preamendment conditions for the subsidy. The plaintiffs would have us read the only with respect to a participant . . . language as simply requiring that a participant satisf[y] (either before or after the amendment) the preamendment conditions for the subsidy to have their benefits protected by the rule. The plaintiffs contend that they have satisfied (or will satisfy) this requirement. The preamendment Plan, they argue, conditioned Golden 80 or 90 benefits on the sum of plaintiffs' years-of-employment plus age equaling 80 or 90, respectively. Because plaintiffs either have seen, or if they continue to age will see, that number equal 80 or 90 and because the Plan has no time limitation within which a participant must reach that number, the preamendment condition, they contend, is or will be satisfied.

The Plan agrees that Golden 80 and 90 Plans are retirement-type subsidies, but insists that § 204(g)(2) contains an implicit continued employment requirement, under which a participant, to be protected by the anti-cutback rule, must have remain [sic] in covered employment until he becomes eligible for the subsidy. The Plan insists that the "only with respect to a participant . . ." language is intended to have a limiting effect on the application of the anti-cutback rule to retirement-type subsidies and that, read literally as the plaintiffs urge, the sentence has none because a participant could never be eligible for a subsidy without satisf[ying] . . . the preamendment conditions for the subsidy. On the basis of this reading, the Plan contends that the scope of the limitation is unclear and can be understood only by resort to the legislative history, which the Plan argues reveals that Congress intended to limit the protection of the anti-cutback rule to current employees. For several reasons, we disagree with the Plan's approach.

Legislative interpretation begins with the plain text of the statute and, where the text is unambiguous, also ends there because the judicial inquiry is complete. We read the provision

> as straightforwardly applying to participants, such as the plaintiffs, who qualified for the subsidy before the amendment or who could do so afterwards. The text says nothing about satisfying the preamendment conditions while employed, or before separating from service, or anything to that effect. To the contrary, the statutory wording cuts against such a requirement. Section 204(g)(2), which requires that a participant satisfy the preamendment conditions of the subsidy in order to enjoy the protections of the anti-cutback rule, is elucidated by the definition of a participant under ERISA as any employee or former employee of an employer, . . . who is or may become eligible to receive a benefit of any type from an employee benefit plan. Consequently, it is immaterial that some plaintiffs had not yet satisfied the preamendment age-level conditions when they left covered employment, because § 204(g)'s prohibition on cutbacks applies to former as well as to current employees.
>
> The Plan's approach would require us to delve into the complex legislative history of ERISA and the REA in search of limiting principles that Congress did not include in the text. This would result not in a construction of the statute, but, in effect, an enlargement of it by the court, so that what was omitted . . . may be included within its scope. Accordingly, we are not inclined to overlook the plaintiffs' straightforward and reasonable interpretation of the statute in favor of one that renders the text ambiguous and resorts to legislative history or policy arguments to give it meaning.[40]

The court joined the Third, Fifth, and Seventh Circuits in rejecting the argument that a participant must be in continued employment to enjoy the anti-cutback rule's protection.[41] Other courts have denied the option

40. *Id.* at *3–4.

41. *Id.* at *5 (citing Bellas v. CBS, Inc., 221 F.3d 517, 521 (3d Cir. 2000); Ahng v. Allsteel, Inc., 96 F.3d 1033, 1036–37 (7th Cir. 1996); Harms v. Cavenham Forest Indus., Inc., 984 F.2d 686, 692 (5th Cir. 1993); Gillis v. Hoechst Celanese Corp., 4 F.3d 1137, 1146 (3d Cir. 1993); Hunger v. AB, 12 F.3d 118, 121 (8th Cir. 1993)).

of growing into benefits in situations where the participant had ceased employment before completing the minimum years of service required for eligibility, or had failed to meet some other preamendment requirement where, regardless of the amendment, the participant would not have qualified for the subsidy.[42]

Statutory Notice Requirements for Prospective Amendments

ERISA does not prohibit prospective reductions in the rate of accrued benefits, but ERISA does require notice of any significant and material reduction in the rate of accrual of plan benefits or when there is a significant reduction in an early retirement or retirement-type subsidy. If a plan provides that retirement benefits at age 65 will be calculated as 3 percent of a participant's average compensation for each year of participation in the plan and a subsequent amendment provides that a participant's accrued benefit at retirement would be only 1.5 percent of average compensation for each year of plan participation both prior to the amendment and postamendment, the amendment would clearly violate the anti-cutback rule. However, if the amendment provided that the benefit would remain at 3 percent of average compensation for each preamendment year and 1.5 percent of average compensation prospectively, the amendment would not run afoul of the anti-cutback rule because the already accrued benefits would remain unaltered. However, in making such a prospective reduction in benefit accruals, the employer would have to comply with the notification requirements of ERISA § 204(h).

Commonly litigated issues under 204(h) include whether the notice concerning plan amendments was deficient and whether such a deficiency was the result of an egregious failure. In determining whether a notice failure was egregious, courts examine various factors, including the number of participants affected, whether the administrator knew that the notice

42. *Id.* (citing Shaver v. Siemens Corp., 670 F.3d 462, 490–91 (3d Cir. 2012); *Hunger*, 12 F.3d at 121; Berger v. Edgewater Steel Co., 911 F.2d 911, 918 (3d Cir. 1990)).

was deficient, and the promptness in correcting the notice failure. A recent example before the United States Court of Appeals for the Fourth Circuit was the unreported case *Brady v. Dow Chemical Company Retirement Board*. *Brady* examined whether the Dow Chemical Company Retirement Board and the plan it administered for employees of the Union Carbide Corporation (UCC) provided adequate notice of substantial amendments to participants and specifically to the claimant Dennis Brady.[43] After concluding that notice was necessary, the court held that the plan had not complied with 204(h).[44] The court reasoned:

> We first consider whether the 204(h) Notice issued by the Dow Retirement Board in this case was deficient. Specifically, Brady alleges that the Dow Board failed to provide adequate notice with respect to the elimination of Table 2 for purposes of the December 31, 2005, grandfather benefit. Section 204(h) requires notice of a significant reduction in the rate of future benefit accrual. A separate ERISA provision makes clear that a plan amendment which eliminates or reduces any early retirement benefit or retirement-type subsidy (within the meaning of subsection (g)(2)(A)) shall be treated as having the effect of reducing the rate of future benefit accrual. The Board does not dispute that the reduction in Brady's benefits that resulted from the elimination of Table 2 constituted a reduction in early retirement benefits or retirement-type subsidies.
>
> In determining whether the reduction in benefits in Brady's case was significant, we compare the amount of the benefit under the plan as amended with the amount of the benefit under the plan prior to the amendment. The parties stipulate that Brady would have been entitled to an additional $281.97 per month under Table 2 of the Prior UCC Plan. Thus, the applicable plan amendments resulted in a 10.7 percent reduction in benefits for Brady. We conclude that a reduction of this magnitude is significant. We also conclude that the

43. Brady v. Dow Chemical Co. Retirement Bd., 311 F. App'x 626, 627 (4th Cir. 2009).
44. *Id.* at 630–31.

Board could anticipate decreases in benefits of this magnitude at the time the amendment was adopted.

Because the elimination of Table 2 caused a significant reduction in retirement benefits, adequate notice was required under ERISA § 204(h). This notice must be written in a manner calculated to be understood by the average plan participant and [must] provide sufficient information . . . to allow applicable individuals to understand the effect of the plan amendment. The Board's 204(h) Notice issued to Brady and other plan participants failed in one respect: it did not provide adequate information about the elimination of Table 2 for purposes of the December 31, 2005, grandfather benefit.

The 204(h) Notice included the following information under the heading, Grandfathered Provisions:

> It is important to note that when you retire on or after February 7, 2003, you will continue to have the right to elect to receive the monthly pension benefit, and associated eligibility dates and payment options you earned under the [Prior UCC Plan] through February 6, 2003. You will not receive a monthly pension benefit less than what you had earned before February 7, 2003.
>
> In addition, to further ease the transition to [the Union Carbide Employees' Pension Plan], you will continue to earn benefit accruals under the [Prior UCC Plan] formulas through December 31, 2005. [Except for two modifications inapplicable to the current dispute that relate to how length of service is calculated and which indicia of earnings is used], [t]his benefit will serve as a minimum monthly pension benefit when you retire.

This provision affirmatively suggests that the formulas used under the Prior UCC Plan will continue to be available through December 31, 2005, with two explicitly identified modifications but no other exceptions. Indeed, the February 6, 2003, grandfather benefit retained Table 2, furthering an understanding that Table 2 is part and parcel of the Prior UCC Plan formulas a plan participant would expect to be used in a grandfathered benefit.

The Dow Retirement Board argues that the language makes clear that only benefit accruals—not early retirement subsidies—continue through December 31, 2005. We disagree that the Board's use of the term benefit accruals meant that early retirement subsidies were excluded. The statutory scheme treats benefit accruals as a term of art that includes retirement subsidies. When Dow used the term benefits accruals, it was incorporating the statutory definition. We therefore conclude that average plan participants would understand the 204(h) Notice language quoted above to grandfather into the December 31, 2005, grandfather benefit the formulas used under the Prior UCC Plan, which incorporate Table 2's reduction factors.

Other provisions of the 204(h) Notice further this understanding. The Questions and Answers section says,

> Q3. What will happen to the pension benefit I earned under the current Union Carbide Retirement Program?
>
> A3. You will not lose the benefit you have already earned under the Union Carbide Retirement Program. In addition, Dow has put transition credits and grandfathered provisions in place to help you transition to UCEPP.

The import of this provision is to assure plan participants that the benefits available under the Prior UCC Plan, which included Table 2, would remain available under the UCEPP during the transition. Certainly, nothing in the 204(h) Notice flags the elimination of Table 2 in the December 1, 2005, grandfather provision. Insofar as the language of the 204(h) Notice is misleading about whether Table 2 is retained, it is inadequate under 29 U.S.C. § 1054(h)(2). At the very least, the 204(h) Notice fails to provide sufficient information from which an average plan participant could understand that Table 2 would not be available under the December 31, 2005, grandfather benefit. We therefore agree with the district court's conclusion that the 204(h) Notice issued in this case was deficient in that respect.[45]

45. *Id.* (citations and quotation marks omitted).

Moreover, the court found that the plan did not qualify for a statutory safe harbor for plans that could demonstrate a good faith effort to comply with 204(h):

> Congress's 2001 amendments to ERISA, which made clear that 204(h) Notice was required for reductions in early retirement benefits and retirement-type subsidies (in addition to benefit accruals for normal retirement benefits), provided for a transitional good faith safe harbor.
>
> > Until such time as the Secretary of the Treasury issues regulations under sections 4980F(e)(2) and (3) of the Internal Revenue Code of 1986, and section 204(h) of the Employee Retirement Income Security Act of 1974, as added by the amendments made by this section, a plan shall be treated as meeting the requirements of such sections if it makes a good faith effort to comply with such requirements.
>
> In the regulations subsequently promulgated, the Secretary of the Treasury similarly provided that for plan amendments taking effect before the September 2, 2003, effective date of the regulations, the requirements of section 204(h), as amended by the Economic Growth and Tax Relief Reconciliation Act, are treated as satisfied if the plan administrator makes a reasonable, good faith effort to comply with those requirements. The Dow Board argues that its efforts to satisfy § 204(h), even if technically deficient, were reasonable, made in good faith, and are thus insulated under the above transitional safe harbor.
>
> The district court concluded that except for the two respects in which it determined that the Board egregiously violated § 204(h), it cannot be said that Defendants failed to make a reasonable, good faith effort to comply with the statutory requirements. Our review is therefore limited to whether there was an unreasonable or bad faith effort to comply with § 204(h) as a result of the two egregious violations identified by the district court. It is further limited by our conclusion above that there was not sufficient evidence in the record to allow a determination that the Dow Board failed to provide most of the individuals with most of the information they are entitled to

receive. Summary judgment is nevertheless appropriate if the Dow Board's failure to promptly rectify its deficient 204(h) Notice was tantamount to an unreasonable or bad faith effort to comply with § 204(h)'s requirements.

The district court concluded that there was a failure to provide notice after the plan administrator discovered an inadvertent deficiency in the plan's 204(h) Notice. The district court expressly declined to conclude that there was an intentional failure in the first instance. We must thus determine whether the failure that did occur is sufficient to establish that the plan failed to make[] a reasonable, good faith effort to comply with [the] requirements [of section 204(h)]. We conclude that it does.

The Board is not protected under the good faith safe harbor unless it acted in good faith in its efforts to comply with all of § 204(h)'s requirements. Those requirements include a continuing obligation to supplement a deficient § 204(h) notice. The statutory safe harbor provides that [u]ntil such time [as regulations are issued interpreting IRC § 4980F and ERISA § 204(h)] a plan shall be treated as meeting the requirements of such sections if it makes a good faith effort to comply with such requirements. This language indicates that the good faith effort contemplated by Congress was an ongoing obligation. It is not enough to have made a good faith effort at the outset of a plan amendment. The text of § 204(h) further supports this understanding:

> [T]here is an egregious failure to meet the requirements of this subsection [§ 204(h)] if [there is a] failure to promptly provide the required notice or information after the plan administrator discovers an unintentional failure to meet the requirements of this subsection [§ 204(h)].

This provision affirms that there is a continuing obligation to correct a deficient § 204(h) notice. An act constituting an egregious failure to meet the requirements of § 204(h) necessarily constitutes a violation of § 204(h). Congress may have been concerned about the ability of pension plans to satisfy the requirements of § 204(h) before Treasury clarified those requirements, but it apparently concluded that it was affording pension plans sufficient protection by placing any pension plan acting in good faith into its safe harbor.

We affirm the district court's conclusion that irrespective of whether the Board acted in good faith when it originally published its 204(h) Notice, it was no longer acting in good faith when it failed to promptly supplement its 204(h) Notice upon discovering a deficiency. The plan administrator received a coherent and compelling explanation that the 204(h) Notice was misleading with respect to whether the December 31, 2005, grandfather benefit retained Table 2's benefits. The language of the 204(h) Notice patently failed to provide sufficient information for an average plan participant to glean that Table 2's benefits would be eliminated with respect to the December 31, 2005, grandfather benefit. The record also contains undisputed evidence that the Board knew that multiple employees were in fact confused about this aspect of the plan amendment. This evidence supports the district court's determination that the Board failed to act in good faith when it declined to clarify its misleading (and thus deficient) 204(h) Notice.[46]

Vesting Protections and Minimum Participation

ERISA ensures that participants in private pension plans have a nonforfeitable right to their retirement benefits at normal retirement age, and to their own contributions.[47] ERISA sets forth minimum vesting schedules to which plans must adhere.[48] The vesting schedules allow some degree of forfeiture, which can be justified on the grounds that the use of the schedules allows employers to experience some degree of employee retention. Statutory exceptions permit forfeitures of accrued benefits derived from employer contributions typically where there is an actionable statutory "break in service."[49] In certain cases, courts have permitted the forfeiture

46. *Id.* at 634–35 (citations and quotation marks omitted).
47. 29 U.S.C. § 1053(a) (2012).
48. *Id.*
49. *Id.*

of benefit schedules that were more generous than the minimum vesting allowed under the statute.[50]

ERISA contains minimum participation standards that limit a pension plan's use of age or length-of-service as a condition for participating in the plan.[51] Federal regulation has elaborated: "Plan provisions which have the effect of requiring an age or service requirement with the employer or employers maintaining the plan will be treated as if they imposed an age or service requirement."[52] This prevents a plan from evading ERISA's minimum participation standards through creative plan design.

Limiting participation in the plan to salaried workers does not violate the minimum participation standards. In *Bauer v. Summit Bancorp*, the United States Court of Appeals for the Third Circuit observed:

> [The employer] had no duty to create the Plan in this case. It also had no duty to provide benefits to every employee. [The employer] could limit plan participation to certain groups or classifications of employees, as long as that limitation was not based upon age or length of service.[53]

Antialienation

Assignment and alienation are distinct terms; assignment refers to a voluntary act with respect to plan benefits, and alienation refers to an involuntary interference with plan benefits. Pension plans must provide that plan benefits may not be assigned or alienated.[54] Both the IRC and ERISA impose antialienation and antiassignment provisions on covered plans in order to protect plan assets from creditors and to ensure participants' benefits are actually available upon retirement and not dissipated due to premature consumption.

50. Montgomery v. Pension Ben. Guar. Corp., 601 F.Supp.2d 139, 140 (D. D.C. 2009) (citing Fremont v. McGraw-Edison Co., 606 F.2d 752, 755 (7th Cir. 1979)).
51. 29 U.S.C. § 1052(a)(1) (2012).
52. 26 C.F.R. § 1.410(a)–3 (2013).
53. Bauer v. Summit Bancorp, 325 F. 3d 155, 166 (3d Cir. 2003) (citations omitted).
54. 29 U.S.C. § 1056(d)(1) (2012).

Whereas vesting protects the employee from employer conduct by prohibiting forfeiture of pension benefits once an employee meets certain requirements, antialienation protects the employee and the employees' dependents from the employee's own spending. Private creditors face an absolute prohibition on alienation of pension benefits. In *Patterson v. Shumate*, the Supreme Court held that ERISA's antialienation provision exempted pension benefits from the bankruptcy estate because the pension benefits fell within the Bankruptcy Code's exclusion of property that was restricted from transfer under "applicable nonbankruptcy law."[55] The Court explained:

> First, our decision today ensures that the treatment of pension benefits will not vary based on the beneficiary's bankruptcy status. We previously have declined to recognize any exceptions to ERISA's antialienation provision outside the bankruptcy context. Declining to recognize any exceptions to that provision within the bankruptcy context minimizes the possibility that creditors will engage in strategic manipulation of the bankruptcy laws in order to gain access to otherwise inaccessible funds.
>
> Our holding also gives full and appropriate effect to ERISA's goal of protecting pension benefits. This Court has described that goal as one of ensuring that if a worker has been promised a defined pension benefit upon retirement—and if he has fulfilled whatever conditions are required to obtain a vested benefit—he actually will receive it. In furtherance of these principles, we recently declined in *Guidry*, notwithstanding strong equitable considerations to the contrary, to recognize an implied exception to ERISA's antialienation provision that would have allowed a labor union to impose a constructive trust on the pension benefits of a corrupt union official. We explained:
>
>> Section 206(d) reflects a considered congressional policy choice, a decision to safeguard a stream of income for pensioners (and their dependents, who may be, and perhaps usually are, blameless), even if that decision prevents others from securing

55. Patterson v. Shumate, 504 U.S. 753, 765 (1992).

> relief for the wrongs done them. If exceptions to this policy are to be made, it is for Congress to undertake that task.
>
> These considerations apply with equal, if not greater, force in the present context.
>
> Finally, our holding furthers another important policy underlying ERISA: uniform national treatment of pension benefits. Construing applicable nonbankruptcy law to include federal law ensures that the security of a debtor's pension benefits will be governed by ERISA, not left to the vagaries of state spendthrift trust law.[56]

In *Guidry v. Sheet Metal Workers National Pension Fund*, the Supreme Court overturned the imposition of a constructive trust on a participant's pension benefits from which funds could be recouped after the participant had pled guilty to embezzling union funds.[57] The petitioner in *Guidry* pled guilty to embezzling over $377,000 from Sheet Metal Workers International Association, Local 9 (Union) while serving as the Union's chief executive officer but then initiated suit for his pension benefits while incarcerated for his violation of § 501(c) of the Labor-Management Reporting and Disclosure Act of 1959 (LMRDA).[58] The Court found that the imposition of a constructive trust to recoup embezzled funds violated ERISA's prohibition against alienation.[59] As a result, the Court rejected the findings of *Guidry*'s lower courts:

> The Court of Appeals, in holding that the district court's use of a constructive trust to redress breaches of ERISA was proper, indicated that an exception to the anti-alienation provision can be made when a pension plan fiduciary breaches a duty owed to the plan itself. The court relied on § 409(a) of ERISA, which provides that a faithless pension plan fiduciary shall be personally liable to make good to such plan any losses to the plan resulting from each such breach, and shall be subject to such other equitable or remedial relief as the court may

56. *Id.* at 764–65 (citations and quotation marks omitted).
57. Guidry v. Sheet Metal Workers Nat'l Pension Fund, 493 U.S. 365, 377 (1990).
58. *Id.* at 367–68.
59. *Id.* at 377.

deem appropriate. We need not decide whether the remedial provisions contained in § 409(a) supersede the bar on alienation in § 206(d)(1), since petitioner has not been found to have breached any fiduciary duty to the pension plans. Respondents contend that, due to the nature of petitioner's scheme, there exists continuing uncertainty as to how much money was stolen from the Union and how much was taken from the pension funds. It is clear, however, that petitioner was convicted of stealing money only from the Union. Moreover, petitioner has negotiated a settlement with the fund of which he was a fiduciary, and only the Union has a judgment against him. Respondents' argument plays on the natural tendency to blur the distinctions between a fund and its related union (since an injury to either will hurt the union's membership). Respondents, however, cannot avoid the fact that the funds here and the Union are distinct legal entities. (Indeed, at an earlier stage of the litigation these parties took inconsistent positions: the funds argued that petitioner's benefits were subject to forfeiture, while the Union contended that petitioner retained his right to benefits but that the benefits should be placed in constructive trust). Although petitioner's actions may have harmed the Union's members who are the beneficiaries of the funds, petitioner has not been found to have breached any duty to the plans themselves. In our view, therefore, the Court of Appeals erred in invoking § 409(a)'s remedial provisions.

. . .

Recognizing the problem with the Court of Appeals' approach, respondents, like the District Court, rely principally on the remedial provisions of the LMRDA. Section 501(a) of that Act states that a union's officers occupy positions of trust in relation to such organization and its members as a group and therefore have a duty to hold its money and property solely for the benefit of the organization and its members. Section 501(b) provides, under certain conditions, a private right of action to recover damages or secure an accounting or other appropriate relief for the benefit of the labor organization. We assume, without deciding, that the statutory provision for other appropriate relief may authorize, in some circumstances, the imposition of a constructive trust. The question is whether that authorization may override ERISA's prohibition on the alienation of pension benefits.

Respondents point to § 514(d) of ERISA. It states: "Nothing in this title shall be construed to alter, amend, modify, invalidate, impair, or supersede any law of the United States . . . or any rule or regulation issued under any such law." In respondents' view, application of ERISA's anti-alienation provision to preclude a remedy that would otherwise be available would modify, impair or supersede the LMRDA. We do not believe, however, that the LMRDA will be modified, impaired, or superseded by our refusal to allow ERISA pension plans to be used to effectuate the remedial goals of the LMRDA. Were we to accept respondents' position, ERISA's anti-alienation provision would be inapplicable whenever a judgment creditor relied on the remedial provisions of a federal statute. Such an approach would eviscerate the protections of § 206(d), and we decline to adopt so broad a reading of § 514(d).

It is an elementary tenet of statutory construction that [w]here there is no clear intention otherwise, a specific statute will not be controlled or nullified by a general one . . . . We do not believe that congressional intent would be effectuated by reading the LMRDA's general reference to other appropriate relief as overriding an express, specific congressional directive that pension benefits not be subject to assignment or alienation. In our view, the two statutes are more persuasively reconciled by holding that the LMRDA determines what sort of judgment the aggrieved party may obtain, while ERISA governs the narrow question whether that judgment may be collected through a particular means—a constructive trust placed on the pension.

. . .

Nor do we think it appropriate to approve any generalized equitable exception—either for employee malfeasance or for criminal misconduct—to ERISA's prohibition on the assignment or alienation of pension benefits. Section 206(d) reflects a considered congressional policy choice, a decision to safeguard a stream of income for pensioners (and their dependents, who may be, and perhaps usually are, blameless), even if that decision prevents others from securing relief

> for the wrongs done them. If exceptions to this policy are to be made, it is for Congress to undertake that task.
>
> As a general matter, courts should be loath to announce equitable exceptions to legislative requirements or prohibitions that are unqualified by the statutory text. The creation of such exceptions, in our view, would be especially problematic in the context of an antigarnishment provision. Such a provision acts, by definition, to hinder the collection of a lawful debt. A restriction on garnishment therefore can be defended only on the view that the effectuation of certain broad social policies sometimes takes precedence over the desire to do equity between particular parties. It makes little sense to adopt such a policy and then to refuse enforcement whenever enforcement appears inequitable. A court attempting to carve out an exception that would not swallow the rule would be forced to determine whether application of the rule in particular circumstances would be especially inequitable. The impracticability of defining such a standard reinforces our conclusion that the identification of any exception should be left to Congress.
>
> Understandably, there may be a natural distaste for the result we reach here. The statute, however, is clear. In addition, as has been noted above, the malefactor often is not the only beneficiary of the pension.[60]

The interest of other beneficiaries in a participant's benefits remains a potent argument in support of strict adherence to the antialienation provisions.

Following remand by the Supreme Court, the United States Court of Appeals for the Tenth Circuit held that ERISA's antialienation provision did not prohibit garnishment of pension benefits following receipt by the beneficiary, although state law prevented the garnishment in the Tenth Circuit's postremand opinion.[61] Welfare benefits are not protected by the antialienation rule.[62] The Supreme Court and lower courts have allowed the garnishment of welfare benefits.[63]

60. *Id.* at 372–77 (citations and quotation marks omitted).

61. Guidry v. Sheet Metal Workers Nat'l Pension Fund, 39 F.3d 1078, 1083 (10th Cir. 1994).

62. 29 U.S.C. § 1056(d)(1) (2012).

63. *See* Mackey v. Lanier Collection Agency & Serv., Inc. 486 U.S. 825, 831 (1988); St. Francis Reg'l Med. Ctr. v. Blue Cross & Blue Shield of Kan., Inc., 49 F.3d 1460, 1464 (10th Cir. 1995); Davidowitz v. Delta Dental Plan of Cal., 946 F.2d 1476, 1478 (9th Cir. 1991).

Exceptions to Antialienation

There are statutory exceptions to the antialienation rules, however Courts have maintained that any equitable exceptions to the antialienation rules must come from Congress.[64] The United States Court of Appeals for the Tenth Circuit explained in *Martorana v. Board of Trustees of Steamfitters Local Union 420 Health, Welfare and Pension Fund*:

> As a general matter, courts should be loath to announce equitable exceptions to legislative requirements or prohibitions that are unqualified by the statutory text. The creation of such exceptions, in our view, would be especially problematic in the context of an antigarnishment provision. Such a provision acts, by definition, to hinder the collection of a lawful debt. A restriction on garnishment therefore can be defended only on the view that the effectuation of certain broad social policies sometimes takes precedence over the desire to do equity between particular parties. It makes little sense to adopt such a policy and then to refuse enforcement whenever enforcement appears inequitable. A court attempting to carve out an exception that would not swallow the rule would be forced to determine whether application of the rule in particular circumstances would be "especially" inequitable. The impracticability of defining such a standard reinforces our conclusion that the identification of any exception should be left to Congress.[65]

In its 2013 decision *Hakim v. Accenture U.S. Pension Plan*, the United States Court of Appeals for the Seventh Circuit found that contested pension claims are not subject to the same antialienation rules as pension entitlements.[66] The court reasoned:

---

64. Guidry v. Sheet Metal Workers Nat'l Pension Fund, 493 U.S. 365, 377 (1990).
65. Martorana v. Bd. of Trs. of Steamfitters Local Union 420 Health, Welfare and Pension Fund, 404 F.3d 797, 803 (10th Cir. 2005).
66. Hakim v. Accenture U.S. Pension Plan, 718 F.3d 675, 681–82 (7th Cir. 2013).

> Pension entitlements are, without exception, subject to the anti-alienation provision of ERISA. A pension entitlement arises under the terms of the pension plan itself. In other words, an entitlement, as its name would suggest, refers to vested benefits to which a plaintiff is entitled under the terms of the pension plan itself. In *Lynn*, the plaintiff sought to protect military service benefits to which he believe[d] he [was] entitled to under the terms of the plan. We held that the plaintiff was asking the court to interpret the pension plan itself and thus the plaintiff's suit involved a pension entitlement, which subjected it to the anti-alienation provision.
>
> Contested pension claims, however, are simply outside the realm of the [antialienation] provision. We have previously explained that a contested claim is one that the claimant had actual or constructive knowledge of . . . at the time of the signing of the release, such that it could have been contested and resolved at the time the release was entered into (but was not). A contested claim does not seek benefits to which the plaintiff believes he is entitled under the terms of the pension plan itself, but rather for additional benefits above and beyond the benefits to which he was entitled under the terms of the plan. For example, a plaintiff might . . . claim that he deserves more benefits than he accrued under the terms of the plan on the grounds that the plan administrator failed to provide adequate notice of a reduction in benefits or that the plan administrator somehow violated his fiduciary duty. Such claims could be resolved before a plaintiff signs a release of those claims, and this is critical because general releases of claims are valid as long as the signing party has actual knowledge of the claims (or could have discovered those claims with a reasonable inquiry) he or she is giving up.[67]

ERISA does not preempt other federal laws.[68] Accordingly, the Mandatory Victims Restitution Act of 1996 (MVRA) has been used to access a criminal defendant's retirement benefits. In *United States v. Novak*, the

67. *Id.* (citations and quotation marks omitted).
68. 29 U.S.C. § 1144 (2012).

United States Court of Appeals for the Ninth Circuit confronted whether the government may put a criminal defendant's retirement benefits toward restitution for crime victims.[69] Specifically, *Novak* concerned an order of restitution pursuant to MVRA entered against Raymond Novak, who had pled guilty to Conspiracy to Transport Stolen Goods and Filing a False Tax Return after engaging in a scheme to steal telephone equipment from Nestle Food Company.[70] The court was forced to reconcile "two federal statutory schemes—one, the Mandatory Victims Restitution Act of 1996 . . . governing the payment of restitution to crime victims, and the other, the Employee Retirement Income Security Act of 1974. . . regulating private pension plans."[71] The court determined that Novak's retirement funds could be put toward restitution:

> Our effort to reconcile the broad MVRA enforcement provision and ERISA's stringent prohibition on alienation of pension benefits begins with the language of MVRA, allowing the enforcement of criminal restitution orders against all property or rights to property, [n]otwithstanding any other Federal law.
>
> By its use of the all property or rights to property language, Congress has made quite clear that the totality of defendants' assets will be subject to restitution orders. The Supreme Court emphasized the breadth of the all property or rights to property phrase in the context of tax collection statutes: The statutory language all property and rights to property . . . is broad and reveals on its face that Congress meant to reach every interest in property . . . . This language, so read, requires that retirement plan benefits can be garnished to fulfill criminal restitution orders. Because ERISA's anti-alienation provision conflicts with this crystal clear command of § 3613(a), we must determine how to square the statutory conflict.
>
> The MVRA statutory language not only establishes this conflict but also provides guidance on how to resolve it, by specifying that all property is covered [n]otwithstanding any other Federal law. The Supreme

69. United States v. Novak, 476 F.3d 1041, 1043 (9th Cir. 2007).
70. *Id.* at 1043–44.
71. *Id.*

Court has indicated as a general proposition that statutory notwithstanding clauses broadly sweep aside potentially conflicting laws.

In examining specific statutes, we have not, however, always accorded universal effect to the notwithstanding language, standing alone. Instead, we have determined the reach of each such notwithstanding clause by taking into account the whole of the statutory context in which it appears.

The overall context of MVRA dictates giving full effect to its use of the notwithstanding language as applied to ERISA's anti-alienation requirement. In particular, two contextual aspects of the restitution enforcement provision found in 18 U.S.C. § 3613(a)—its treatment of other types of otherwise inalienable property and, most importantly, its replication of the language authorizing tax levies—make it clear that MVRA's criminal restitution enforcement orders do override ERISA's alienation restrictions. Our interpretation also accords with case law concerning how to reconcile statutes enacted at different times.

. . .

Section 3613(a) specifies that one of the federal laws includ[ed] within the notwithstanding clause is section 207 of the Social Security Act. Similar to ERISA's anti-alienation provision, section 207 of the Social Security Act dictates that [t]he right of any person to any future payment . . . shall not be transferable or assignable, at law or in equity, and none of the moneys paid or payable or rights existing . . . shall be subject to execution, levy, attachment, garnishment, or other legal process, or to the operation of any bankruptcy or insolvency law. Unlike ERISA, however, the Social Security Act further specifies that [n]o other provision of law . . . may be construed to limit, supersede, or otherwise modify the provisions of this section except to the extent that it does so by express reference to this section. MVRA supplies that express reference, stating that the [n]otwithstanding any other Federal law override includ[es] section 207 of the Social Security Act.

There was no need similarly to specify other anti-alienation statutes, such as section 206(d) of ERISA, that do not mandate a clear statement for override. The all property and notwithstanding clauses, taken together, were sufficient to accomplish that end. Indeed, Congress has afforded greater protections to Social Security benefits against alienation than those afforded to retirement plans covered by ERISA. It would thus be anomalous to interpret § 3613(a) as abandoning the protection of Social Security benefits but not of retirement plans covered by ERISA. We conclude that by making clear that the notwithstanding clause includes the one federal anti-alienation provision that demands explicit statutory override, Congress manifested that § 3613(a) means what it says—that it reaches all property or rights to property not excepted, including property otherwise covered by federally mandated anti-alienation provisions.

This conclusion is reinforced by another structural feature of § 3613(a): Not only did Congress expressly override the one anti-alienation provision that it could remove only through such a reference, but it also specified that restitution orders could not be enforced against certain retirement plans even though those plans were already covered by anti-alienation statutes.

Four narrow types of federally-authorized pensions—Railroad Retirement Act pensions, Railroad Unemployment Insurance Act benefits, pensions received by those on the Armed Forces Medal of Honor rolls, and certain pensions paid to military service members in lieu of retirement pay—are excluded from the notwithstanding language of the restitution enforcement provision. The federal statutes that establish all four of those pension programs already contain anti-alienation provisions similar to that found in ERISA. By carving out these retirement plans from the operation of § 3613(a), Congress indicated that, in light of the notwithstanding clause and the breadth of the all property language, the anti-alienation provisions in the federal pension statutes would not suffice to protect retirement benefits from garnishment and similar orders enforcing criminal fines and restitution orders. Except on this understanding the explicit exclusion of the referenced pensions was unnecessary, as the exclusion would have been accomplished by the anti-alienation provisions in the statutes establishing the pension plans.

We avoid whenever possible statutory interpretations that result in superfluous language. Applying that precept, we regard the express

> and specific § 3613(a)(1) retirement plan exclusions as indicating that other federally regulated pension plans containing anti-alienation provisions, such as those covered by ERISA, are covered by the statutory trump worked by the broad all property and notwithstanding guidance.
>
> The inclusion of Social Security benefits and exclusion of certain retirement plans from the operation of § 3613(a) is important to our inquiry for another, related reason: Inclusion of these two references in § 3613(a) demonstrates that Congress focused quite directly upon the problem of allowing the enforcement of restitution orders against retirement plan assets and determined to allow such enforcement except as specified. The failure to include retirement plans covered by ERISA on the list of excluded retirement plans thus has substantial significance.
>
> In sum, the treatment in § 3613(a) of other federal statutory anti-alienation provisions indicates that Congress intended to override ERISA's anti-alienation provision and allow the government to reach defendants' ERISA-covered retirement plan benefits when enforcing criminal restitution orders.[72]

Every federal circuit court to consider whether the government may garnish pension plans to satisfy criminal restitution has agreed with the Ninth Circuit in *Novak*.[73]

Outside the criminal context, ERISA provides three exceptions to the antialienation rule: one for federal tax liens, one for judgments arising from fiduciary misconduct, and, as discussed in the prior chapter, one for qualified domestic relations orders (QDROs).[74] Other exceptions allow participants access to the benefits under very controlled, statutorily defined situations.

Federal tax liens can attach to ERISA pension plans. The United States Court of Appeals for the Ninth Circuit observed in *U.S. I.R.S. v. Snyder*:

72. *Id.* (citations and quotation marks omitted).

73. *See* United States v. Decay, 620 F.3d 534, 540–41 (5th Cir. 2010); United States v. Irving, 452 F.3d 110, 126 (2d Cir. 2006).

74. The United States Court of Appeals concluded in Brown v. Continental Airlines, Inc. that a plan administrator could not determine "that an otherwise valid DRO is not a QDRO because it is based on a 'sham' divorce," thus extending this spousal protection to unmarried individuals. Brown v. Cont'l Airlines, Inc., 647 F.3d 221, 228 (5th Cir. 2011).

> ERISA expressly provides that it shall [not] be construed to alter, amend, modify, invalidate, impair, or supercede any law of the United States, including federal tax law. Section 6321 of the Internal Revenue Code provides that the United States shall have a lien upon all property and rights to property, whether real or personal, belonging to any person liable to pay any tax who neglects or refuses to do the same after demand; and § 6331 authorizes the IRS to levy upon all property or rights to property of such person in order to execute the lien.[75]

The priority of the IRS's lien depends on when the IRS has perfected its lien in relation to other lienholders.[76]

Subsequent to *Guidry*, Congress enacted a fiduciary-misconduct exception to the antialienation rule. This codified the United States Court of Appeals' decision in *Coar v. Kazimir* that to restore plan funds due to a fiduciary breach, ERISA permitted attachment of or setoff against a breaching fiduciary-participant's pension benefits.[77] Now, ERISA expressly limits its antialienation rule so that it does not protect the benefits of a wrongdoer when:

> (A) the order or requirement to pay arises—
>
> (i) under a judgment of conviction for a crime involving such plan,
>
> (ii) under a civil judgment (including a consent order or decree) entered by a court in an action brought in connection with a violation (or alleged violation) of [an ERISA fiduciary responsibility], or
>
> (iii) pursuant to a settlement agreement between the Secretary and the participant, or a settlement agreement between the Pension Benefit Guaranty Corporation and the participant, in connection with a violation (or alleged violation) of [an ERISA fiduciary responsibility] by a fiduciary or any other person,

75. U.S. I.R.S. v. Snyder, 343 F.3d 1171, 1175 (9th Cir. 2003) (citations and quotation marks omitted).

76. *See generally* United States v. Taylor, 338 F.3d 947, 951–52 (8th Cir. 2003).

77. Coar v. Kazimir, 990 F.3d 1413, 1420 (3d Cir. 1993).

(B) the judgment, order, decree, or settlement agreement expressly provides for the offset of all or part of the amount ordered or required to be paid to the plan against the participant's benefits provided under the plan, and

(C) in a case in which the survivor annuity requirements . . . apply with respect to distributions from the plan to the participant, if the participant has a spouse at the time at which the offset is to be made—

(i) either—

(I) such spouse has consented in writing to such offset and such consent is witnessed by a notary public or representative of the plan (or it is established to the satisfaction of a plan representative that such consent may not be obtained by reason of circumstances [required by ERISA], or

(II) an election to waive the right of the spouse to a qualified joint and survivor annuity or a qualified preretirement survivor annuity is in effect in accordance with the requirements of [ERISA],

(ii) such spouse is ordered or required in such judgment, order, decree, or settlement to pay an amount to the plan in connection with a violation of [an ERISA fiduciary responsibility], or

(iii) in such judgment, order, decree, or settlement, such spouse retains the right to receive the survivor annuity under a qualified joint and survivor annuity . . . .[78]

The interest of the spouse is protected with a 50 percent survival annuity,[79] which many would argue is hardly a generous protection.

Antialienation protection does not extend beyond distribution. As previously discussed, the Supreme Court held in *Kennedy v. Plan Administrator for DuPont Savings & Investment Plan* that beneficiaries are entitled to ERISA plan benefits regardless of state-law waivers.[80] *Kennedy* left open whether the estate could recover benefits after distribution.[81] The Third

78. 29 U.S.C. § 1056 (2012).
79. *Id.*
80. Kennedy v. Plan Adm'r for DuPont Savings & Inv. Plan, 555 U.S. 285, 288 (2009).
81. *Id.* at 299 n.10.

Circuit ruled in *Estate of Kensinger v. URL Pharma, Inc.*[82] and the Fourth Circuit ruled in *Andochick v. Byrd*[83] that the estate could recover the benefits from the former spouse after distribution, as have multiple state courts.[84]

Antiassignment

An employee cannot assign his or her interest prior to actual distribution even if the assignment is executed after the termination of the plan. However, unless doing so to defray administrative costs, the plan may provide for a voluntary, revocable assignment not to exceed 10 percent after a benefit is in pay status.[85] While a garnishment or levy is not to be considered a voluntary assignment, vested benefits may be used as collateral for reasonable loans from a plan where the fiduciary requirements of the law are not violated.[86] The loan must be "secured by the participant's accrued non-forfeitable benefit,"[87] and must satisfy certain rules under the IRC in order not to be taxed as a distribution.[88] Although loans to interested parties of a pension plan are generally prohibited by ERISA, secured loans are permissible.[89] The exceptions for loans and the voluntary revocable assignment can be justified on the grounds that loan availability encourages plan participation and the 10 percent limitation on assignment is a de minimis amount that should not threaten plan benefits.

As previously noted, it is clear that areas under IRS enforcement and regulation generate less litigation. This may be due in part to the parties of interest in such cases, constraints on government resources, and the speed and effectiveness of tax penalties, which include loss of treasured tax incentives and loss of tax qualified plan status.

82. Estate of Kensinger v. URL Pharma, Inc., 674 F.3d 131, 134 (3d Cir. 2012).
83. Andochick v. Byrd, 709 F.3d 296, 299 (4th Cir. 2013).
84. Sweebe v. Sweebe, 712 N.W.2d 708 (Mich. 2006); Alcorn v. Appleton, 708 S.E.2d 390 (Ga. App. 2011); Pardee v. Pardee, 112 P.3d 308 (Okla. Civ. App. 2004).
85. 29 U.S.C. § 1056 (2012).
86. *Id.*
87. *Id.*
88. 26 U.S.C. § 72(p) (2012).
89. 29 U.S.C. § 1108 (2012).

Table of Cases

B

E

Pane v. RCA Corp., 667 F. Supp. 168, 171 (D. N.J. 1987), *aff'd*, 868 F.2d 631 (3d Cir. 1989), 12

Pappas v. Buck Consultants, Inc., 923 F.2d 531 (7th Cir. 1991), 107n8

Pardee v. Pardee, 112 P.3d 308 (Okla. Civ. App. 2004), 238n63, 286n84

Pari-Fasano v. ITT Hartford Life & Accident Ins. Co, 230 F.3d 415 (1st Cir. 2000), 200n92

Partners Healthcare Sys., Inc. v. Sullvan, 497 F. Supp. 2d 42 (D. Mass. 2007), 247, 247n88

Patterson v. Shumate, 504 U.S. 753 (1992), 272, 273n55

Patton v. Denver Post Corp., 326 F.3d 1148 (10th Cir. 2003), 228n29

Paulsen v. CNF Inc., 559 F.3d 1061 (9th Cir. 2009), 99, 99n84

Pegram v. Herdrich, 530 U.S. 211 (2000), 110, 110n32

Penny/Ohlmann/Nieman, Inc. v. Miami Valley Pension Corp., 399 F.3d 692 (6th Cir. 2005), 57, 57n96, 57, 59

Perry v. Simplicity Eng'ring, 900 F.2d 963 (6th Cir. 1990), 89n35

Pettaway v. Teachers Ins. & Annuity Ass'n of Am., 547 F. Supp. 2d 1 (D. D.C. 2008), 104n107

Phelps v. C.T. Enters., Inc., 394 F.3d 213 (4th Cir. 2005), 108n19

Phillips v. Lincoln Nat. Life Ins. Co., 978 F.2d 302 (7th Cir. 1992), 83n23

Physicians HealthChoice, Inc. v. Trustees of Automotive Employee Ben. Trust, 988 F.2d 53 (8th Cir. 1993), 154n47

Pierce Cnty. Hotel Emps. and Restaurant Emps. Health Trust v. Elks Lodge, B.P.O.E. No. 1450, 827 F.2d 1324 (9th Cir. 1987), 103n99

Pierre v. Conn. Gen. Life Ins. Co., 932 F.2d 1552 (5th Cir. 1991), 83, 83n20

Pilot Life Ins. Co. v. Dedeaux, 481 U.S. 41 (1987), 1n4, 35, 40n25, 48, 49n55, 52, 54n85

Pinto v. Reliance Standard Life Ins. Co., 214 F.3d 377 (3d Cir. 2000), 87n31

Pisciotta v. Teledyne Indus., Inc., 91 F.3d 1326 (9th Cir. 1996), 185n30

Postma v. Paul Revere Life Ins. Co., 223 F.3d 533 (7th Cir. 2000), 3n14, 20n128

Powell v. Chesapeake & Potomac Tel. Co. of Va., 780 F.2d 419 (4th Cir. 1985), 43n36

Price v. Provident Life & Accident Ins. Co., 2 F.3d 986 (9th Cir. 1993), 184, 185n27

Provident Life & Accident Ins. Co. v. Waller, 906 F.2d 985 (4th Cir. 1990), 56n89, 98n80

Q

R

S

Y

Z

Index

E